PowerScore®

LSAT® LOGICAL REASONING BIBLE WORKBOOK

The best resource for practicing PowerScore's famous Logical Reasoning methods!

Copyright © 2010-2022 by PowerScore Incorporated.
Copyright © 2023 by PowerScore LLC.

All Rights Reserved. No part of this publication may be reproduced, stored in a retrieval system, or transmitted in any form or by any means electronic, mechanical, photocopying, recording, scanning, or otherwise, without the prior written permission of the Publisher. Parts of this book have been previously published in other PowerScore publications and on the powerscore.com website.

All actual LSAT® content reproduced within this work is used with the permission of Law School Admission Council, Inc., (LSAC) Box 40, Newtown, PA 18940, the copyright owner. LSAC does not review or endorse specific test-preparation materials, companies, or services, and inclusion of licensed LSAT content within this work does not imply the review or endorsement of LSAC. LSAT is a registered trademark of LSAC.

PrepTest is a registered trademark of the Law School Admission Council, Inc.

PowerScore® is a registered trademark. *The Logical Reasoning Bible*™, *The Logic Games Bible*™, *The Reading Comprehension Bible*™, The PowerScore Bible Series™, The Logical Reasoning Primary Objectives™, The Conclusion Identification Method™, The Fact Test™, The Uniqueness Rule of Answer Choices™, The Justify Formula™, The Supporter/Defender Assumption Model™, The Assumption Negation Technique™, The Opposition Construct™, The Logic Ladder™, The Negative Logic Ladder™, The Complete Table of Formal Logic Additive Inferences™, The Elemental Attack™, The Variance Test™, and The Agree/Disagree Test™ are the exclusive service marked property of PowerScore. Any use of these terms without the express written consent of PowerScore is prohibited.

The logical reasoning, logic games, and reading comprehension systems, question classification systems, diagramming systems, and the overall approach to solving each question used in this book were created by PowerScore. Any use or reproduction of any such classifications, systems, or solutions without the express written consent of PowerScore is prohibited.

Published by
PowerScore LLC
12222 Merit Drive
Suite 1340
Dallas, TX 75251

Authors: David M. Killoran

Printed in the United States of America
12 15 20 22

ISBN: 978-1-68561-638-0

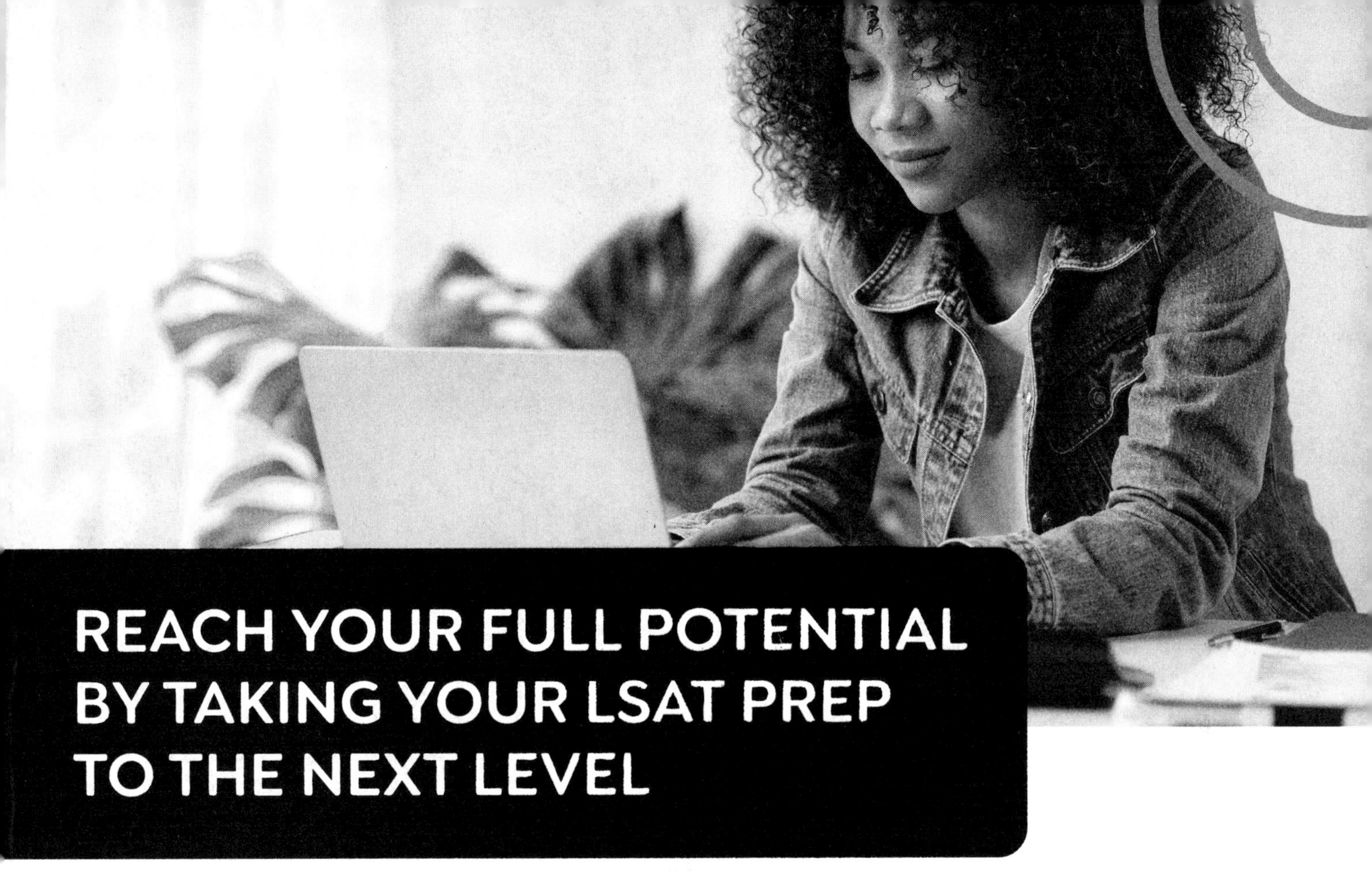

REACH YOUR FULL POTENTIAL BY TAKING YOUR LSAT PREP TO THE NEXT LEVEL

With our LSAT Bibles in hand, you are already building the strong foundation you'll need for LSAT success. The LSAT is manageable with the right plan of attack—and the next logical step is to build on your foundation and focus on making the leap from "good" to "great."

The PowerScore LSAT Course will bolster and refine the skills you're developing and elevate your chances to get into stronger law schools and qualify for favorable financial aid offers.

- Core syllabus, study roadmap, and in-depth LSAT lessons designed by LSAT Bible authors, Dave Killoran & Jon Denning
- Tailored to your learning style with live, interactive online or pre-recorded video lessons
- Digital practice test database containing every available official LSAT
- Full explanations and walkthroughs for all available past LSAT questions
- Insider info about upcoming LSATs and test content predictions

"I decided to go with PowerScore for online LSAT lessons to get an extra edge after receiving the basic groundwork from the LSAT Bibles. My instructor had unique insights and tricks that I couldn't get from the books, and I found the online tools to be outstandingly helpful for practice. Over time my practice scores crept up and I scored a 170 on my official test! I would recommend PowerScore's collection of LSAT prep services to any prospective test taker." —Jack F.

GET YOUR HIGHEST POSSIBLE LSAT SCORE NOW AT
powerscore.com/lsatprep

IT'S YOUR LEGAL EDUCATION JOURNEY. WE'RE YOUR TRUSTED GUIDE.

Get the most out of every step with help from BARBRI Global.

From the hard work of getting accepted and excelling in law school to walking into your bar exam fully confident in your preparation, you want to be sure you're always putting your best foot forward on your journey to a bright legal future. To stay on track, you'll want to take advantage of all the proven assistance BARBRI Global offers with a complete set of tools designed to help you to achieve your legal dreams.

Get pre-law guidance and assistance with PowerScore and Law Preview

West Academic arms you with casebooks, textbooks and online study aids throughout your law school tenure

BARBRI Bar Prep is the global leader, and gives you the confidence and training you need to master the bar exam

Our mission is to make legal professionals better. To make your journey better. And it starts here, with BARBRI Global.

WWW. BARBRI.COM

TAKE THE FIRST STEP TOWARD THE TOP OF THE CLASS

The Law Preview Law School Prep Course is the ultimate course for law school success. With Law Preview, you'll create a 1L game plan that gets you ahead of the competition and allows you to enter law school with the skills and confidence you need to succeed—starting on day one.

Through a series of lectures from the nation's top law professors, you'll navigate core 1L material, learn exam-taking strategies, build academic skills, and more—all in an interactive, engaging format—and all before your first day of law school.

- 48 hours of in-depth learning
- Seven top law professors
- One chance to excel

"I received all As my first semester and am ranked #1 in my class. Law Preview gave me the right mindset entering law school, and I feel the class was a big part of my success. Not only did it help me succeed grades-wise, but the class also gave me a sense of excitement to start law school."

Sean C.,
University of Houston Law Center

ENROLL TODAY!

lawpreview.com

Our Testing & Analytics Package pairs perfectly with LSAC Prep Plus.

- Take full digital tests or practice individual timed sections.
- Master specific question types in drill sets.
- Access additional practice LSATs not available in LSAC's Prep Plus database.
- Track your performance by question type, reasoning type, and time per question.
- Determine your strengths and weaknesses with our detailed scoring and analytical breakdown of your results.
- NEW: Add on our Logical Reasoning Bible Course with video lessons and explanations for just $19.99/month.

SUBSCRIBE NOW!

powerscore.com/lsat/publications/digital-tests/

NEED A HELPING HAND WITH YOUR LSAT PREP?

Our tutors have the answers. Work one-on-one with a top-scoring expert for tutoring sessions tailored to your needs.

- Go further, faster! Customized study plans help you reach your goals quickly and efficiently.
- You're in control—schedule tutoring session times, length, and frequency to fit your unique situation.
- Request a free consultation. Chat with our staff about your goals, timeline, strengths, and weaknesses before making a commitment.

Live Online tutoring means even more flexibility. Match with a tutor no matter where you are!
powerscore.com/lsat/tutoring

PowerScore Admissions Consulting

- Our consultants are admissions experts, many of whom are lawyers and graduates of the top law schools in North America.

- We offer a multitude of packages. Whether you need help from start-to-finish or an in-depth evaluation and critique of your personal statement, we've got you covered.

- Need general guidance or help with specific parts of your application? Hourly admissions consulting is also available.

GET STARTED TODAY! GO ONLINE OR CALL TODAY TO START AN INQUIRY.

powerscore.com/lsat/law-school-admissions

1-800-845-1750

CONTENTS

INTRODUCTION

CHAPTER ONE: PRACTICE DRILLS

CHAPTER TWO: PREPTEST 44 LOGICAL REASONING SECTION I

CHAPTER THREE: PREPTEST 45 LOGICAL REASONING SECTION II

CHAPTER FOUR: PREPTEST 47 LOGICAL REASONING SECTION II

CHAPTER FIVE: PREPTEST 58 LOGICAL REASONING SECTION I

CHAPTER SIX: PREPTEST 58 LOGICAL REASONING SECTION II

GLOSSARY

About PowerScore

PowerScore is one of the nation's fastest growing test preparation companies. Founded in 1997, PowerScore offers LSAT, GMAT, GRE, SAT, and ACT preparation classes in over 150 locations in the U.S. and abroad. Preparation options include In Person courses, Accelerated courses, Live Online courses, On Demand courses, and private tutoring. For more information, please visit our website at powerscore.com or call us at (800) 545-1750.

About the Author

Dave Killoran, a graduate of Duke University, is an expert in test preparation with over 25 years of teaching experience and a 99th percentile score on a LSAC-administered LSAT. In addition to having written PowerScore's legendary LSAT Bible Series, and many other popular publications, Dave has overseen the preparation of thousands of students and founded two national LSAT preparation companies. Find him on Twitter at http://twitter.com/DaveKilloran or on the PowerScore LSAT Forum at http://forum.powerscore.com.

Introduction

Welcome to the *PowerScore LSAT Logical Reasoning Bible Workbook*. This book is designed for use after reading the *PowerScore LSAT Logical Reasoning Bible*; the purpose of the workbook is to help you better understand the ideas presented in the *Logical Reasoning Bible*, and allow you to practice the application of our methods and techniques.

If you are looking for a how-to manual, please refer to the *PowerScore LSAT Logical Reasoning Bible*, which provides the conceptual basis for understanding logical argumentation, recognizing the various question types, approaching the answers, and applying other general strategies you will be practicing here. In the discussions of approaches and techniques in this workbook, we will assume that you have read the *Logical Reasoning Bible* and are familiar with its basic terminology.

This book begins with a chapter of practice drills, designed to reinforce and improve upon the specific skills and approaches necessary to successfully attack the Logical Reasoning section. The set of drills is followed by an answer key explaining each item.

The section of practice drills and explanations is followed by five logical reasoning sections from past LSATs, presented in their entirety, followed by full explanations of each stimulus and every corresponding question. If you choose to do any or all of these sections under timed conditions, this gives you the opportunity to emulate actual testing conditions, allowing you to apply the full range of your Logical Reasoning strategies while also focusing on your pacing under time pressure.

Each of the six sections is easily located using the black sidebars that mark each section.

Section One: Practice Drills and Explanations

Section Two: PrepTest 44: Logical Reasoning Section I

Section Three: PrepTest 45: Logical Reasoning Section II

Section Four: PrepTest 47: Logical Reasoning Section II

Section Five: PrepTest 58: Logical Reasoning Section I

Section Six: PrepTest 58: Logical Reasoning Section II

As you review each item, we suggest that you carefully read the corresponding explanation. Examine the correct answer choice, but also study the incorrect answer choices. Look again at the problem and determine which elements led to the correct answer. Study the explanations provided in the book and check them against your own work to assess and improve vital reasoning skills. By doing so you will greatly increase your chances of performing well on the Logical Reasoning sections of the LSAT.

Finally, in our LSAT courses, in our admissions counseling programs, and in our publications, we always strive to present the most accurate and up-to-date information available. Consequently, we have devoted a section of our website to *Logical Reasoning Bible Workbook* students. This free online resource area offers supplements to the book material and provides updates as needed. There is also an official book evaluation form that we encourage you to use. The exclusive *LSAT Logical Reasoning Bible Workbook* online area can be accessed at:

powerscore.com/lsatprep

Once there, create an account and then use the code on the inside front cover of this book to gain access.

And please connect with us directly via Twitter and our podcast!:

@DaveKilloran

powerscore.com/lsat/podcast

If you would like to discuss the LSAT with our experts, please visit our free LSAT discussion forum at:

forum.powerscore.com

We are happy to assist you in your LSAT preparation in any way, and we look forward to hearing from you!

Chapter One: Practice Drills

Chapter One: Practice Drills

POWERSCORE
BY BARBRI

Chapter Notes

This section contains a set of drills designed to achieve the following goals:

1. Reacquaint you with the language used in the LSAT Logical Reasoning Sections, using the Logical Reasoning question classification system developed by PowerScore.

2. Isolate and test certain skills that are used in Logical Reasoning, and refresh and refine your abilities to apply those skills.

3. Expose you to a variety of Logical Reasoning concepts and challenges.

We believe the best approach is to complete each drill, and then check the answer key in the back, examining both the questions you answered correctly and the ones you answered incorrectly.

These drills have no timing restrictions. Instead of worrying about speed, focus on a complete understanding of the idea under examination.

Identify the Question Stem Drill

Each of the following items contains a sample LSAT question stem. Based upon the discussion in Chapter 3 of the *Logical Reasoning Bible*, categorize each stem into one of the thirteen Logical Reasoning Question Types: Must Be True/Most Strongly Supported, Main Point, Point at Issue/ Point of Agreement, Assumption, Justify the Conclusion, Strengthen, Resolve the Paradox, Weaken, Method of Reasoning, Flaw in the Reasoning, Parallel Reasoning/Parallel Flaw, Evaluate the Argument, or Cannot Be True. Refer to the *Logical Reasoning Bible* as needed. *Answers on page 30*

1. Which of the following can properly be inferred from the statements above?

   Question Type: must be true

2. Which of the following arguments is most similar in its pattern of reasoning to the argument presented above?

   Question Type: parallel reasoning

3. Which one of the following is an assumption required by the argument above?

   Question Type: assumption

4. Which one of the following, if assumed, would allow the writer's conclusion to be properly drawn?

   Question Type: ~~resolve paradox~~ justify conclusion

5. The author of the editorial proceeds by

   Question Type: ~~main point?~~ method of reasoning

6. The answer to which one of the following questions would be most helpful in evaluating the physician's argument?

   Question Type: ______

7. If the statements above are true, which one of the following must be false?

   Question Type: ______

8. Which one of the following, if true, would provide the most support for the politician's conclusion?

   Question Type: ______

9. All of the following, if true, would help to resolve the apparent discrepancy EXCEPT

   Question Type: ______

10. Which one of the following best expresses the main point of the argument?

    Question Type: ______

Identify the Question Stem Drill

11. The argument above is most vulnerable to which one of the following criticisms?

    Question Type: ______________________

12. If the statements above are true, all of the following must be true EXCEPT

    Question Type: ______________________

13. Which one of the following, if true, justifies the conclusion above?

    Question Type: ______________________

14. Which one of the following, if true, would most seriously undermine the argument presented in the editorial?

    Question Type: ______________________

15. The dialogue above supports the claim that Ned and Michelle disagree about which of the following issues?

    Question Type: ______________________

Premise and Conclusion Analysis Drill

For each stimulus, identify the conclusion(s) and supporting premise(s), if any. The answer key will identify the conclusion and premises of each argument, the logical validity of each argument, and also discuss how to identify argument structure. *Answers on page 34*

1. At Umberland University, students given a choice between taking more advanced courses in their major or introductory courses in unrelated disciplines typically chose to take the introductory courses. This shows that, contrary to expectations, students are more interested in broadening their horizons than in concentrating their knowledge in a single field.

   A. What is the conclusion of the argument, if any?

   B. What premises are given in support of this conclusion?

   C. Is the argument strong or weak? If you think that the argument is weak, please explain why.

2. Some researchers claim that many mnemonic devices actually function more as a result of a process called "temporal fixation" and less as a function of long-term memory. But this conclusion is suspect. Research has shown that temporal fixation is simply a short-term memory process that transitions into long-term memory.

   A. What is the conclusion of the argument, if any?

   B. What premises are given in support of this conclusion?

   C. Is the argument strong or weak? If you think that the argument is weak, please explain why.

Premise and Conclusion Analysis Drill

3. The "tiny house" movement advocates living in very small homes in a simple fashion. Although no set standards exist on what defines a tiny house, the focus is on small living spaces utilized in an environmentally-friendly manner. Given the range of benefits offered by tiny homes—a decreased energy and carbon footprint, affordable sheltering for displaced persons, and an increased population density—it is imperative that tax laws and urban codes be altered to allow for tax breaks and other incentives that will increase the building, adoption, and use of tiny homes.

   A. What is the conclusion of the argument, if any?

   B. What premises are given in support of this conclusion?

   C. Is the argument strong or weak? If you think that the argument is weak, please explain why.

Premise and Conclusion Analysis Drill

4. In the feudal system of Medieval Europe, land or a right to work the land was typically offered in exchange for services. A tiered system existed with the King at the apex, providing land to the noble classes of knights and barons, who in exchange pledged fealty and provided soldiers and arms during times of war and unrest. The noble classes in turn provided land rights to lower classes, who often farmed and provided goods and services back to the nobility. Perhaps unsurprisingly, this system often produced poor living conditions for the lowest classes of society, and by the 16th century feudalism had largely disappeared.

   A. What is the conclusion of the argument, if any?

   B. What premises are given in support of this conclusion?

   C. Is the argument strong or weak? If you think that the argument is weak, please explain why.

Premise and Conclusion Analysis Drill

5. Many cultures share taboos concerning watching others eat. Some anthropologists have argued that these taboos arise from concerns about appropriate conduct around relatives, guests, and strangers; others suggest that the taboos relate to historical resource scarcity and famine. Undoubtedly, both hypotheses are correct. Social rules that prohibit certain behaviors are common to nearly all societies, and these prohibitions often arise from practical concerns about maintaining order and self-preservation.

   A. What is the conclusion of the argument, if any?

   B. What premises are given in support of this conclusion?

   C. Is the argument strong or weak? If you think that the argument is weak, please explain why.

Premise and Conclusion Analysis Drill

6. Recent analysis of sugar addiction studies shows that restrictive diets may lead some dieters to binge eat. Animal studies indicate that addiction-type behaviors towards sugar occur only in animals on restrictive diets. Animals with unrestricted access to food exhibited no such behavior. The studies found no chemical mechanism responsible for sugar addiction. Instead, intermittent access to sweet foods correlated with bouts of excessive sugar consumption.

   A. What is the conclusion of the argument, if any?

   B. What premises are given in support of this conclusion?

   C. Is the argument strong or weak? If you think that the argument is weak, please explain why.

Conditional Reasoning Diagramming Drill

Each of the following represents a conditional statement, providing both a sufficient condition and a necessary condition. Based upon the discussion of conditional diagrams in Chapter Six of the *Logical Reasoning Bible*, write the proper arrow diagram for each, followed by the proper arrow diagram for the contrapositive of each conditional relationship. Refer to the text of the *LSAT Logical Reasoning Bible* as needed. *Answers on page 40*

Example:

In order to pass the test, one must study.

original diagram: Pass ⟶ Study

contrapositive: ~~Study~~ ⟶ ~~Pass~~

---

1. To be eligible for the drawing, entries must be postmarked by May 1.

   ______ ⟶ ______

   ______ ⟶ ______

2. You cannot pass airport security without a valid boarding pass.

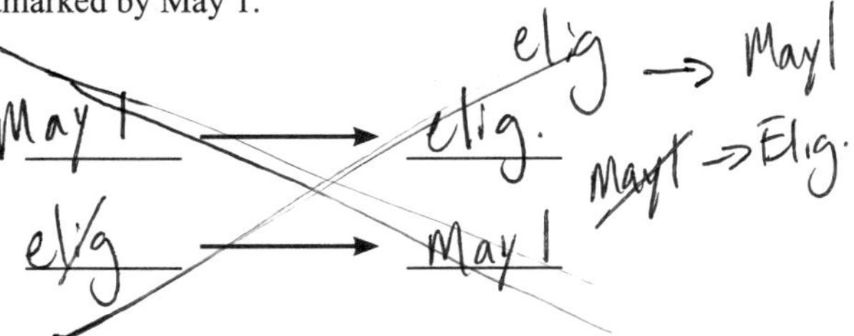

   ______ ⟶ ______

   ______ ⟶ ______

3. Car seatbelts are required for all children over the age of 7.

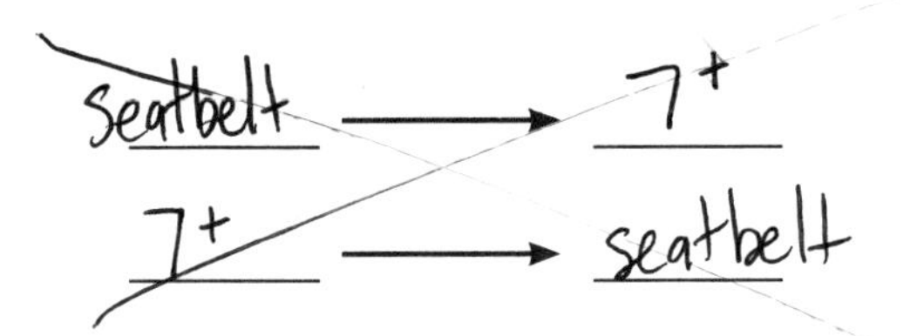

   ______ ⟶ ______

   ______ ⟶ ______

4. No student who fails the test will be admitted to the school.

   ______ ⟶ ______

   ______ ⟶ ______

5. You cannot find cheap airfare to Barcelona unless you book your tickets months in advance.

   ______ ⟶ ______

   ______ ⟶ ______

6. The amendment to the bill will pass only if some members of the opposition party vote for it.

   ______ ⟶ ______

   ______ ⟶ ______

Conditional Reasoning Diagramming Drill

7. Further Lane is the only way to reach the marina.

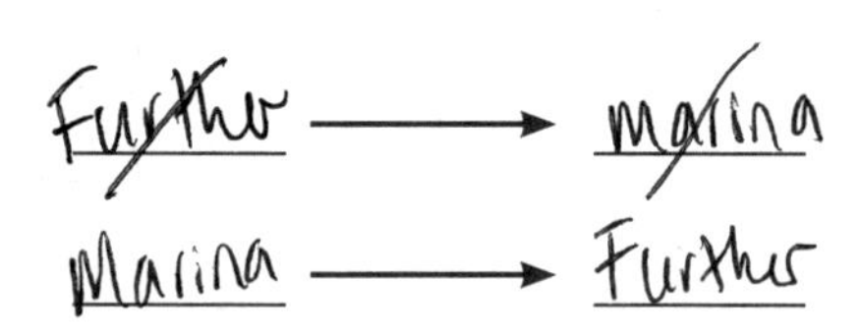

8. In order to park at the beach, residents must first obtain a beach pass.

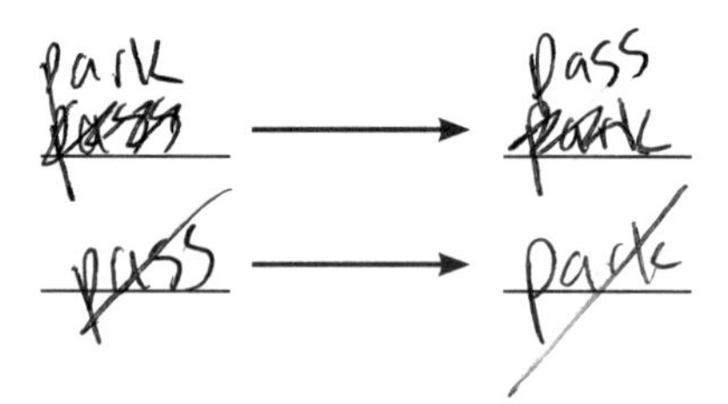

9. To win with honor, one must not cheat.

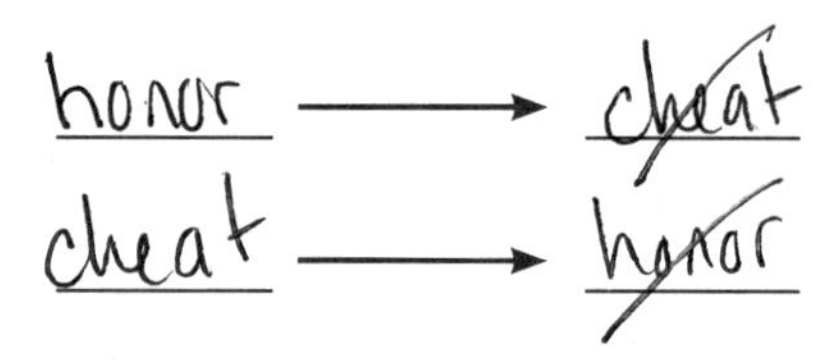

10. Either Patrick or Miranda will win the literary contest.

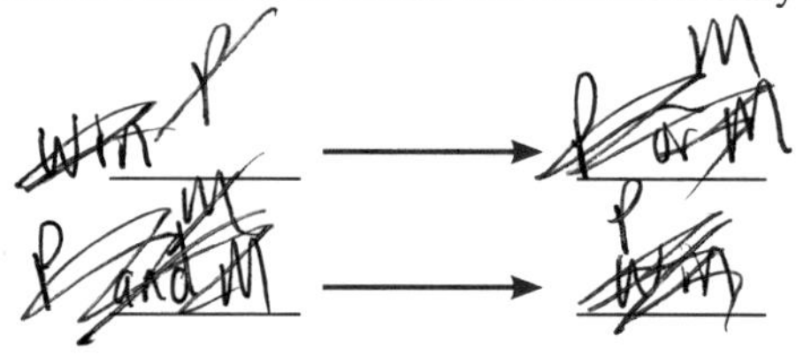

11. Whenever a package is shipped, the system generates a unique tracking number.

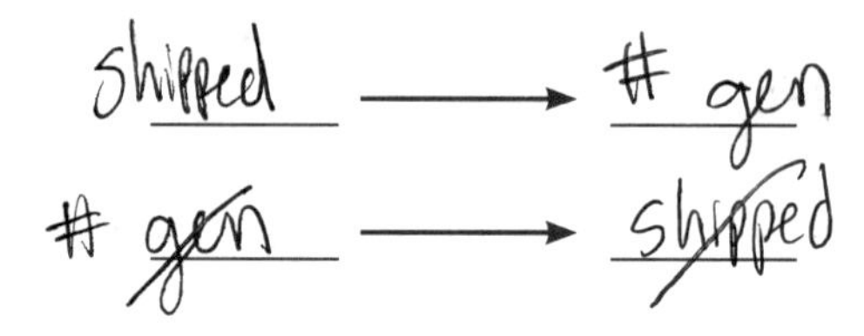

12. The only way for a company to maintain its stock price is by paying a dividend.

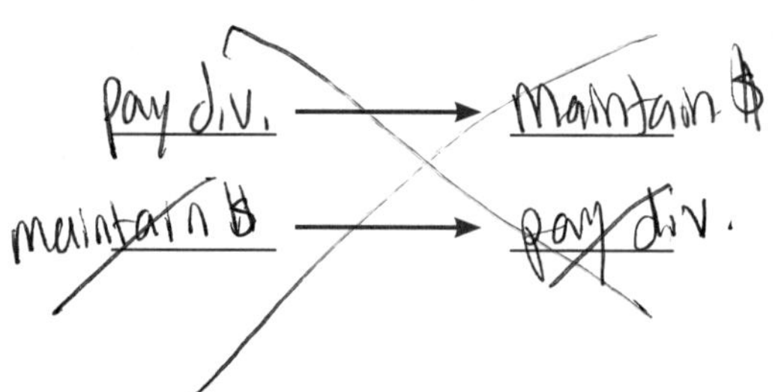

13. Students will not receive diplomas until all requirements for graduation have been satisfied.

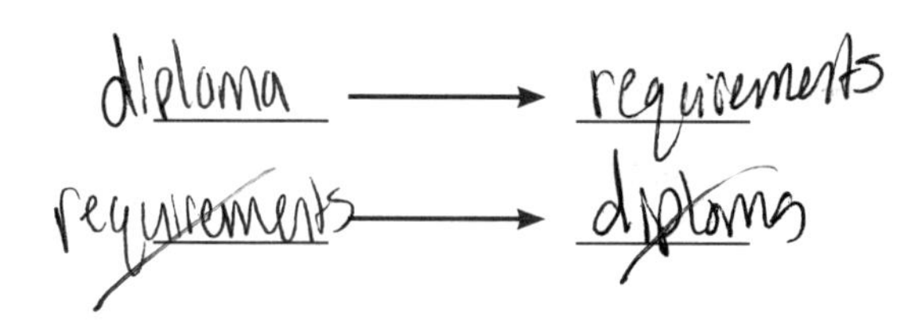

14. Taxpayers must either declare all received income or face a penalty.

declare → penalty
penalty → declare

15. No one without sufficient exposure to linear algebra can enroll in this seminar.

algebra → enroll
enroll → algebra

16. Suspects shall be presumed innocent until proven guilty.

presumed innocent → proven guilty
proven guilty → presumed innocent

Conditional Reasoning Diagramming Drill

17. Extraordinary ideas require innovative minds.

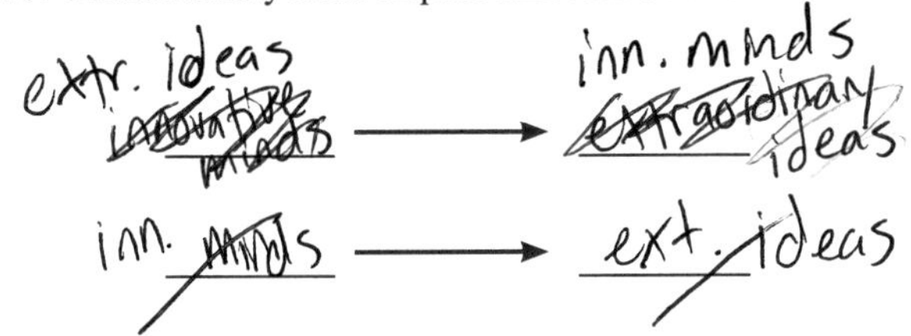

18. You cannot lose if you do not play.

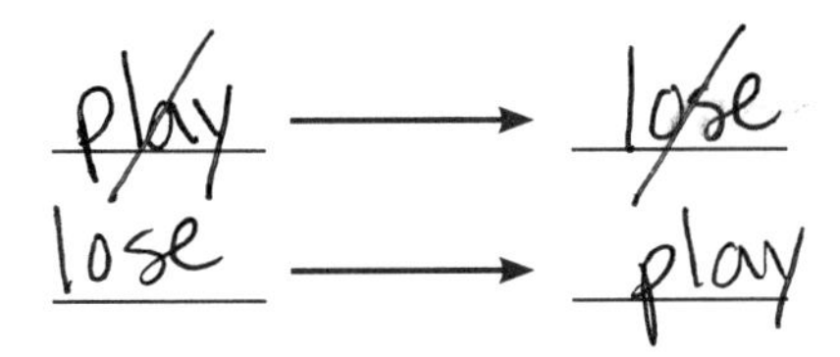

19. Except for Mary, everyone came to the party.

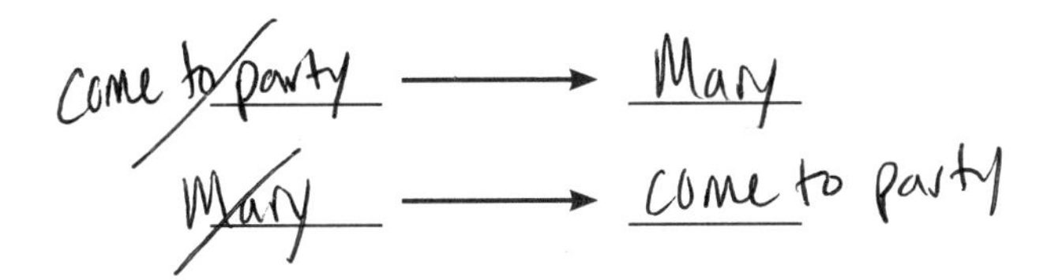

20. No student can receive high honors unless he or she has submitted a senior thesis.

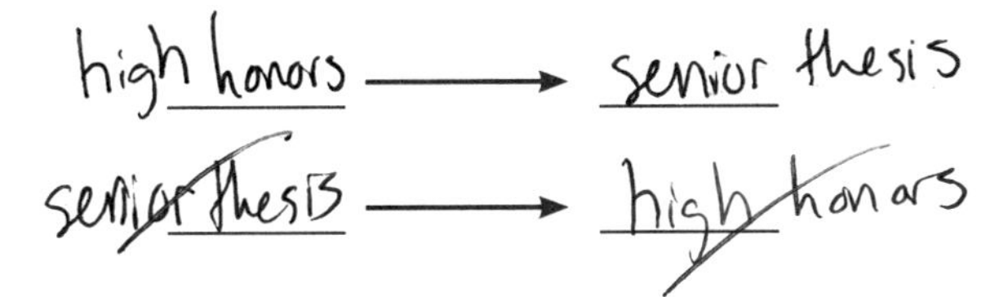

PRACTICE DRILLS

Either/Or, Multiple Condition, and Double Arrow Diagramming Drill

Each of the following statements contains at least one sufficient condition and at least one necessary condition; therefore, each of the following statements can be described as a "conditional statement." In the spaces provided, write the proper arrow diagram for each of the following conditional statements. Then write the proper arrow diagram for the contrapositive of each of the following conditional statements. In some cases you may have to modify the given arrow to indicate that a double arrow is present. *Answers on page 49*

1. The proposal will pass if and only if there is no opposition.

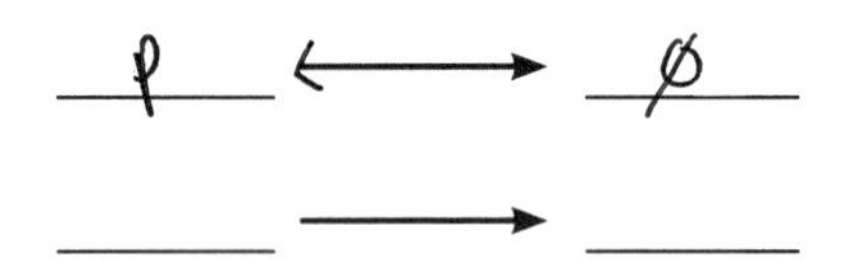

2. We will go to the beach only if the weather is nice and we can get the day off.

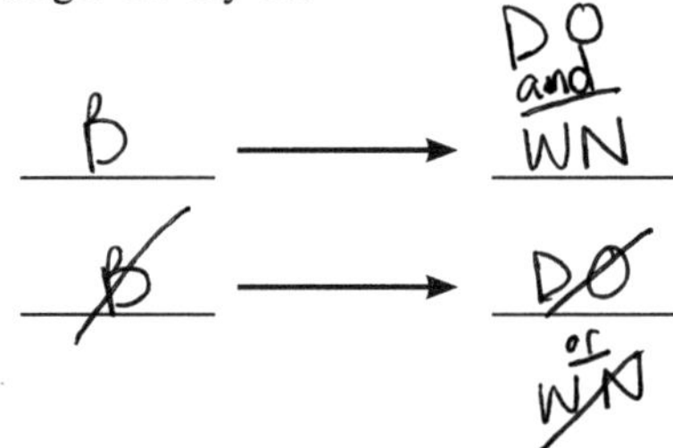

3. The concert will be cancelled if ticket sales are insufficient or if it rains.

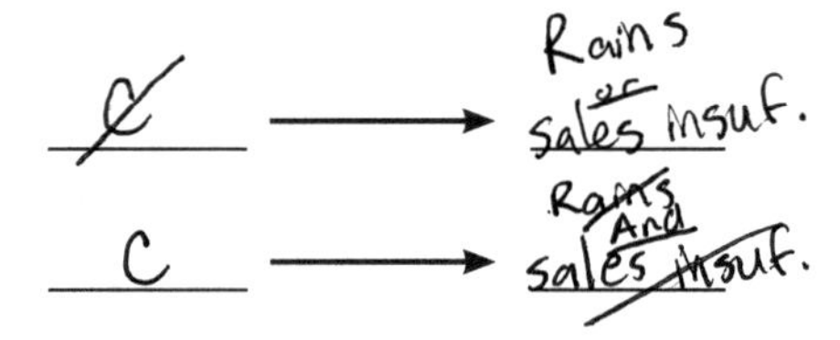

4. Unless private donations increase or ticket sales go up, the museum will raise admission fees.

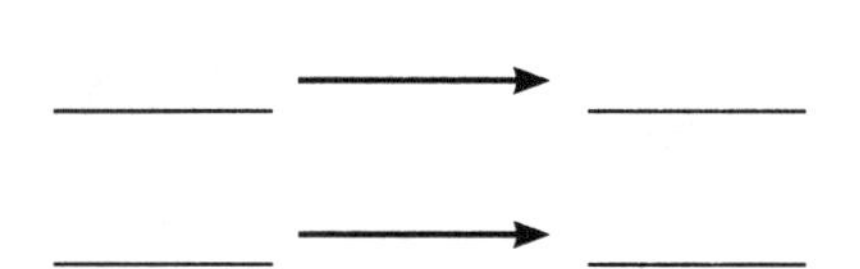

5. Either Scott *or* Michelle will drive the carpool on Sunday.

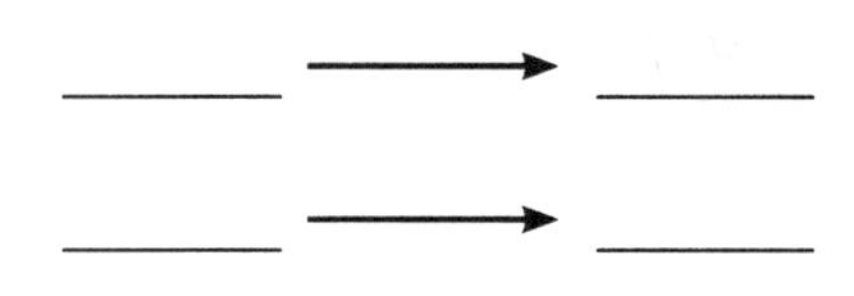

6. When the parties agree and the details have been finalized, we will sign the contract.

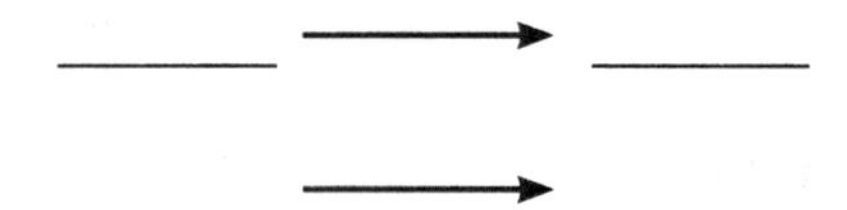

PRACTICE DRILLS

Either/Or, Multiple Condition, and Double Arrow Diagramming Drill

7. In order to be prepared for the test, you must study and get plenty of sleep.

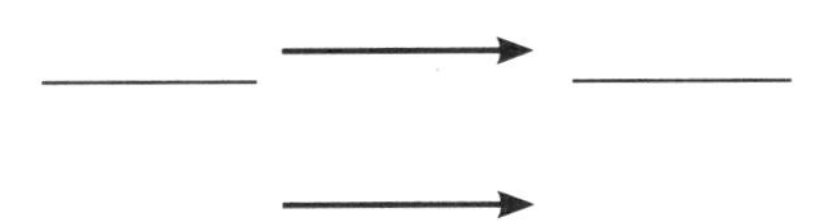

8. The class cannot go on the field trip until transportation has been secured and all permission slips have been signed.

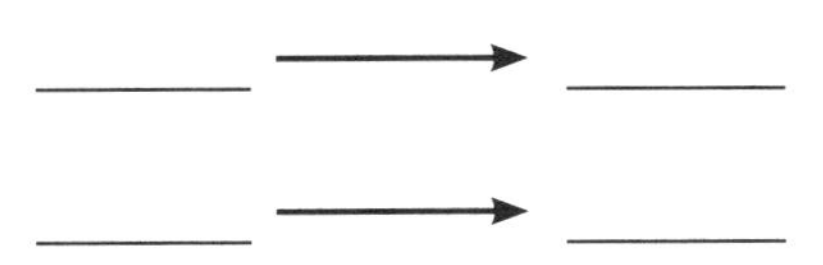

9. If the plan is approved and the finances are secured, we can move forward.

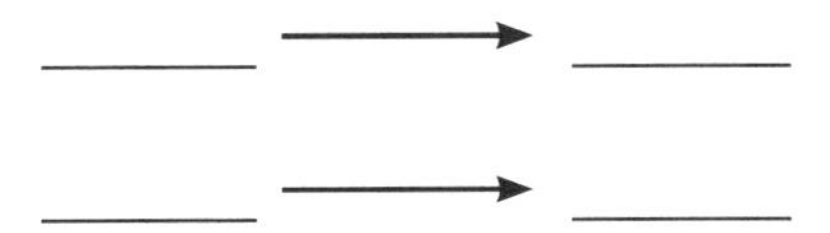

10. It's either fight or flight.

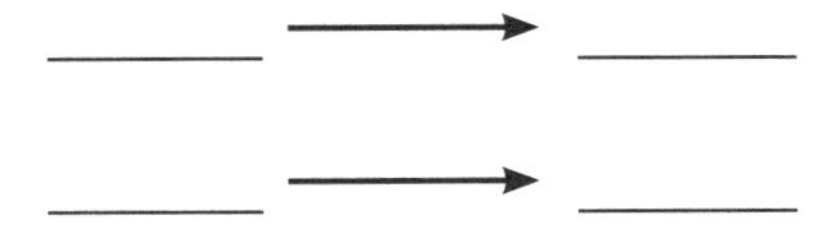

Statement Negation Drill

This drill tests the ability to apply the Assumption Negation Technique™, as discussed in Chapter Eleven of the *Logical Reasoning Bible*, which allows you to assess whether an argument relies on a given assumption. Negate each of the following in the spaces provided. *Answers on page 53*

1. The president could veto the bill.

____

2. All of the teams played well.

____

3. Only one witness was present when the robbery took place.

____

4. If Smith gets elected, he will serve only one term as mayor.

____

5. The weather in this area is very predictable.

____

6. The winner will not necessarily be determined during the first half of the game.

____

7. The detrimental effects of global warming can be felt everywhere.

____

8. You cannot enter unless you pay admission.

____

9. Early to bed and early to rise makes a person healthy, wealthy and wise.

____

10. New methods of warfare led to increased casualty rates.

____

Justify Formula Drill

Each of the following items presents a premise and a conclusion. Supply the missing statement that would, when added to the premise, force the conclusion to be true. In other words, supply the missing element which satisfies the Justify Formula, as discussed in Chapter Ten of the *Logical Reasoning Bible*. *Answers on page 55*

1. Premise: Every professor at McClellan University with tenure has been published extensively.

   Conclusion: Dr. Daktari has been published extensively.

   Justifying statement: ______________________________

   ____

   ____

2. Premise: The combination of poor management and poor customer service causes sales to go down.

   Conclusion: Sales at Xmark Corporation declined last year.

   Justifying statement: ______________________________

   ____

   ____

3. Premise: Some DaytonWilson drugs have been found to have dangerous side effects.

   Conclusion: DaytonWilson will be fined by the Food and Drug Administration.

   Justifying statement: ______________________________

   ____

   ____

Justify Formula Drill

4. Premise: If Carlos attends the meeting, then Hiroshi attends the meeting.

   Conclusion: Carlos does not attend the meeting.

   Justifying statement: ______________________________

   ____

   ____

5. Premise: This month there was an increase in the percentage of callers who made a purchase compared to last month.

   Conclusion: More callers made a purchase this month than made a purchase last month.

   Justifying statement: ______________________________

   ____

   ____

Identify the Flaw in the Argument Drill

Each of the following problems contains an error of reasoning. Based on the discussion in Chapter 15 of the *Logical Reasoning Bible*, identify the error of reasoning. Refer back to the text in the *Logical Reasoning Bible* as needed. *Answers on page 57*

1. After several periods of record sales increases, the Janacek Group relocated their offices to the new Industrial Pointe complex and chose one of the most expensive office suites in the city. Despite the significant financial investment required, Janacek executives defended the move by noting the benefits to Janacek's image that would come with a location in a complex which, they concluded, must house all of the city's most expensive office space.

____

____

____

2. Offshore oil drilling has long been a risky endeavor, but oil companies and related industries argue strenuously that no further restrictions should be placed on such drilling due to our country's need for energy resources, and the possible serious consequences if such energy reserves are not located and explored now. Of course, the vast sums of money the oil companies stand to make from such drilling automatically make their arguments suspect.

____

____

____

3. Supporters of the theory of global warming claim that carbon emissions are causing our environment to slowly warm, which will eventually produce catastrophic results. However, this past winter was one of the coldest on record. Therefore, the claim that global warming is accelerating is false.

____

____

____

Identify the Flaw in the Argument Drill

4. When temperatures drop just below freezing, the plant pathogen *Pseudomonas syringae* produces certain proteins that force ice to form on the surface of a plant. The damage caused by the freezing process releases plant nutrients that are then available to the *Pseudomonas syringae* bacteria. Although this fruit grove contains *Pseudomonas syringae* bacteria, temperatures have not dropped below freezing at any point during the last 30 days, so there should be no concern over *Pseudomonas syringae*-related frost damage during that period.

____

____

____

5. Will executor: The maker of this will left a number of antiques as gifts to her descendants. I recently attempted to have each antique evaluated for value by a local university professor who is an international expert in the valuation and authentication of antiques. This month, however, she will be too busy to examine all of the pieces. Therefore, I must take all of the antiques to the local appraising firm for valuation.

____

____

____

6. Last year, within the sales division of the company, the salespeople with highest average number of miles driven each week had the highest sales figures. Thus, we should immediately implement a policy requiring all salespeople to begin driving more miles each week.

____

____

____

Identify the Flaw in the Argument Drill

7. Each member of Dr. Martin's research team is now well-known among the particle physics scientific community. We know this because the team recently published a ground breaking physics paper on baryon asymmetry. The paper created great excitement among those who study particle physics, and there has been intense debate on what the results of the paper mean for the science of particle physics. Consequently, the work of Dr. Martin's team of researchers has become world-renowned.

____

____

____

8. Car Advertisement: The new Electra Argive is among the best-driving cars on the road today. A recent poll at our dealerships of interested drivers who had test-driven the Argive rated it among the top cars they had driven, and over 80% of those drivers indicated they would be buying an Argive in the near future.

____

____

____

9. Thompson has rightly been lauded for his academic achievements at this school, but Thompson is also an excellent overall athlete and he is obviously the school's best runner. This claim is decisively proven in those instances when Thompson does lose a race, because Thompson obviously would not lose unless the other runners cheated.

____

____

____

Identify the Flaw in the Argument Drill

10. New restaurant manager: Several employees complained about the firing of a recently trained waiter after his very first erroneous order. They claim that the previous manager had been quite lenient with regard to the first few mistakes made by any recent trainee, but this claim is clearly false. I know the previous manager, and she would not have tolerated countless errors without any repercussions, even if those errors were made by recent trainees.

____

____

____

11. Within certain library departments, established practice dictates that seniority be used as the main criterion for job advancement. Thereby, the employee who has worked the most years has priority in the promotion process. However, this process is patently unfair. Janet Watson, the local mayor, recently spoke out against this process and strongly criticized the library administration for adhering to what she called "a completely obsolete system."

____

____

____

12. Veterinarian: There is serious cause for concern with the cattle herds in this state. Yesterday I treated two cows for listeriosis, a disease of the central nervous system, and the day before that I treated two different cows for the very same malady. We need to immediately begin testing all cows in the state for this disease, and take curative action on any cow exhibiting signs of illness.

____

____

____

Identify the Flaw in the Argument Drill

13. Board member: The protesters who recently criticized the Board for taking advantage of a loophole in the city charter are falsely informed. Although the Board agreed to provide further financing to the city transit system, the Board did not use the bank owned by one of the Board members. Thus, as the protesters have failed to show that any board member gained any benefit from the action we took, their claim is false.

____

____

____

14. Richardson recently claimed that we must do something in response to the university's current economic crisis. I have repeatedly proposed that we layoff a percentage of all workers and simultaneously reduce all budgets to last year's levels. If we are to follow Richardson's advice, and actually do something, we must implement my program of action immediately.

____

____

____

15. Company Travel Manager: Although we had originally planned for the eight marketing department employees to drive the 250 miles to this week's advertising meeting, our car rental firm informed us today that no van will be available for rent until next week. Thus, we have no choice but to postpone the meeting.

____

____

____

Numbers and Percentages Practice Drill

The scenarios below are each followed by three statements, any or all of which may be possible. After considering the limited information presented in each case, select all statements that apply. Please see Chapter 17 of the *Logical Reasoning Bible* for a complete review of Numbers and Percentages concepts as applied on the LSAT. *Answers on page 64*

1. The Mercantile Corporation increased its national market share last year by 5% compared to its market share two years ago.

   Which of the following could be true of the overall unit sales of the Mercantile Corporation? Select all that apply.

   I. Mercantile Corporation sold fewer units last year than it had sold the prior year.
   II. Mercantile Corporation sold the same number of units each of the last two years.
   III. Mercantile Corporation sold more units last year than it had sold the prior year.

2. In today's mayoral election, West received 1500 votes, compared with the 1000 votes that he had received in last year's election.

   Which of the following could be true of the percentage of the vote Mayor West won in today's election compared to the percentage he won in the last election? Select all that apply.

   I. West received a greater percentage of the vote today than in the last election.
   II. West received a smaller percentage of the vote today than in the last election.
   III. West received the same percentage of the vote today as in the last election.

3. Halstead's and McGrady's are competing furniture stores, each of which carries exactly one type of couch. Next week Halstead's will have its annual holiday sale, during which every piece of furniture in the store is to be marked down by 60%. McGrady's has just announced a competing sale, in which various products will be marked down by 30%.

   Which of the following could be true of Halstead's couch price compared with McGrady's during next week's sale? Select all that apply.

   I. A couch purchased at Halstead's will cost less than a couch at McGrady's.
   II. A couch purchased at Halstead's will cost more than a couch at McGrady's.
   III. A couch purchased at Halstead's will cost the same as a couch at McGrady's.

Numbers and Percentages Practice Drill

4. In response to brisk sales, a certain car dealership increased the price of the Cheetah, its best-selling sport utility vehicle, by 25% on January 1. In February, after no other price changes had been implemented, the dealership held a special sale during which the price of every car was marked down by 20%.

   Which of the following could be true of the price of the Cheetah during the February sale compared with the price on December 31 (just prior to the January 1 price change)?

   I. The price of the Cheetah was higher during the sale than it had been on December 31.
   II. The price of the Cheetah was lower during the sale than it had been on December 31.
   III. The price of the Cheetah was the same during the sale as it had been on December 31.

5. Last year, Davis, Acme Company's top salesperson, was responsible for 25% of Acme's total sales. This year Davis is credited with 35% of Acme's total sales, which have decreased overall compared to last year's total sales.

   Which of the following could be true of Davis' sales this year as compared with Davis' sales from last year? Select all that apply.

   I. Davis' total sales at Acme were greater this year.
   II. Davis' total sales at Acme were greater last year.
   III. Davis' total sales at Acme were the same over the last two years.

Formal Logic Additive Inference Drill

Each of the following statements has three or more elements linked in a relationship. First, diagram the relationship, and then list each additive inference, if any, that result from the relationship. Inherent inferences will not appear in the answer key. For a complete discussion of Formal Logic as applied to the LSAT, please review Chapter 13 of the *Logical Reasoning Bible*. *Answers on page 68*

Example: Some Rs are Ss
All Ss are Ts

Diagram: R ←s→ S ⟶ T

Inference(s): R ←s→ T

---

1. All Es are Fs.
Some Fs are Gs
No Gs are Hs

Diagram:

Inference(s):

2. Some As are Bs
Some Bs are Cs
Most Cs are Ds

Diagram:

Inference(s):

3. Some Ws are Xs
All Xs are Ys
Most Ys are Zs

Diagram:

Inference(s):

4. Some Hs are Is
No Is are Js
No Js are Ks

Diagram:

Inference(s):

Formal Logic Additive Inference Drill

5. No Ts are Us
   All Us are Vs
   Most Vs are Ws

   Diagram:

   Inference(s):

6. More than half of Ms are Ns
   Some Ns are Os
   All Os are Ps

   Diagram:

   Inference(s):

7. All Qs are Rs
   Most Rs are Ss
   Some Ss are Ts

   Diagram:

   Inference(s):

Identify the Question Stem Drill Answer Key—page 6

1. Which of the following can properly be inferred from the statements above?

Question Type: Must Be True

On the LSAT, when an answer choice can be "properly inferred," that means that it Must Be True.

---

2. Which of the following arguments is most similar in its pattern of reasoning to the argument presented above?

Question Type: Parallel Reasoning

Here you are asked to find the choice which is "most similar" in its reasoning to the argument presented in the stimulus. Since the task here is to parallel the argumentative pattern presented, this is a Parallel Reasoning question.

---

3. Which one of the following is an assumption required by the argument above?

Question Type: Assumption

This question is fairly straightforward: when we are looking for an assumption required by the author's conclusion, we are dealing with an Assumption question.

---

4. Which one of the following, if assumed, would allow the writer's conclusion to be properly drawn?

Question Type: Justify the Conclusion

In this case you are asked to find the answer choice which allows the conclusion to be "properly drawn" or fully justified—that is, the choice which, if true, will Justify the Conclusion.

Identify the Question Stem Drill Answer Key—page 6

5. The author of the editorial proceeds by

Question Type: Method of Reasoning

The question here asks how the author "proceeds," or what method the author chooses to develop the argument presented, so this is a Method of Reasoning question.

---

6. The answer to which one of the following questions would be most helpful in evaluating the physician's argument?

Question Type: Evaluate the Argument

Here you are asked to choose the question which would be most helpful in evaluating an argument presented in the stimulus. From the wording of the question we can determine that this is an Evaluate the Argument question.

---

7. If the statements above are true, which one of the following must be false?

Question Type: Cannot Be True

The correct answer choice here is "must be false," which is the same as saying that it "cannot be true." So among the five answer choices, the four wrong answer choices will fall under the category of "could be true" and only one answer choice will be provably false, based on the information provided in the stimulus.

---

8. Which one of the following, if true, would provide the most support for the politician's conclusion?

Question Type: Strengthen

The phrase, "Which of the following, if true…" indicates that this question belongs to either the second or third question family. In this case, since we are looking for the answer choice which lends support, we are dealing with a Strengthen question.

Identify the Question Stem Drill Answer Key—page 6

9. All of the following, if true, would help to resolve the apparent discrepancy EXCEPT

Question Type: Resolve the ParadoxX

The use of the term "resolve" should alert you to the fact that your task will be to resolve the paradox. Since this is an EXCEPT question, every answer choice will provide resolution except for one. That is, the four incorrect answer choices will effectively resolve the discrepancy, and the correct answer choice will be the one which fails to do so.

---

10. Which one of the following best expresses the main point of the argument?

Question Type: Main Point

Some questions are easier to classify than others. When a question requires you to find the main point of the argument presented, you will probably recognize it as a Main Point question.

---

11. The argument above is most vulnerable to which one of the following criticisms?

Question Type: Flaw in the Reasoning

When a question stem describes an argument as being "vulnerable to criticism," this means that the argument presented in the stimulus is not a perfect argument. Because you are charged with the task of finding the flaw, this question type is Flaw in the Reasoning.

---

12. If the statements above are true, all of the following must be true EXCEPT

Question Type: Must Be True Except

For Must questions, we generally need to find the answer choice which is confirmed by the stimulus. Since this is a Must Except question, that means that the four incorrect answer choices must be true, and can all be confirmed by the information in the stimulus. The one correct answer choice will be the only one that is not dictated to be true—the one which is not necessarily true.

Identify the Question Stem Drill Answer Key—page 6

13. Which one of the following, if true, justifies the conclusion above?

Question Type: Justify the Conclusion

This example is clearly recognizable as a Justify the Conclusion question stem, so the correct answer choice will allow complete confidence in the validity of the conclusion drawn by the author.

---

14. Which one of the following, if true, would most seriously undermine the argument presented in the editorial?

Question Type: Weaken

Since this question stem begins with "Which of the following, if true…" we know that this question belongs to either the second or third family. Since the correct answer choice will in this case undermine the argument, this must be a Weaken question.

---

15. The dialogue above supports the claim that Ned and Michelle disagree about which of the following issues?

Question Type: Point at Issue

This question stem is likely to follow a dialogue, and the phrase "disagree about" tells us that it is a Point at Issue question. To find the correct answer choice, which will reflect the point of contention between the speakers, we can apply the Agree/Disagree Test.

Premise and Conclusion Analysis Drill Answer Key—page 8

1. At Umberland University, students given a choice between taking more advanced courses in their major or introductory courses in unrelated disciplines typically chose to take the introductory courses. This shows that, contrary to expectations, students are more interested in broadening their horizons than in concentrating their knowledge in a single field.

Conclusion: Students are more interested in broadening their horizons than in concentrating their knowledge in a single field.

Premise: At Umberland University, students given a choice between taking more advanced courses in their major or introductory courses in unrelated disciplines typically chose to take the introductory courses.

Premise: Contrary to expectations [implies that expectations were that the students would take the advanced courses in their major].

The conclusion is introduced by the phrase "This shows that."

The argument is weak. The conclusion assumes that the cause of the course is a preference for broadening one's horizons, when in fact there could have been other causes, such as better schedule availability, better professors, or a desire to maximize grade point average.

Premise and Conclusion Analysis Drill Answer Key—page 8

2. Some researchers claim that many mnemonic devices actually function more as a result of a process called "temporal fixation" and less as a function of long-term memory. But this conclusion is suspect. Research has shown that temporal fixation is simply a short-term memory process that transitions into long-term memory.

Conclusion:	But this conclusion is suspect.
Premise:	Some researchers claim that many mnemonic devices actually function more as a result of a process called "temporal fixation" and less as a function of long-term memory.
Premise:	Research has shown that temporal fixation is simply a short-term memory process that transitions into long-term memory.

Note the use of the "Some researchers claim..." device. This construction raises a viewpoint that the author eventually argues against.

The argument is strong. The author provides evidence that suggests that the claim may be questionable, and on that basis concludes that the claim may be "suspect." Had the author stated that the claim was false, then the conclusion would have been too strong and the argument would have been weak.

Premise and Conclusion Analysis Drill Answer Key—page 8

3. The "tiny house" movement advocates living in very small homes in a simple fashion. Although no set standards exist on what defines a tiny house, the focus is on small living spaces utilized in an environmentally-friendly manner. Given the range of benefits offered by tiny homes—a decreased energy and carbon footprint, affordable sheltering for displaced persons, and an increased population density—it is imperative that tax laws and urban codes be altered to allow for tax breaks and other incentives that will increase the building, adoption, and use of tiny homes.

Conclusion: It is imperative that tax laws and urban codes be altered to allow for tax breaks and other incentives that will increase the building, adoption, and use of tiny homes.

Premise: The "tiny house" movement advocates living in very small homes in a simple fashion.

Premise: Although no set standards exist on what defines a tiny house, the focus is on small living spaces utilized in an environmentally-friendly manner.

Premise: Given the range of benefits offered by tiny homes—a decreased energy and carbon footprint, affordable sheltering for displaced persons, and an increased population density—…

The conclusion is not introduced by a traditional indicator, but is instead contained in a sentence that begins with a premise indicator ("given that") and transitions to the conclusion with the factual declarative "it is."

The conclusion is too strong, and makes this a weak argument. The word "imperative" means "required" or "absolutely must occur," and the author has only shown that it may be advisable that laws and codes be altered, not that it is absolutely necessary. There could be considerations that are not addressed here that counter the benefits of the tiny house movement.

Premise and Conclusion Analysis Drill Answer Key—page 8

4. In the feudal system of Medieval Europe, land or a right to work the land was typically offered in exchange for services. A tiered system existed with the King at the apex, providing land to the noble classes of knights and barons, who in exchange pledged fealty and provided soldiers and arms during times of war and unrest. The noble classes in turn provided land rights to lower classes, who often farmed and provided goods and services back to the nobility. Perhaps unsurprisingly, this system often produced poor living conditions for the lowest classes of society, and by the 16th century feudalism had largely disappeared.

Premise: In the feudal system of Medieval Europe, land or a right to work the land was typically offered in exchange for services.

Premise: A tiered system existed with the King at the apex, providing land to the noble classes of knights and barons, who in exchange pledged fealty and provided soldiers and arms during times of war and unrest.

Premise: The noble classes in turn provided land rights to lower classes, who often farmed and provided goods and services back to the nobility.

Premise: Perhaps unsurprisingly, this system often produced poor living conditions for the lowest classes of society, and by the 16th century feudalism had largely disappeared.

Be careful, there is no conclusion here! This is simply a set of factual statements, and no conclusion or summary thought is provided. Thus, no argument analysis can be made.

Premise and Conclusion Analysis Drill Answer Key—page 8

5. Many cultures share taboos concerning watching others eat. Some anthropologists have argued that these taboos arise from concerns about appropriate conduct around relatives, guests, and strangers; others suggest that the taboos relate to historical resource scarcity and famine. Undoubtedly, both hypotheses are correct. Social rules that prohibit certain behaviors are common to nearly all societies, and these prohibitions often arise from practical concerns about maintaining order and self-preservation.

Conclusion:	Undoubtedly, both hypotheses are correct.
Premise:	Many cultures share taboos concerning watching others eat.
Premise:	Some anthropologists have argued that these taboos arise from concerns about appropriate conduct around relatives, guests, and strangers;
Premise:	Others suggest that the taboos relate to historical resource scarcity and famine.
Premise:	Social rules that prohibit certain behaviors are common to nearly all societies, and these prohibitions often arise from practical concerns about maintaining order and self-preservation.

Notice the way the argument introduces two viewpoints in the second sentence ("Some anthropologists…"). The LSAT often presents the viewpoint of some person or group at the beginning of an argument that the author eventually argues against. However, here the author synthesizes the two viewpoints into the conclusion that both are correct. This is a very "modern" LSAT construction.

The argument is somewhat weak as given, but needn't have been. One issue is the author's use of "undoubtedly" in the conclusion. Language of likelihood is always worth noting, and here the near-absolute nature of "undoubtedly" overstates the case: while the author does offer evidence that both hypotheses *may* explain taboos about watching others eat, and suggest a way the hypotheses *could* be related to each other, the conclusion itself is too strong. If the author had lessened the degree of certainty in the conclusion the argument would be far easier to accept. For instance, the author would be better served concluding "it is possible that both hypotheses are correct," or even "it is likely that both hypotheses are correct."

Premise and Conclusion Analysis Drill Answer Key—page 8

6. Recent analysis of sugar addiction studies shows that restrictive diets may lead some dieters to binge eat. Animal studies indicate that addiction-type behaviors towards sugar occur only in animals on restrictive diets. Animals with unrestricted access to food exhibited no such behavior. The studies found no chemical mechanism responsible for sugar addiction. Instead, intermittent access to sweet foods correlated with bouts of excessive sugar consumption.

Conclusion: Recent analysis of sugar addiction studies shows that restrictive diets may lead some dieters to binge eat.

Premise: Animal studies indicate that addiction-type behaviors towards sugar occur only in animals on restrictive diets.

Premise: Animals with unrestricted access to food exhibited no such behavior.

Premise: The studies found no chemical mechanism responsible for sugar addiction.

Premise: Instead, intermittent access to sweet foods correlated with bouts of excessive sugar consumption.

The argument is relatively strong, mainly because the language used in the conclusion is fairly broad ("may lead") and does not absolutely commit the author to the conclusion's claim. In leaving open the possibility that the conclusion may not be entirely true, or that exceptions could exist, the author increases the likelihood that the argument is a reasonable one.

That said, is the argument airtight? No. Due to the use of both statistical evidence as well as causal reasoning there are still ways you could weaken (or strengthen) the conclusion. There could be an alternate cause for the binge eating. There could be other studies that the analysis did not consider that present counterevidence and thus suggest a different conclusion. Further, it could be claimed that animal studies may not be applicable to human behavior. The list of potential objections is enough to prevent the argument from being completely unassailable.

However, because the author couches the conclusion in relatively soft terms, a defense against these counter-claims remains possible and the argument could theoretically survive them.

Conditional Reasoning Diagramming Drill Answer Key—page 13

1. To be eligible for the drawing, entries must be postmarked by May 1.

Diagram: Eligible for Drawing ⟶ Postmark May 1

Contrapostive: Postmark May 1 ⟶ Eligible for Drawing

Diagram: For eligibility, it is *necessary* that entrees are postmarked by May 1. Note that an entry that is postmarked by May 1 is not *guaranteed* eligibility (this would represent a mistaken reversal of the rule).

Contrapositive: If a letter is not postmarked by May 1, it will not be eligible for the drawing.

---

2. You cannot pass airport security without a valid boarding pass.

Diagram: Pass security ⟶ Valid boarding pass

Contrapositive: Valid boarding pass ⟶ Pass security

Diagram: If someone has successfully passed through the airport security gate, we know that person must have a valid boarding pass.

Contrapositive: If you don't have a valid boarding pass, you cannot pass security.

---

3. Car seatbelts are required for all children over the age of 7.

Diagram: Over age 7 ⟶ Car seat belt required

Contrapositive: Car seat belt required ⟶ Over age 7

Diagram: Since "required" refers to car seatbelts, the seatbelts must be the necessary condition. In other words, for every person over the age of 7, car seatbelts are a necessity.

Contrapositive: If one is not required to wear a seat belt, one must not be over the age of 7.

Conditional Reasoning Diagramming Drill Answer Key—page 13

4. No student who fails the test will be admitted to the school.

Diagram: Fail ⟶ ~~Admit~~

Contrapositive: Admit ⟶ ~~Fail~~

Diagram: As a rule of thumb, expressions such as "no A is a B" can be represented as "if A, then not B" (and "if B, then not A"). So, failing the test is sufficient to guarantee rejection. In other words: If you fail the test, you will not be admitted.

Contrapositive: If a student is admitted, that student must not have failed the test (i.e., that student must have passed the test).

---

5. You cannot find cheap airfare to Barcelona unless you book your tickets months in advance.

Diagram: Find cheap airfare to BCN ⟶ Book months in advance

Contrapositive: ~~Book months in advance~~ ⟶ ~~Find cheap airfare to BCN~~

Diagram: Since "unless" modifies "book your tickets months in advance," we can apply the Unless Formula: scheduling in advance becomes the necessary condition. The remainder ("it is impossible to find cheap airfare to Barcelona") can be negated by changing the word "impossible" to "possible." Thus, if anyone is going to be able to find cheap airfare, they must book their tickets months in advance.

Contrapositive: If you don't book months in advance, you will not be able to find cheap airfare.

Conditional Reasoning Diagramming Drill Answer Key—page 13

6. The amendment to the bill will pass only if some members of the opposition party vote for it.

Diagram: Amendment passes ⟶ Opposition votes

Contrapositive: Opposi~~ti~~on votes ⟶ Amend~~m~~ent passes

Diagram: Since "only if" refers to "some members of the opposition party vote for the amendment," the opposition votes are a necessary condition for the passage of the amendment. So, if the amendment passes, it is clear that some members of the opposition party voted for it.

Contrapositive: If no members of the opposition party vote for the bill, it will not pass.

---

7. Further Lane is the only way to reach the marina.

Diagram: Reach the marina ⟶ Further Lane

Contrapositive: Furthe~~r L~~ane ⟶ Reach ~~t~~he marina

Diagram: Since Further Lane is the only way to reach the marina, we know that anyone who has reached the marina must have taken Further Lane.

You must be sure to note what part of the sentence is modified by the word "only." In this case, because taking Further Lane is the only way to reach the marina, "only" refers to Further Lane. Further Lane is thus the necessary condition, and reaching the marina is the sufficient.

Contrapositive: If one does not take Further Lane, one cannot reach the marina.

Conditional Reasoning Diagramming Drill Answer Key—page 13

8. In order to park at the beach, residents must first obtain a beach pass.

Diagram: Park at the beach ⟶ Obtain pass

Contrapostive: Obtain pass ⟶ Park at the beach

Diagram: Since "in order to" refers to "park at the beach", parking at the beach becomes the sufficient condition. Likewise, because "must" refers to "obtain a beach pass," securing a beach pass is the necessary condition. So, if someone is parking on the beach, it is clear that a pass has been obtained.

Contrapositive: If one does not obtain a beach pass, one cannot park at the beach.

---

9. To win with honor, one must not cheat.

Diagram: Win with Honor ⟶ Cheat

Contrapositive: Cheat ⟶ Win with Honor

Diagram: If one wishes to win with honor, it is *necessary* that one avoid cheating.

Contrapositive: If you cheat, you cannot win with honor.

Conditional Reasoning Diagramming Drill Answer Key—page 13

10. Either Patrick or Miranda will win the literary contest.

Diagram: ~~Patrick~~ ⟶ Miranda

Contrapositive: ~~Miranda~~ ⟶ Patrick

Diagram: The formulation "Either A or B" essentially means "if not A, then B" (and "if not B, then A"). In other words, if Patrick does not win the literary contest, then we know that Miranda surely will.

Contrapositive: If Miranda does not win the contest, Patrick will win.

Note: "either…or" does not preclude the possibility of both events occurring at the same time: it is entirely possible that Patrick and Miranda could both win the contest. Either way, if one of them does not win, the other one will.

---

11. Whenever a package is shipped, the system generates a unique tracking number.

Diagram: Shipped ⟶ Unique tracking number

Contrapositive: ~~Unique tracking number~~ ⟶ ~~Shipped~~

Diagram: Since "whenever" is a sufficient condition indicator, shipping a package is sufficient to guarantee that a unique number has been generated.

Contrapositive: Based on the conditional rule that was provided, if a package has not been issued a unique tracking number, it has not shipped.

Conditional Reasoning Diagramming Drill Answer Key—page 13

12. The only way for a company to maintain its stock price is by paying a dividend.

Diagram: Maintain stock price ——→ Pay dividend

Contrapositive: Pay dividend (negated) ——→ Maintain stock price (negated)

Diagram: In this case, because paying a dividend is the only way to maintain a stock price, "only" refers to paying the dividend (the only way to maintain the price). Therefore, paying dividends is the necessary condition, and maintaining the stock price – the sufficient. Thus, if the company is to maintain its stock price, it is necessary to pay the dividend.

Contrapositive: If this company chooses not to pay a dividend, the company will not be able to maintain its stock price.

---

13. Students will not receive their diplomas until all requirements for graduation have been satisfied.

Diagram: Diploma ——→ Grad requirements satisfied

Contrapositive: Grad requirements satisfied (negated) ——→ Diploma (negated)

Diagram: "Until" works like "unless," so we can use the Unless Formula to create the conditional diagram. Since "until" modifies "satisfying all requirements for graduation," that becomes the necessary condition. If a student has received his or her diploma, we know that all requirements for graduation have been satisfied.

Contrapositive: If a student has not satisfied all requirements for graduation, that student cannot receive a diploma.

Conditional Reasoning Diagramming Drill Answer Key—page 13

14. Taxpayers must either declare all received income or face a penalty.

Diagram: Declare all income ⟶ Face a penalty

Contrapositive: Face penalty ⟶ Declare all income

Diagram: The formulation "Either A or B" essentially means "if not A, then B" (and "if not B, then A"). If tax payers do not declare all income, they must face a penalty.

Contrapositive: If a tax payer is not facing penalties, we know that the tax payer must have declared all of his or her income.

---

15. No one without sufficient exposure to linear algebra can enroll in this seminar.

Diagram: Sufficient algebra exposure ⟶ Enroll

Contrapositive: Enroll ⟶ Sufficient algebra exposure

Diagram: A simpler and clearer way to rephrase this conditional sentence would be, "If one does not have sufficient exposure to linear algebra, one cannot enroll in this seminar."

Contrapositive: Thus, if one is allowed to enroll in this seminar, we know that person must have sufficient algebra exposure.

Conditional Reasoning Diagramming Drill Answer Key—page 13

16. Suspects shall be presumed innocent until proven guilty.

Diagram: Presumed innocent ⟶ Proven guilty

Contrapositive: Proven guilty ⟶ Presumed innocent

Diagram: Again we can use the Unless Formula to create the conditional diagram. In this case, since "until" modifies "proven guilty," proving someone guilty becomes the necessary condition. Thus, if a suspect is not presumed innocent, he or she must be guilty.

Contrapositive: If a suspect is not proven guilty, he or she must be presumed innocent.

---

17. Extraordinary ideas require innovative minds.

Diagram: Extraordinary Ideas ⟶ Innovative minds

Contrapositive: Innovative minds ⟶ Extraordinary ideas

Diagram: Because innovative minds are a requirement for extraordinary ideas, the minds become the necessary condition and the ideas – the sufficient. "A requires B" essentially means "If A, then B." That is, if we are to have extraordinary ideas, we will require innovative minds.

Contrapositive: If we do not have the required innovative minds, we will not have extraordinary ideas.

Conditional Reasoning Diagramming Drill Answer Key—page 13

18. You cannot lose if you do not play.

Diagram: ~~Play~~ ⟶ ~~Lose~~

Contrapositive: Lose ⟶ Play

Diagram: Do not be misled by the order of presentation here: because the sufficient condition "if" modifies "do not play," the second part of the sentence is the sufficient condition ("not play") and the first part is the necessary ("cannot lose"). In other words, a more straightforward version of this sentence would be, "If you do not play, you cannot lose."

Contrapositive: If you lose, then you must have played.

---

19. Except for Mary, everyone came to the party.

Diagram: ~~Come to the party~~ ⟶ Mary

Contrapositive: ~~Mary~~ ⟶ Come to the party

Diagram: Since "except" modifies "Mary," Mary becomes the necessary condition. The remainder is negated to produce "not come to the party." Thus, if anyone did not come to the party, then that person must be Mary.

Contrapositive: If a person is not Mary, that person must have come to the party.

---

20. No student can receive high honors unless he or she has submitted a senior thesis.

Diagram: High honors ⟶ Senior thesis

Contrapositive: ~~Senior thesis~~ ⟶ ~~High honors~~

Diagram: Because "unless" modifies writing a senior thesis, "senior thesis" becomes the necessary condition. The remainder ("no student can receive high honors") is negated. Thus, if any student receives high honors, that student must have submitted a senior thesis.

Contrapositive: If one has not submitted a senior thesis, one cannot receive high honors.

Either/Or, Multiple Condition, and Double Arrow Diagramming Drill Answer Key—page 16

The answer key for each problem contains a duplicate of the problem with the conditional indicators in italics, a legend for the symbols used to represent each condition, a diagrammatic representation of the statement and its contrapositive, and occasional notes for each problem.

Note: Because a conditional statement and its contrapositive are identical in meaning, the order in which the two arrow diagrams appear is not important.

1. The proposal will pass *if and only if* there is no opposition.

   Pass = proposal will pass   O = opposition

   P ⟷ ~~O~~

---

2. We will go to the beach *only if* the weather is nice *and* we can get the day off.

   GB = go to the beach
   WN = weather is nice
   DO = we can get the day off

   GB ⟶ WN and DO

   ~~WN~~ or ~~DO~~ ⟶ ~~GB~~

Either/Or, Multiple Condition, and Double Arrow Diagramming Drill Answer Key—page 16

3. The concert will be cancelled *if* ticket sales are insufficient *or* if it rains.

CC = Concert Cancelled
TSI = Ticket sales insufficient
R = Rain

~~CC~~ ⟶ ~~TSI~~ and ~~R~~

---

4. Unless private donations increase *or* ticket sales go up, the museum will raise admission fees.

PDI = Private donations increase
TSU = Ticket sales go up
MRA = Museum will raise admission fees

~~MRA~~ ⟶ PDI or TSU

~~PDI~~ and ~~TSU~~ ⟶ MRA

---

5. *Either* Scott *or* Michelle will drive the carpool on Sunday.

S = Scott will drive
M = Michelle will drive

~~S~~ ⟶ M

~~M~~ ⟶ S

Note: If we also were told that the carpool could have only one driver, then a second set of diagrams would also apply, indicating that if Scott drives, Michelle does not, and vice-versa.

Either/Or, Multiple Condition, and Double Arrow Diagramming Drill Answer Key—page 16

6. When the parties agree and the details have been finalized, we will sign the contract.

PA = Parties agree
DF = Details have been finalized
SC = We will sign the contract

PA and DF ⟶ SC

~~SC~~ ⟶ ~~PA~~ or ~~DF~~

---

7. In order to be prepared for the test, you *must* study *and* get plenty of sleep.

PT = prepared for the test
ST = study
PS = plenty of sleep

PT ⟶ ST and PS

~~PS~~ or ~~ST~~ ⟶ ~~PT~~

Either/Or, Multiple Condition, and Double Arrow Diagramming Drill Answer Key—page 16

8. The class cannot go on the field trip *until* transportation has been secured *and* all permission slips have been signed.

FT = field trip
TS = transportation secured
PSS = permission slips signed

FT ⟶ TS and PSS

~~TS~~ or ~~PSS~~ ⟶ ~~FT~~

---

9. If the plan is approved and the finances are secured, we will move forward.

PA = plan is approved
FS = finances are secured
MF = we will move forward

PA and FS ⟶ MF

~~MF~~ ⟶ ~~PA~~ or ~~FS~~

---

10. It's either fight or flight.

FI = fight
FL = flight

~~FI~~ ⟶ FL

~~FL~~ ⟶ FI

Statement Negation Drill Answer Key—page 18

The correct answer is listed below, with the negating elements italicized.

1. The president could veto the bill.

   The president *cannot* veto the bill.

   "Cannot" is the opposite of "could."

---

2. All of the teams played well.

   Not all of the teams played well.

---

3. Only one witness was present when the robbery took place.

   Not only one witness was present during the robbery.

---

4. If Smith gets elected, he will serve only one term as mayor.

   If Smith gets elected, he *might not* serve only one term as mayor.

   You can negate the necessary condition using "won't necessarily" or "might not."

---

5. The weather in this area is very predictable.

   The weather in this area is *not* very predictable.

---

6. The winner will not necessarily be determined during the first half of the game.

   The winner *will* be determined during the first half of the game.

Statement Negation Drill Answer Key—page 18

7. The detrimental effects of global warming can be felt everywhere.

   The detrimental effects of global warming *cannot* be felt everywhere.

   Note that we must be sure to negate the right words; changing "detrimental" to "beneficial" would not logically negate the statement.

---

8. You cannot enter unless you pay admission.

   Note that this is a conditional statement, and changing to an "if...then" construction can often be helpful. Here, the original statement could be restated as "If you do not pay admission, then you cannot enter."

   Thus the **negated** version of the original statement would be:

   (Even) if you do not pay admission, you *can* enter.

---

9. Early to bed and early to rise makes a person healthy, wealthy and wise.

   Early to bed and early to rise does *not necessarily* make a person healthy, wealthy and wise.

---

10. New methods of warfare led to increased casualty rates.

    New methods of warfare *did not* lead to increased casualty rates.

Justify Formula Drill—page 19

Note that any answer that contains the items below is correct. So, in the case of #1, an answer such as "Dr. Daktari is a professor at McClellan University with tenure, and she is also an outstanding public speaker," would also be correct. Justify questions are different from Assumption questions in that Justify questions can contain extraneous information in addition to the element that justifies the conclusion. If an answer does not make sense to you, simply add the premise to the correct answer, and you will see that when combined they produce the conclusion in each item.

1. Premise: Every professor at McClellan University with tenure has been published extensively.

   Conclusion: Dr. Daktari has been published extensively.

   Dr. Daktari is a professor at McClellan University with tenure.

   This problem is in the format of: Premise: A ⟶ B

   Conclusion: B

   Justifying statement: A

---

2. Premise: The combination of poor management and poor customer service causes sales to go down.

   Conclusion: Sales at Xmark Corporation declined last year.

   Xmark Corporation had a combination of poor management and poor customer service last year.

   This problem uses a causal premise. The conclusion asserts that the effect has occurred in a particular company last year, so the correct answer simply needs to indicate that the cause occurred in that company last year.

Justify Formula Drill—page 19

3. Premise: Some DaytonWilson drugs have been found to have dangerous side effects.

   Conclusion: DaytonWilson will be fined by the Food and Drug Administration.

   If any of DaytonWilson's drugs have been found to have side effects, then DaytonWilson will be fined by the Food and Drug Administration.

   This problem is in the format of: Premise: A

   Conclusion: B

   Justifying statement: A ⟶ B

---

4. Premise: If Carlos attends the meeting, then Hiroshi attends the meeting.

   Conclusion: Carlos does not attend the meeting.

   Hiroshi does not attend the meeting.

   This problem is in the format of: Premise: A ⟶ B

   Conclusion: $\not{A}$

   Justifying statement: $\not{B}$

---

5. Premise: This month there was an increase in the percentage of callers who made a purchase compared to last month.

   Conclusion: More callers made a purchase this month than made a purchase last month.

   The number of callers did not decrease from the last month.

   This problem features numbers and percentages. The test makers could have used an answer that roughly is equivalent to "the rate of decrease of callers did not exceed the rate of increase of purchase percentage," but this is less likely to occur without some knowledge of the size of the groups.

Identify the Flaw in the Argument Drill Answer Key—page 21

1. After several periods of record sales increases, the Janacek Group relocated their offices to the new Industrial Pointe complex and chose one of the most expensive office suites in the city. Despite the significant financial investment required, Janacek executives defended the move by noting the benefits to Janacek's image that would come with a location in a complex which, they concluded, must house all of the city's most expensive office space.

Error of Composition

An error of composition occurs when a person attributes a characteristic of part of the group or entity to the group or entity as a whole or to each member of the group. In this instance, the Janacek executives make the mistake of thinking that because their office suite is among the most expensive in the city, that the office building must contain all of the city's most expensive office space.

---

2. Offshore oil drilling has long been a risky endeavor, but oil companies and related industries argue strenuously that no further restrictions should be placed on such drilling due to our country's need for energy resources, and the possible serious consequences if such energy reserves are not located and explored now. Of course, the vast sums of money the oil companies stand to make from such drilling automatically make their arguments suspect.

Source Argument

Although the oil companies apparently make an argument in favor of continued drilling based on the energy needs of the country, the author calls their position suspect because the oil companies stand to make a considerable sum of money from drilling. This is a form of Source Argument, where the author imputes a motive or action to the source as opposed to addressing factual reasons for rejecting the proposal.

Identify the Flaw in the Argument Drill Answer Key—page 21

3. Supporters of the theory of global warming claim that carbon emissions are causing our environment to slowly warm, which will eventually produce catastrophic results. However, this past winter was one of the coldest on record. Therefore, the claim that global warming is accelerating is false.

Error in the Use of Evidence

Some evidence against a position is taken to prove that the position is false or invalid. Note that this argument does not contain a causal error although causal language is used. There is no causal error because the author simply describes a position involving causal reasoning held by another group (the supporters of the global warming theory); the author does not draw a causal conclusion in this argument.

---

4. When temperatures drop just below freezing, the plant pathogen *Pseudomonas syringae* produces certain proteins that force ice to form on the surface of a plant. The damage caused by the freezing process releases plant nutrients that are then available to the *Pseudomonas syringae* bacteria. Although this fruit grove contains *Pseudomonas syringae* bacteria, temperatures have not dropped below freezing at any point during the last 30 days, so there should be no concern over *Pseudomonas syringae*-related frost damage during that period.

Error of Conditional Reasoning—Mistaken Negation

In the first sentence, the argument establishes a conditional relationship between below freezing temperatures and *Pseudomonas syringae* frost damage:

Temperatures below freezing ——→ *Pseudomonas syringae* cause plant damage

The last sentence indicates that the sufficient condition about temperatures has not been met during the last 30 days, and then concludes that the necessary condition about bacteria damage also has not been met. This error is a Mistaken Negation, which arises when the lack of occurrence of a sufficient condition is used to conclude that a necessary condition will not occur.

Identify the Flaw in the Argument Drill Answer Key—page 21

5. Will executor: The maker of this will left a number of antiques as gifts to her descendants. I recently attempted to have each antique evaluated for value by a local university professor who is an international expert in the valuation and authentication of antiques. This month, however, she will be too busy to examine all of the pieces. Therefore, I must take all of the antiques to the local appraising firm for valuation.

False Dilemma

The will executor indicates that one option for the appraisal of the antiques—a local university expert—is unavailable, and on that basis concludes that the antiques must be taken to a local appraisal firm. Thus, by eliminating one choice and then concluding that another choice must be made, the argument assumes there are only two choices. This error is known as a False Dilemma because other options for appraisal may exist.

---

6. Last year, within the sales division of the company, the salespeople with highest average number of miles driven each week had the highest sales figures. Thus, we should immediately implement a policy requiring all salespeople to begin driving more miles each week.

Error of Causal Reasoning—Mistaking a Correlation for Causation

The argument describes a correlation: salespeople who drive more miles have greater sales figures. On the basis of this information, the author assumes that the higher mileage is causing the greater sales figures, and draws a conclusion advocating that all salespeople drive more miles every week. As with all LSAT causal conclusions, this one is flawed because the correlation does not have to be causal, or the relationship could be different from one where miles driven raises sales figures (for example, perhaps the relationship is reversed: the more lucrative territories have more companies, and visiting each requires more driving).

Identify the Flaw in the Argument Drill Answer Key—page 21

7. Each member of Dr. Martin's research team is now well-known among the particle physics scientific community. We know this because the team recently published a ground breaking physics paper on baryon asymmetry. The paper created great excitement among those who study particle physics, and there has been intense debate on what the results of the paper mean for the science of particle physics. Consequently, the work of Dr. Martin's team of researchers has become world-renowned.

Error of Division

An error of division occurs when the author attributes a characteristic of the whole of a group to each member of the group. In this case, the first sentence is the main conclusion of the argument, namely that "Each member of Dr. Martin's research team is now well-known among the particle physics scientific community." This is supported by the premise/subconclusion in the final sentence that "the work of Dr. Martin's team of researchers has become world-renowned." Note as always the critical importance of understanding that a conclusion in an argument can be the main conclusion, or just a subsidiary conclusion.

---

8. Car Advertisement: The new Electra Argive is among the best-driving cars on the road today. A recent poll at our dealerships of interested drivers who had test-driven the Argive rated it among the top cars they had driven, and over 80% of those drivers indicated they would be buying an Argive in the near future.

Survey Error—Biased Sample

The advertisement states that the new Argive is "among the best-driving cars on the road today." The basis for this claim are the results of a survey of individuals who have test-driven the Argive. However, these individuals constitute a biased sample as they were at the dealership, had just test-driven the car, and were ostensibly "interested" in purchasing the car. The Argive may indeed be a car that drives well, but an independent panel of experts would provide better proof for that claim.

Identify the Flaw in the Argument Drill Answer Key—page 21

9. Thompson has rightly been lauded for his academic achievements at this school, but Thompson is also an excellent overall athlete and he is obviously the school's best runner. This claim is decisively proven in those instances when Thompson does lose a race, because Thompson obviously would not lose unless the other runners cheated.

Circular Reasoning

The latter part of the conclusion of the argument is that Thompson is the school's best runner. The author attempts to support this conclusion by saying that if Thompson loses, someone must have cheated (*since Thompson, the school's best runner, would not lose!*) As this premise assumes the conclusion that the author is attempting to establish, the argument is circular and therefore flawed.

---

10. New restaurant manager: Several employees complained about the firing of a recently trained waiter after his very first erroneous order. They claim that the previous manager had been quite lenient with regard to the first few mistakes made by any recent trainee, but this claim is clearly false. I know the previous manager, and she would not have tolerated countless errors without any repercussions, even if those errors were made by recent trainees.

Straw Man

In a Straw Man argument, the author distorts the opposition argument, thereby making it easier to attack. In this argument, several employees claimed that the previous manager "had been quite lenient with regard to the first few mistakes made by any recent trainee." The author recasts this position later, stating that the previous manager "would not have tolerated countless errors without any repercussions." This is a different position than the one made by the employees, and one that makes their position seem less defensible.

Identify the Flaw in the Argument Drill Answer Key—page 21

11. Within certain library departments, established practice dictates that seniority be used as the main criterion for job advancement. Thereby, the employee who has worked the most years has priority in the promotion process. However, this process is patently unfair. Janet Watson, the local mayor, recently spoke out against this process and strongly criticized the library administration for adhering to what she called "a completely obsolete system.

Appeal Fallacy—Appeal to Authority

In this case, the authors' evidence for the conclusion that "this process is patently unfair" are the statements of the local mayor. This is a classic Appeal Fallacy because the opinion of an authority is used to attempt to persuade the reader.

---

12. Veterinarian: There is serious cause for concern with the cattle herds in this state. Yesterday I treated two cows for listeriosis, a disease of the central nervous system, and the day before that I treated two different cows for the very same malady. We need to immediately begin testing all cows in the state for this disease, and take curative action on any cow exhibiting signs of illness.

Exceptional Case/Overgeneralization

The conclusion that all cows in the state need to be tested is based on just four examples. Given that the claim is made regarding the testing of "all cows in the state," more cases would be needed to justify a program that broad.

---

13. Board member: The protesters who recently criticized the Board for taking advantage of a loophole in the city charter are falsely informed. Although the Board agreed to provide further financing to the city transit system, the Board did not use the bank owned by one of the Board members. Thus, as the protesters have failed to show that any board member gained any benefit from the action we took, their claim is false.

Error in the Use of Evidence

Lack of evidence for a position is taken to prove that the position is false. In this instance, the Board member states that there is no proof that "any board member gained any benefit from the action we took," and on the basis of this lack of evidence, concludes that the protesters' claim is false.

Identify the Flaw in the Argument Drill Answer Key—page 21

14. Richardson recently claimed that we must do something in response to the university's current economic crisis. I have repeatedly proposed that we layoff a percentage of all workers and simultaneously reduce all budgets to last year's levels. If we are to follow Richardson's advice, and actually do something, we must implement my program of action immediately.

Uncertain Use of a Term

This is a tricky argument that may at first appear to be an Appeal to Authority. But Richardson is not cited as an authority, so that is unlikely to be the flaw. Instead, the author's conclusion is based on a shift in meaning within the argument of the word "something." Richardson's initial comment takes "something" to mean "some action or solution," which would typically refer to the best solution; at the least, Richardson takes "something" to mean that a minimal action must occur. The author shifts the meaning of "something" to refer to his proposal specifically, as in "something" means "this thing."

---

15. Company Travel Manager: Although we had originally planned for the eight marketing department employees to drive the 250 miles to this week's advertising meeting, our car rental firm informed us today that no van will be available for rent until next week. Thus, we have no choice but to postpone the meeting.

False Dilemma

The Company Travel Manager states that because one option for travel is unavailable (driving a rented van), the conclusion is that the meeting must be postponed. This is a False Dilemma because other options most likely exist (e.g., an employee could drive his or her car, or the employees could take a bus or train, etc.).

Numbers and Percentages Practice Drill Answer Key—page 26

1. The Mercantile Corporation increased its national market share last year by 5% compared to its market share two years ago.

   Which of the following could be true of the overall unit sales of the Mercantile Corporation? Select all that apply.

   I. Mercantile Corporation sold fewer units last year than it had sold the prior year.
   II. Mercantile Corporation sold the same number of units each of the last two years.
   III. Mercantile Corporation sold more units last year than it had sold the prior year.

All three scenarios listed are plausible. The only information provided is a comparison of the corporation's market share from one year to the next. Without further information, regarding either the size of the overall market or Mercantile's unit sales, any of the scenarios presented are plausible.

<u>Statement I Hypothetical</u>:
Two years ago Mercantile Corporation had a 30% market share, having sold 30,000 out of a total 100,000 units sold by all producers nationally. Last year Mercantile had a 35% market share, having sold 3,500 out of a total of only 10,000 units sold by all producers nationally. In this scenario, thanks to a significant decrease in the overall market, the Mercantile Corporation's higher market share represented lower unit sales.

<u>Statement II Hypothetical</u>:
Two years ago Mercantile Corporation had a 20% market share, having sold 20,000 of 100,000 units sold by all producers nationally. Last year, Mercantile increased its market share to 25%, having sold 20,000 of 80,000 units sold by all producers nationally.

<u>Statement III Hypothetical</u>:
If the total number of units sold by all producers nationally remained constant over the past two years, e.g., the 5% increase in market share would clearly translate to a greater number of unit sales.

Numbers and Percentages Practice Drill Answer Key—page 26

2. In today's mayoral election, West received 1500 votes, compared with the 1000 votes that he had received in last year's election.

   Which of the following could be true of the percentage of the vote Mayor West won in today's election compared to the percentage he won in the last election? Select all that apply.

   I. West received a greater percentage of the vote today than in the last election.
   II. West received a smaller percentage of the vote today than in the last election.
   III. West received the same percentage of the vote today as in the last election.

The information provided is limited to the number of votes West received. Without further information about either the total number of residents who voted, or alternatively the number of votes received by the other candidates, I, II and III are all possible.

Statement I Hypothetical:
If the same number of residents voted in the two elections, then today's total of 1500 would, of course, represent a higher percentage of the total vote for West.

Statement II Hypothetical:
Today, West received 1500 out of 15000 total votes, representing 10% of all votes cast. In last year's election, he received 1000 out of 2000 total votes cast, representing 50% of all votes cast.

Statement III Hypothetical:
Today, West received 1500 out of 15000 total votes, representing 10% of all votes cast. In last year's election, West received 1000 out of 10000 total votes, requiring fewer votes to earn 10% of all votes cast.

Numbers and Percentages Practice Drill Answer Key—page 26

3. Halstead's and McGrady's are competing furniture stores, each of which carries exactly one type of couch. Next week Halstead's will have its annual holiday sale, during which every piece of furniture in the store is to be marked down by 60%. McGrady's has just announced a competing sale, in which various products will be marked down by 30%.

   Which of the following could be true of Halstead's couch price compared with McGrady's during next week's sale? Select all that apply.

   I. A couch purchased at Halstead's will cost less than a couch at McGrady's.
   II. A couch purchased at Halstead's will cost more than a couch at McGrady's.
   III. A couch purchased at Halstead's will cost the same as a couch at McGrady's.

Once again, of course, with such limited information, all things are possible. As we see in the real world, the impressive sounding sale doesn't always provide the best deals. Halstead's sale certainly sounds impressive; if the two stores normally charge the same prices, then of course Halstead's couch price will be lower during the sale. But if Halstead's prices generally start out significantly higher, then the 60% sale might result in a price that is equal to, or possibly even greater than, the price of McGrady's couch at 30% off.

Numbers and Percentages Practice Drill Answer Key—page 26

4. In response to brisk sales, a certain car dealership increased the price of the Cheetah, its best-selling sport utility vehicle, by 25% on January 1. In February, after no other price changes had been implemented, the dealership held a special sale during which the price of every car was marked down by 20%.

   Which of the following could be true of the price of the Cheetah during the February sale compared with the price on December 31 (just prior to the January 1 price change)?

   I. The price of the Cheetah was higher during the sale than it had been on December 31.
   II. The price of the Cheetah was lower during the sale than it had been on December 31.
   III. The price of the Cheetah was the same during the sale as it had been on December 31.

   Statement III presents the only plausible scenario given the information provided. Regardless of the price on December 31, a 25% increase followed by a 20% decrease has no net effect—the price charged for the Cheetah during the sale will be the same as the price charged on December 31.

---

5. Last year, Davis, Acme Company's top salesperson, was responsible for 25% of Acme's total sales. This year Davis is credited with 35% of Acme's total sales, which have decreased overall compared to last year's total sales.

   Which of the following could be true of Davis' sales this year as compared with Davis' sales from last year? Select all that apply.

   I. Davis' total sales at Acme were greater this year.
   II. Davis' total sales at Acme were greater last year.
   III. Davis' total sales at Acme were the same over the last two years.

   Without knowing more about the decrease in total sales from last year to this year, once again all scenarios listed are plausible.

Formal Logic Additive Inference Drill Answer Key—page 28

1. All Es are Fs.
   Some Fs are Gs
   No Gs are Hs

   Diagram: E ⟶ F ←s→ G ←|→ H

   Inferences: F ←s→ ~~H~~

---

2. Some As are Bs
   Some Bs are Cs
   Most Cs are Ds

   Diagram: A ←s→ B ←s→ C —M→ D

   Inferences: None

---

3. Some Ws are Xs
   All Xs are Ys
   Most Ys are Zs

   Diagram: W ←s→ X ⟶ Y —M→ Z

   Inferences: W ←s→ Y

---

4. Some Hs are Is
   No Is are Js
   No Js are Ks

   Diagram: H ←s→ I ←|→ J ←|→ K

   Inferences: H ←s→ ~~I~~

Formal Logic Additive Inference Drill Answer Key—page 28

5. No Ts are Us
   All Us are Vs
   Most Vs are Ws

   Diagram:

   Inferences: V ←—S—→ ~~T~~

---

6. More than half of Ms are Ns
   Some Ns are Os
   All Os are Ps

   Diagram: M —M→ N ←—S—→ O ——→ P

   Inferences: N ←—S—→ P

---

7. All Qs are Rs
   Most Rs are Ss
   Some Ss are Ts

   Diagram: Q ——→ R —M→ S ←—S—→ T

   Inferences: None

2

Chapter Two: PrepTest 44 Logical Reasoning Section I

Chapter Two: PrepTest 44 Logical Reasoning Section I

POWERSCORE
BY BARBRI

Chapter Notes

Each of the next five chapters contains a complete LSAT Logical Reasoning section. We recommend taking each as a timed exercise by allotting yourself 35 minutes to complete the section. Then, check your work against the answer key that immediately follows the section, and compare your answers to the answers and explanations provided.

As you begin this section, remember to consider your overall time and pacing strategy, and keep in mind that you are not required to complete the questions in the order they are presented to you. Take control of your performance, be focused, and stay calm to ensure your best performance. Good luck!

PrepTest 44

Logical Reasoning Section I

SECTION I
Time-35 minutes
25 Questions

Directions: The questions in this section are based on the reasoning contained in brief statements or passages. For some questions, more than one of the choices could conceivably answer the question. However, you are to choose the best answer; that is, the response that most accurately and completely answers the question. You should not make assumptions that are by commonsense standards implausible, superfluous, or incompatible with the passage. After you have chosen the best answer, blacken the corresponding space on your answer sheet.

1. The tidal range at a particular location is the difference in height between high tide and low tide. Tidal studies have shown that one of the greatest tidal ranges in the world is found in the Bay of Fundy and reaches more than seventeen meters. Since the only forces involved in inducing the tides are the sun's and moon's gravity, the magnitudes of tidal ranges also must be explained entirely by gravitational forces.

   Which one of the following most accurately describes a flaw in the reasoning above?

   (A) It gives only one example of a tidal range.
   (B) It fails to consider that the size of a tidal range could be affected by the conditions in which gravitational forces act.
   (C) It does not consider the possibility that low tides are measured in a different way than are high tides.
   (D) It presumes, without providing warrant, that most activity within the world's oceans is a result of an interplay of gravitational forces.
   (E) It does not differentiate between the tidal effect of the sun and the tidal effect of the moon.

2. Cardiologist: Coronary bypass surgery is commonly performed on patients suffering from coronary artery disease when certain other therapies would be as effective. Besides being relatively inexpensive, these other therapies pose less risk to the patient since they are less intrusive. Bypass surgery is especially debatable for single-vessel disease.

   The cardiologist's statements, if true, most strongly support which one of the following?

   (A) Bypass surgery is riskier than all alternative therapies.
   (B) Needless bypass surgery is more common today than previously.
   (C) Bypass surgery should be performed when more than one vessel is diseased.
   (D) Bypass surgery is an especially expensive therapy when used to treat single-vessel disease.
   (E) Sometimes there are equally effective alternatives to bypass surgery that involve less risk.

3. In the past, combining children of different ages in one classroom was usually a failure; it resulted in confused younger children, who were given inadequate attention and instruction, and bored older ones, who had to sit through previously learned lessons. Recently, however, the practice has been revived with excellent results. Mixed-age classrooms today are stimulating to older children and enable younger children to learn much more efficiently than in standard classrooms.

   Which one of the following, if true, most helps to resolve the apparent discrepancy in the passage?

   (A) On average, mixed-age classrooms today are somewhat larger in enrollment than were the ones of the past.
   (B) Mixed-age classrooms of the past were better equipped than are those of today.
   (C) Today's mixed-age classrooms, unlike those of the past, emphasize group projects that are engaging to students of different ages.
   (D) Today's mixed-age classrooms have students of a greater range of ages than did those of the past.
   (E) Few of the teachers who are reviving mixed-age classrooms today were students in mixed-age classrooms when they were young.

GO ON TO THE NEXT PAGE.

4. The top 50 centimeters of soil on Tiliga Island contain bones from the native birds eaten by the islanders since the first human immigration to the island 3,000 years ago. A comparison of this top layer with the underlying 150 centimeters of soil—accumulated over 80,000 years—reveals that before humans arrived on Tiliga, a much larger and more diverse population of birds lived there. Thus, the arrival of humans dramatically decreased the population and diversity of birds on Tiliga.

Which one of the following statements, if true, most seriously weakens the argument?

(A) The bird species known to have been eaten by the islanders had few natural predators on Tiliga.
(B) Many of the bird species that disappeared from Tiliga did not disappear from other, similar, uninhabited islands until much later.
(C) The arrival of a species of microbe, carried by some birds but deadly to many others, immediately preceded the first human immigration to Tiliga.
(D) Bones from bird species known to have been eaten by the islanders were found in the underlying 150 centimeters of soil.
(E) The birds that lived on Tiliga prior to the first human immigration generally did not fly well.

5. The corpus callosum—the thick band of nerve fibers connecting the brain's two hemispheres—of a musician is on average larger than that of a nonmusician. The differences in the size of corpora callosa are particularly striking when adult musicians who began training around the age of seven are compared to adult nonmusicians. Therefore, musical training, particularly when it begins at a young age, causes certain anatomic brain changes.

Which one of the following is an assumption on which the argument depends?

(A) The corpora callosa of musicians, before they started training, do not tend to be larger than those of nonmusicians of the same age.
(B) Musical training late in life does not cause anatomic changes to the brain.
(C) For any two musicians whose training began around the age of seven, their corpora callosa are approximately the same size.
(D) All musicians have larger corpora callosa than do any nonmusicians.
(E) Adult nonmusicians did not participate in activities when they were children that would have stimulated any growth of the corpus callosum.

6. Chai: The use of the word "tree" to denote both deciduous and coniferous plant forms, while acceptable as a lay term, is scientifically inadequate; it masks the fact that the two plant types have utterly different lineages.

Dodd: But the common name highlights the crucial fact that both are composed of the same material and have very similar structures; so it is acceptable as a scientific term.

The conversation provides the strongest grounds for holding that Chai and Dodd disagree over whether

(A) it is advisable to use ordinary terms as names for biological forms in scientific discourse
(B) using the same term for two biological forms with different lineages can be scientifically acceptable
(C) both deciduous and coniferous plant forms evolved from simpler biological forms
(D) it is important that the lay terms for plant forms reflect the current scientific theories about them
(E) biological forms with similar structures can have different lineages

7. Increases in the occurrence of hearing loss among teenagers are due in part to their listening to loud music through stereo headphones. So a group of concerned parents is recommending that headphone manufacturers include in their product lines stereo headphones that automatically turn off when a dangerous level of loudness is reached. It is clear that adoption of this recommendation would not significantly reduce the occurrence of hearing loss in teenagers, however, since almost all stereo headphones that teenagers use are bought by the teenagers themselves.

Which one of the following, if true, provides the most support for the argument?

(A) Loud music is most dangerous to hearing when it is played through stereo headphones.
(B) No other cause of hearing loss in teenagers is as damaging as their listening to loud music through stereo headphones.
(C) Parents of teenagers generally do not themselves listen to loud music through stereo headphones.
(D) Teenagers who now listen to music at dangerously loud levels choose to do so despite their awareness of the risks involved.
(E) A few headphone manufacturers already plan to market stereo headphones that automatically turn off when a dangerous level of loudness is reached.

GO ON TO THE NEXT PAGE.

8. Most plants have developed chemical defenses against parasites. The average plant contains about 40 natural pesticides-chemical compounds toxic to bacteria, fungi, and other parasites. Humans ingest these natural pesticides without harm every day. Therefore, the additional threat posed by synthetic pesticides sprayed on crop plants by humans is minimal.

Each of the following, if true, weakens the argument EXCEPT:

(A) Humans have been consuming natural plant pesticides for millennia and have had time to adapt to them.
(B) The concentrations of natural pesticides in plants are typically much lower than the concentrations of synthetic pesticides in sprayed crop plants.
(C) Natural plant pesticides are typically less potent than synthetic pesticides, whose toxicity is highly concentrated.
(D) Natural plant pesticides generally serve only as defenses against specific parasites, whereas synthetic pesticides are often harmful to a wide variety of organisms.
(E) The synthetic pesticides sprayed on crop plants by humans usually have chemical structures similar to those of the natural pesticides produced by the plants.

9. In addition to the labor and materials used to make wine, the reputation of the vineyard where the grapes originate plays a role in determining the price of the finished wine. Therefore, an expensive wine is not always a good wine.

Which one of the following is an assumption on which the argument depends?

(A) The price of a bottle of wine should be a reflection of the wine's quality.
(B) Price is never an accurate indication of the quality of a bottle of wine.
(C) The reputation of a vineyard does not always indicate the quality of its wines.
(D) The reputation of a vineyard generally plays a greater role than the quality of its grapes in determining its wines' prices.
(E) Wines produced by lesser-known vineyards generally are priced to reflect accurately the wines' quality.

10. Before their larvae hatch, each parental pair of *Nicrophorus* beetles buries the carcass of a small vertebrate nearby. For several days after the larvae hatch, both beetles feed their voracious larvae from the carcass, which is entirely consumed within a week. Since both parents help with feeding, larvae should benefit from both parents' presence; however, removing one parent before the hatching results in larvae that grow both larger and heavier than they otherwise would be.

Which one of the following, if true, best helps to explain why removing one parent resulted in larger, heavier larvae?

(A) Two beetles can find and bury a larger carcass than can a single beetle.
(B) Both parents use the carcass as their own food supply for as long as they stay with the larvae.
(C) Beetle parents usually take turns feeding their larvae, so that there is always one provider available and one at rest.
(D) After a week, the larvae are capable of finding other sources of food and feeding themselves.
(E) Two parents can defend the carcass from attack by other insects better than a single parent can.

11. For many centuries it was believed that only classical Euclidean geometry could provide a correct way of mathematically representing the universe. Nevertheless, scientists have come to believe that a representation of the universe employing non-Euclidean geometry is much more useful in developing certain areas of scientific theory. In fact, such a representation underlies the cosmological theory that is now most widely accepted by scientists as accurate.

Which one of the following is most strongly supported by the statements above?

(A) Scientists who use Euclidean geometry are likely to believe that progress in mathematical theory results in progress in natural science.
(B) Scientists generally do not now believe that classical Euclidean geometry is uniquely capable of giving a correct mathematical representation of the universe.
(C) Non-Euclidean geometry is a more complete way of representing the universe than is Euclidean geometry.
(D) An accurate scientific theory cannot be developed without the discovery of a uniquely correct way of mathematically representing the universe.
(E) The usefulness of a mathematical theory is now considered by scientists to be more important than its mathematical correctness.

GO ON TO THE NEXT PAGE.

12. Experts hired to testify in court need to know how to make convincing presentations. Such experts are evaluated by juries in terms of their ability to present the steps by which they arrived at their conclusions clearly and confidently. As a result, some less expert authorities who are skilled at producing convincing testimony are asked to testify rather than highly knowledgeable but less persuasive experts.

    Which one of the following most closely conforms to the principle illustrated by the passage above?

    (A) Successful politicians are not always the ones who best understand how to help their country. Some lack insight into important political issues but are highly skilled at conducting an election campaign.
    (B) Trial lawyers often use the techniques employed by actors to influence the emotions of jurors. Many lawyers have studied drama expressly for the purpose of improving their courtroom skills.
    (C) The opera singer with the best voice is the appropriate choice even for minor roles, despite the fact that an audience may be more affected by a singer with greater dramatic ability but a lesser voice.
    (D) It is often best to try to train children with gentle reinforcement of desired behavior, rather than by simply telling them what to do and what not to do. This results in children who behave because they want to, not because they feel compelled.
    (E) Job applicants are usually hired because their skills and training best meet a recognized set of qualifications. Only rarely is a prospective employer convinced to tailor a position to suit the skills of a particular applicant.

13. The solution to any environmental problem that is not the result of government mismanagement can only lie in major changes in consumer habits. But major changes in consumer habits will occur only if such changes are economically enticing. As a result, few serious ecological problems will be solved unless the solutions are made economically enticing.

    The conclusion drawn in the argument above follows logically if which one of the following is assumed?

    (A) Few serious ecological problems are the result of government mismanagement.
    (B) No environmental problems that stem from government mismanagement have solutions that are economically feasible.
    (C) Major changes in consumer habits can be made economically enticing.
    (D) Most environmental problems that are not the result of government mismanagement are major ecological problems.
    (E) Few serious ecological problems can be solved by major changes in consumer habits.

14. The economy is doing badly. First, the real estate slump has been with us for some time. Second, car sales are at their lowest in years. Of course, had either one or the other phenomenon failed to occur, this would be consistent with the economy as a whole being healthy. But, their occurrence together makes it quite probable that my conclusion is correct.

    Which one of the following inferences is most strongly supported by the information above?

    (A) If car sales are at their lowest in years, then it is likely that the economy is doing badly.
    (B) If the economy is doing badly, then either the real estate market or the car sales market is not healthy.
    (C) If the real estate market is healthy, then it is likely that the economy as a whole is healthy.
    (D) If the economy is in a healthy state, then it is unlikely that the real estate and car sales markets are both in a slump.
    (E) The bad condition of the economy implies that both the real estate and the car sales markets are doing badly.

GO ON TO THE NEXT PAGE.

15. According to current geological theory, the melting of ice at the end of the Ice Age significantly reduced the weight pressing on parts of the earth's crust. As a result, lasting cracks in the earth's crust appeared in some of those parts under the stress of pressure from below. At the end of the Ice Age Sweden was racked by severe earthquakes. Therefore, it is likely that the melting of the ice contributed to these earthquakes.

Which one of the following, if true, most strengthens the argument above?

(A) The earth's crust tends to crack whenever there is a sudden change in the pressures affecting it.
(B) There are various areas in Northern Europe that show cracks in the earth's crust.
(C) Evidence of severe earthquakes around the time of the end of the Ice Age can be found in parts of northern Canada.
(D) Severe earthquakes are generally caused by cracking of the earth's crust near the earthquake site.
(E) Asteroid impacts, which did occur at the end of the Ice Age, generally cause severe earthquakes.

16. Sociologist: Some economists hold that unregulated markets should accompany democratic sovereignty because they let people vote with their money. But this view ignores the crucial distinction between the private consumer and the public citizen. In the marketplace the question is, "What do I want?" At the voting booth the question is always, "What do we want?" Hence, supporters of political democracy can also support marketplace regulation.

Which one of the following most accurately expresses the conclusion drawn by the sociologist?

(A) Voters think of themselves as members of a community, rather than as isolated individuals.
(B) Unregulated markets are incompatible with democratic sovereignty.
(C) Where there is democratic sovereignty there should be unregulated markets.
(D) Private consumers are primarily concerned with their own self-interest.
(E) Opposition to unregulated markets is consistent with support for democracy.

17. The tiny hummingbird weighs little, but its egg is 15 percent of the adult hummingbird's weight. The volume and weight of an adult goose are much greater than those of a hummingbird, but a goose's egg is only about 4 percent of its own weight. An adult ostrich, much larger and heavier than a goose, lays an egg that is only 1.6 percent of its own weight.

Which one of the following propositions is best illustrated by the statements above?

(A) The eggs of different bird species vary widely in their ratio of volume to weight.
(B) The smaller and lighter the average adult members of a bird species are, the larger and heavier the eggs of that species are.
(C) The ratio of egg weight of a species to body weight of an adult member of that species is smaller for larger birds than for smaller ones.
(D) The size of birds' eggs varies greatly from species to species but has little effect on the volume and weight of the adult bird.
(E) Bird species vary more in egg size than they do in average body size and weight.

18. Bram Stoker's 1897 novel *Dracula* portrayed vampires—the "undead" who roam at night to suck the blood of living people—as able to turn into bats. As a result of the pervasive influence of this novel, many people now assume that a vampire's being able to turn into a bat is an essential part of vampire myths. However, this assumption is false, for vampire myths existed in Europe long before Stoker's book.

Which one of the following is an assumption on which the argument depends?

(A) At least one of the European vampire myths that predated Stoker's book did not portray vampires as strictly nocturnal.
(B) Vampire myths in Central and South America, where real vampire bats are found, portray vampires as able to turn into bats.
(C) Vampire myths did not exist outside Europe before the publication of Stoker's *Dracula*.
(D) At least one of the European vampire myths that predated Stoker's book did not portray vampires as able to turn into bats.
(E) At the time he wrote *Dracula*, Stoker was familiar with earlier European vampire myths.

GO ON TO THE NEXT PAGE.

19. It is unlikely that the world will ever be free of disease. Most diseases are caused by very prolific microorganisms whose response to the pressures medicines exert on them is predictable: they quickly evolve immunities to those medicines while maintaining their power to infect and even kill humans.

Which one of the following most accurately describes the role played in the argument by the claim that it is unlikely that the world will ever be free of disease?

(A) It is a conclusion that is claimed to follow from the premise that microorganisms are too numerous for medicines to eliminate entirely.
(B) It is a conclusion for which a description of the responses of microorganisms to the medicines designed to cure the diseases they cause is offered as support.
(C) It is a premise offered in support of the claim that most disease-causing microorganisms are able to evolve immunities to medicines while retaining their ability to infect humans.
(D) It is a generalization used to predict the response of microorganisms to the medicines humans use to kill them.
(E) It is a conclusion that is claimed to follow from the premise that most microorganisms are immune to medicines designed to kill them.

20. Scientist: My research indicates that children who engage in impulsive behavior similar to adult thrill-seeking behavior are twice as likely as other children to have a gene variant that increases sensitivity to dopamine. From this, I conclude that there is a causal relationship between this gene variant and an inclination toward thrill-seeking behavior.

Which one of the following, if true, most calls into question the scientist's argument?

(A) Many impulsive adults are not unusually sensitive to dopamine.
(B) It is not possible to reliably distinguish impulsive behavior from other behavior.
(C) Children are often described by adults as engaging in thrill-seeking behavior simply because they act impulsively.
(D) Many people exhibit behavioral tendencies as adults that they did not exhibit as children.
(E) The gene variant studied by the scientist is correlated with other types of behavior in addition to thrill-seeking behavior.

21. It is highly likely that Claudette is a classical pianist. Like most classical pianists, Claudette recognizes many of Clara Schumann's works. The vast majority of people who are not classical pianists do not. In fact, many people who are not classical pianists have not even heard of Clara Schumann.

The reasoning in the argument above is flawed in that it

(A) ignores the possibility that Claudette is more familiar with the works of other composers of music for piano
(B) presumes, without providing justification, that people who have not heard of Clara Schumann do not recognize her works
(C) presumes, without providing justification, that classical pianists cannot also play other musical instruments
(D) relies for its plausibility on the vagueness of the term "classical"
(E) ignores the possibility that the majority of people who recognize many of Clara Schumann's works are not classical pianists

GO ON TO THE NEXT PAGE.

22. All the evidence so far gathered fits both Dr. Grippen's theory and Professor Heissmann's. However, the predictions that these theories make about the result of the planned experiment cannot both be true. Therefore, the result of this experiment will confirm one of these theories at the expense of the other.

The argument above exhibits an erroneous pattern of reasoning most similar to that exhibited by which one of the following?

(A) David and Jane both think they know how to distinguish beech trees from elms, but when they look at trees together they often disagree. Therefore, at least one of them must have an erroneous method.
(B) Although David thinks the tree they saw was a beech, Jane thinks it was an elm. Jane's description of the tree's features is consistent with her opinion, so this description must be inconsistent with David's view.
(C) David and Jane have been equally good at identifying trees so far. But David says this one is an elm, whereas Jane is unsure. Therefore, if this tree turns out to be an elm, we'll know David is better.
(D) David thinks that there are more beeches than elms in this forest. Jane thinks he is wrong. The section of forest we examined was small, but examination of the whole forest would either confirm David's view or disprove it.
(E) David thinks this tree is a beech. Jane thinks it is an elm. Maria, unlike David or Jane, is expert at tree identification, so when Maria gives her opinion it will verify either David's or Jane's opinion.

23. Columnist: The relief from the drudgery of physical labor that much modern technology affords its users renders them dependent on this technology, and, more importantly, on the elaborate energy systems required to run it. This leads to a loss of self-sufficiency. Clearly, then, in addition to undermining life's charm, much modern technology diminishes the overall well-being of its users.

Which one of the following is an assumption required by the columnist's argument?

(A) Physical labor is essential to a fulfilling life.
(B) Self-sufficiency contributes to a person's well-being.
(C) People are not free if they must depend on anything other than their own capacities.
(D) Anything causing a loss in life's charm is unjustifiable unless this loss is compensated by some gain.
(E) Technology inherently limits the well-being of its users.

GO ON TO THE NEXT PAGE.

24. Psychologist: Some psychologists mistakenly argue that because dreams result from electrical discharges in the brain, they must be understood purely in terms of their physiological function. They conclude, against Freud, that dreams reveal nothing about the character of the dreamer. But since dream content varies enormously, then even if electrical discharges provide the terms of the physiological explanation of dreams, they cannot completely explain the phenomenon of dreaming.

The claim that dream content varies enormously plays which one of the following roles in the argument?

(A) It is used to support the anti-Freudian conclusion that some psychologists draw concerning dreams.
(B) It is used to support the explicitly stated conclusion that a fully satisfactory account of dreams must allow for the possibility of their revealing significant information about the dreamer.
(C) It is used to suggest that neither Freud's theory nor the theory of anti-Freudian psychologists can completely explain the phenomenon of dreaming.
(D) It is used to illustrate the difficulty of providing a complete explanation of the phenomenon of dreaming.
(E) It is used to undermine a claim that some psychologists use to argue against a view of Freud's.

25. The first bicycle, the Draisienne, was invented in 1817. A brief fad ensued, after which bicycles practically disappeared until the 1860s. Why was this? New technology is accepted only when it coheres with the values of a society. Hence some change in values must have occurred between 1817 and the 1860s.

The reasoning in the argument is flawed because the argument

(A) presumes, without giving justification, that fads are never indicative of genuine acceptance
(B) fails to recognize that the reappearance of bicycles in the 1860s may have indicated genuine acceptance of them
(C) offers no support for the claim that the Draisienne was the first true bicycle
(D) poses a question that has little relevance to the argument's conclusion
(E) ignores, without giving justification, alternative possible explanations of the initial failure of bicycles

S T O P

IF YOU FINISH BEFORE TIME IS CALLED, YOU MAY CHECK YOUR WORK ON THIS SECTION ONLY.
DO NOT WORK ON ANY OTHER SECTION IN THE TEST.

PREPTEST 44 LOGICAL REASONING SECTION I

1. B	8. E	15. D	22. E
2. E	9. C	16. E	23. B
3. C	10. B	17. C	24. E
4. C	11. B	18. D	25. E
5. A	12. A	19. B	
6. B	13. A	20. B	
7. D	14. D	21. E	

PrepTest 44 Logical Reasoning Section I Explanations

Question #1: Flaw in the Reasoning—CE. The correct answer choice is (B)

This stimulus provides a definition of the term "tidal range," followed by information about one particularly large one. The author then makes the following causal argument:

Premise:	The only forces involved in causing *tides* are gravitational in nature.
Conclusion:	Thus the *magnitude* of tidal ranges must be entirely caused by those same gravitational forces.

Note that the argument jumps from a premise that deals with the cause of *tides* to a conclusion about the cause of *the magnitude of tidal ranges*. That leap is unjustified; although tides are induced by gravity, tidal range size may be affected by other factors. Since the question asks us to identify the flaw, we should look for a response that discusses this leap (or any answer choice that points out the failure to consider alternative causes of a tidal range's magnitude).

Answer choice (A): The use of only one example is not a flaw in the reasoning; the example was used to illustrate how big tidal ranges can get, so more examples wouldn't be necessarily required in this context.

Answer choice (B): This is the correct answer choice, as it points out the author's failure to consider other conditions (alternative causes) that might affect the size of a tidal range.

Answer choice (C): The author discusses what causes the actual magnitude of tidal ranges, not their measurement. This choice does not describe a flaw, so it is incorrect.

Answer choice (D): The author does not discuss *most* activity in the world's oceans, only tides and tidal ranges, so this choice is wrong.

Answer choice (E): Since the argument concludes only that gravitational forces account for the magnitude of tidal ranges, it is not important to differentiate between the tidal effects of the moon's gravity and those of the sun's.

Question #2: Must Be True. The correct answer choice is (E)

In this stimulus, the cardiologist presents observations about whether bypass surgery is always the best remedy for coronary artery disease:

1. Coronary bypass surgery is commonly performed when certain less expensive and less risky procedures would be as effective.

2. Bypass surgery is especially debatable for single-vessel disease.

The stimulus, which presents a basic fact set rather than an argument, is followed by a Must Be True question, which means that the answer choice must pass the Fact Test, meaning that it can be confirmed by the facts presented in the stimulus.
Answer choice (A): The operative term in this choice is "all." The stimulus does not support the idea that coronary bypass surgery is riskier than *all* other therapies, so this choice can be eliminated.

Answer choice (B): We cannot infer from the use of "common" that there has been any increase in frequency over time, especially since the stimulus does not concern different time periods. Furthermore, it is wrong to infer that bypass surgery is "needless," just because alternative (or even superior) remedies exist.

Answer choice (C): The cardiologist says that bypass surgery is *especially* debatable when only one vessel is involved, which does not necessarily mean that such surgery is desirable when more than one vessel is involved.

Answer choice (D): While bypass surgery is especially debatable for single-vessel disease, the cardiologist does not say that it is particularly expensive.

Answer choice (E): This is the correct answer choice. The stimulus states that bypass surgery is commonly performed when other equally effective, less risky remedies are available.

Question #3: Resolve the Paradox. The correct answer choice is (C)

This stimulus presents the following paradox:

Premise:	In the past, combining different age groups caused confusion and boredom.
Premise:	Now, mixed-age classrooms are turning out to be stimulating and beneficial.

In Resolve the Paradox questions, we must look for the answer choice which is compatible with the two apparently contradictory premises in the stimulus. Sometimes we can prephrase the resolution of this paradox. For example, the shift from "confusion and boredom" to "more efficient learning and stimulation" suggests a possible change in teaching style, materials, etc. It is also possible that certain subjects are better suited to combined age groups.

Answer choice (A): It is unclear that a larger classroom could resolve the "confusion and boredom." Even if we felt that the "larger enrollment" was indicative of the current, better situation, that increase would not resolve the apparent discrepancy.

Answer choice (B): The present classes are the good ones, but this response says that the past classes were better equipped. This Opposite answer would serve to broaden the apparent discrepancy.

Answer choice (C): This is the correct answer choice, as it offers an explanation for the improvements that come with the shift from old classrooms to the new ones: A new emphasis on group projects. This idea is consistent with both premises in the stimulus and explains why modern mixed-age classrooms enjoy greater success.

Answer choice (D): A greater range of ages would seem likely to result in more confusion and boredom. This choice appears to broaden the paradox and is therefore incorrect.

Answer choice (E): This choice might help to explain why the learning environment has changed, but without other information there would be no reason to assume this would cause an improved learning environment.

Question #4: Weaken—CE. The correct answer choice is (C)

In this stimulus, the author considers two variables which are correlated, and jumps to the conclusion that there is a causal relationship:

Premise:	Human arrival on Tiliga Island coincided with decrease in population and diversity of bird species on the island.
Conclusion:	Therefore humans must have *caused* this decrease.

This is a Cause/Effect stimulus with a weaken question. As we know, there are several specific ways to weaken a Cause/Effect argument. Since we know the supposed effect in this case (diminishing bird population and diversity), we might want to keep alternative causes in mind as we consider the answer choices.

Answer choice (A): This answer choice actually strengthens the argument in the stimulus. If there were no other natural predators of this species, it seems more likely that the decrease was attributable to the human presence on the island.

Answer choice (B): This choice strengthens the causal argument, by pointing out that when humans were not present, species apparently did not disappear as quickly.

Answer choice (C): This is the correct answer choice. A deadly microbe could serve as an alternate cause for the bird extinctions, thus weakening the causal argument in the stimulus.

Answer choice (D): The birds that the islanders ate likely lived on the island before the islanders' arrival, so evidence of the birds' earlier existence has no effect on the causal argument. This response does not weaken the author's argument.

Answer choice (E): The inability to fly would likely make these birds an easier target for their new human predators, so this answer choice would seem to strengthen the argument in the stimulus. This choice certainly does not weaken the argument and is therefore incorrect.

Question #5: Assumption—CE. The correct answer choice is (A)

In this stimulus, the author discusses the correlation of two variables and incorrectly concludes that a causal relationship exists:

Premise:	Musician adults trained from childhood have, on average, larger corpora callosa than adult non-musicians.
Conclusion:	Therefore musical training must *cause* these differences in the brain.

This argument is flawed, because the author attempts to draw a causal conclusion (that musical training increases corpus callosum size), where only a correlation between the two variables has been shown. Since this is a Cause/Effect question, we should consider other possibilities. Perhaps there is some other variable at work, causing both an enlarged corpus and a predisposition to music. Or perhaps cause and effect have been reversed, and in reality having a larger corpus callosum *predisposes* one to take up music.

Since this is an assumption question, we can apply the Assumption Negation technique by seeking a response which, when negated, weakens the causal argument.

Answer choice (A): This is the correct answer choice. Negating this choice, if the corpora callosa of musicians were naturally larger, the argument would fail. Thus the argument must assume that the corpora callosa are initially similarly sized.

Answer choice (B): The argument concludes that musical training *in general* causes changes in the brain, and that the effect is *particularly pronounced* when training begins at an early age. This response states that music training at older ages cannot cause anatomic brain changes, which is somewhat contrary to the author's argument. Therefore this cannot be an assumption required by the argument.

Answer choice (C): The argument compares musicians to non-musicians, so it does not matter whether two similarly trained musicians have roughly equal corpora callosa, only whether those musicians in general have larger corpora callosa than non-musicians.

Answer choice (D): The argument specifically stated that, *on average*, the corpus callosum of a musician is larger than that of a non-musician, so the argument would not make the needless assumption that *all* musicians have larger corpora callosa. Applying the Assumption Negation Technique, we would see that the argument is unaffected by the assertion that "*not* all musicians have larger corpora callosa than any non-musicians."

Answer choice (E): By logically negating this answer choice, we get, "adult non-musicians *did* participate in stimulating activities when they were children." This negated version does nothing to weaken the author's argument, so we know this choice does not reflect an assumption required by the argument.

Question #6: Point at Issue. The correct answer choice is (B)

The dialogue presented in this stimulus reflects Chai's belief that the term "tree" is *scientifically inadequate*, because this one term is used to describe plants with different lineages. Dodd responds that use of the term "tree" does highlight some important structural similarities between the two, making the term *scientifically acceptable*.

With a dialogue stimulus, we can often glean more about the point at issue from the words of the second speaker, who is more likely to spell out the point of contention between the two. In this case the pair is arguing about the scientific adequacy of the term "tree."

Answer choice (A): The dialogue does not reflect either speaker's opinion on the general advisability of using ordinary terms; the discussion surrounds the acceptability of a term for a specific context.

Answer choice (B): This is the correct answer choice. Chai claims that because of the different lineages, "tree" is unacceptable. Dodd argues that "tree" is acceptable, so the two disagree on this issue.

Answer choice (C): We are not given enough information in the stimulus to assess either speaker's perspective on this issue, so this choice is incorrect.

Answer choice (D): Neither Chai nor Dodd is concerned about lay terminology; they are interested in whether certain terms are scientifically adequate.

Answer choice (E): Both Chai and Dodd would agree with this statement, given that Chai accepts Dodd's definition. Even if Chai did not accept that coniferous and deciduous plants were similar in structure, he might still agree with this general assertion.

Question #7: Strengthen. The correct answer choice is (D)

This stimulus concerns plans for a controlled volume headphone, recommended to reduce hearing loss among teenagers. The author concludes that the plan will not work, based on the premise that teenagers are the ones who purchase the headphones. The apparent assumption in this case is that teenagers prefer not to have the volume of their music controlled in this way, despite the risks involved.

Answer choice (A): Even if stereo headphones pose the greatest threat, that does not strengthen the case that teenagers will refuse to buy the safer headphones.

Answer choice (B): Even if no other cause is as damaging as loud music through stereo headphones, this does not help to demonstrate that teenagers will continue to buy the unsafe headphones. This choice is irrelevant to the argument and therefore incorrect.

Answer choice (C): The fact that parents do not tend to listen to loud music through headphones does not strengthen the argument that teenagers would avoid volume control, so this choice is incorrect.

Answer choice (D): This is the correct answer choice. If teenagers choose the louder levels despite the risk, they would not be likely to purchase the new, volume-controlled headphones.

Answer choice (E): This choice offers a different type of headphone than the one already being planned. This is irrelevant to the argument in the stimulus.

Question #8: WeakenX. The correct answer choice is (E)

The argument in this stimulus is fairly straightforward, though clearly flawed:

Premise: Natural pesticides aren't harmful.

Conclusion: Thus the additional threat from *synthetic* pesticides is minimal.

This reasoning is weak, because it neglects the potential dissimilarities between natural and synthetic pesticides. Since this is an Except question, we should eliminate the four choices that *do* weaken the argument, in search of the single answer choice that *does not weaken* the argument.

Answer choice (A): This response weakens the argument by pointing out that humans have had a long time to get used to natural pesticides, the author strengthens the contrast between natural and synthetic pesticides.

Answer choice (B): This response points out that spraying with synthetic pesticides leads to higher relative concentrations, which makes it more likely that spraying with synthetics could be dangerous. This response weakens the argument, and is incorrect.

Answer choice (C): If synthetic pesticides have a more highly concentrated toxicity, they might be more dangerous, so this is another response which weakens the argument.

Answer choice (D): If synthetic pesticides affect a wider variety of species, this would increase the likelihood that humans might be affected, so this choice weakens the author's argument.

Answer choice (E): This is the correct answer choice. If the synthetic pesticides are similar in chemical structure to the natural pesticides, that would strengthen the claim that we might expect the same degree of harmlessness in synthetic pesticides as in their natural counterparts. This response does not weaken the argument and is therefore correct.

Question #9: Assumption. The correct answer choice is (C)

The conclusion in this case is presented in the last sentence of the stimulus: "an expensive wine is not always a good wine." In other words, an expensive wine is sometimes not a good wine. This conclusion is based on the premise that vineyard reputation is a factor in wine pricing:

Premise: **High Price** ⟶ **Based on good reputation**

Conclusion: **High Price** ←s→ ***~~Good wine~~***

When we diagram these two conditional statements, the variable present in both is "**High Price**." For the conclusion above to be properly drawn, there must be some other premise that is not explicitly stated; this is our supporter assumption, which fills in the gap between the premise and the conclusion. We should thus seek the answer choice that somehow links the remaining two variables: "Based on reputation" and "***~~Good wine~~***."

Answer choice (A): The author concludes that price is not always a good indicator of a wine's quality, not that some breach of justice has occurred because of that discrepancy. What *should* occur is irrelevant, so this choice is wrong.

Answer choice (B): The author concludes that expense is *not always* a good indicator of quality, so the claim that price is *never* a good indicator is not an assumption required by the argument. Furthermore, referring back to our prephrase, since this answer choice makes no reference to reputation, we know that it cannot be correct.

Answer choice (C): This is the correct answer choice. This answer choice links the two variables as discussed above. If we add this premise to those provided in the stimulus, we can see that the conclusion can then be properly drawn:

Premise: **High Price** ⟶ **Based on good reputation**

Assumption: ***Good reputation*** ←s→ ***~~Good wine~~***

Thus, we can link the two statements:

High Price ⟶ **Based on good reputation** ←s→ ***~~Good wine~~***

This allows us to properly draw the inference which is the author's conclusion:

High Price ←s→ ***~~Good wine~~***

Answer choice (D): This answer choice does not link the variables discussed above, and instead introduces the new variable, grape quality. Since this choice does not involve the quality of the *wine*, it cannot be the supporter assumption required by the argument.

Answer choice (E): We cannot glean anything about the pricing methods of reputed wines based on the pricing of lesser-known vineyards. Logically, this choice has no effect on the argument, so it is incorrect.

Question #10: Resolve the Paradox. The correct answer choice is (B).

The paradox in this case involves nicrophorus beetle parents, who remain in pairs to feed their larvae, leading to the expectation that the larvae benefit from the presence of both parents. Surprisingly, however, the larvae grow larger when one parent is removed.

Since we've been presented with a potential discrepancy, and the question asks us to explain the situation, we should consider why the larvae might fare better with only one parent. If we can prephrase an answer, we should do so. Otherwise we should look for the answer choice that is consistent with the apparently contrary premises in the stimulus.

Answer choice (A): This answer choice actually broadens the paradox, making it more difficult to explain why the larvae would grow larger with only one parent present.

Answer choice (B): This is the correct answer choice. If both parent beetles would normally consume the family food supply, the absence of one would mean more food for the larvae.

Answer choice (C): This is another answer choice which broadens the paradox. If there is a parent resting while the other one is providing, there would be more reason to expect that the larvae with two parents might be better off.

Answer choice (D): Since the stimulus concerns the first week, and this response concerns occurrences from after this period, this choice cannot help to resolve the discrepancy and is therefore incorrect.

Answer choice (E): If this is the case, we might expect greater results from the pair. This broadens the paradox, rather than explaining it.

Question #11: Must Be True. The correct answer choice is (B)

This stimulus consists of several observations and no conclusion, so a Must Be True question is likely to follow. A few facts are introduced:

1. Scientists once thought classical Euclidean geometry was *essential* to mathematically representing the universe.

2. Scientists came to feel *non*-Euclidean geometries were more useful in developing certain areas of scientific theory.

3. One most widely accepted theory is based on non-Euclidean geometry.

The suggestion is that most scientists believe that Euclidean geometry may be inessential to the formation of a correct mathematical representation of the universe, because other geometries might provide better bases for certain theories. If a non-Euclidean geometry is *sufficient*, then Euclidean geometry is *not necessary*.

Answer choice (A): There is no suggestion about scientists' beliefs concerning the progression of science relative to that of math.

Answer choice (B): This is the correct answer choice. The author suggests that most scientists do not believe that Euclidean geometry is essential to creating a correct mathematical representation of the universe.

Answer choice (C): The stimulus concerns *accurate, useful*, theories, and never discusses *completeness*. This choice is unsupported by the stimulus, and therefore incorrect.

Answer choice (D): This choice discusses "uniquely correct" methods, which is not a concept presented in the stimulus. Furthermore, the stimulus never argues that *all* accurate scientific theories *require* mathematical bases, just that *certain* scientific theories find some mathematical bases *useful*.

Answer choice (E): The stimulus does not establish that Euclidean geometry was the only mathematically correct means of representing the universe. The inference that scientists currently prefer useful theories to correct theories is thus unsupported.

Question #12: Must Be True—PR. The correct answer choice is (A)

In this stimulus, we are told that lawyers will sometimes employ authorities with less expertise, simply because these people sound more convincing in court. Since we are asked to choose a scenario that most closely conforms to the reflected principle, we can apply the *test of abstraction*. We might abstract as follows: "In some cases, persuasiveness can be more important than knowledge as a criterion for selection."

Answer choice (A): This is the correct answer choice. Some politicians win on the basis of public perception; they can run a persuasive campaign, without necessarily having particular expertise with regard to political issues. This is a case in which persuasiveness is more important than knowledge.

Answer choice (B): This response might appear slightly attractive, because it involves persuasiveness. It is not perfectly analogous, however because it doesn't involve a contrast to any other criterion.

Answer choice (C): This choice is an Opposite answer, because it involves selection on the basis of the merit of a singer's voice, and recommends that public perception be ignored. This principle is contrary to the one reflected in the stimulus.

Answer choice (D): The stimulus does not concern coercion, with or without reinforcement, nor does the stimulus prescribe any particular course of action, so this choice is incorrect.

Answer choice (E): This answer choice provides that companies generally try to fit the person to the job rather than vice versa. This is different from the principle reflected in the stimulus, which is more focused on selection criteria.

Question #13: Justify the Conclusion. The correct answer choice is (A)

In this stimulus, we are given several conditional statements:

1. The solution to any *non-government-caused* serious environmental problem can *only* lay in major consumer habit changes (MC). This can be diagrammed as follows:

   $S_{\not G} \longrightarrow MC$

2. These major changes will *only* occur with economic enticement (EE):

   $MC \longrightarrow EE$

3. Therefore (i.e., in *conclusion*), few problems of any kind will be solved without enticement. In other words, if there is no enticement, not many problems will be solved:

   $\not{EE} \longrightarrow \not{\text{many problems solved}}$.

   (contrapositive: many problems solved $\longrightarrow$ EE)

The leap between the premises is subtle, but important: The argument begins with the premise that economic enticement is needed to bring about consumer changes necessary to solve *non-government-caused problems*. The author then jumps to the conclusion that without these economic enticements, few environmental *problems* will be solved (whether or not government-caused). When we notice a leap like this one and are asked to justify the conclusion, we should seek the answer choice which fills in this gap and allows for the conclusion to be properly drawn.

Answer choice (A): This is the correct answer choice. The premises in the stimulus only offer information about non-government-caused problems. If we assume, as this answer choice provides, that most problems fall into this category (of non-government-caused problems), then the premises in the stimulus justify the author's conclusion.

This answer choice can be diagrammed as follows:

Major problem —M→ Not Due to Government

If we add this to the premises from the stimulus, we arrive at the following logic chain:

Major problem —M→ Not Due to Government ——→ S$_{\not{S}}$ ——→ MC ——→ EE

In other words, we can now properly conclude that most major problems will indeed require economic enticement, which is another way to phrase the conclusion in the stimulus.

Answer choice (B): This answer choice concerns environmental problems that *are* the result of government mismanagement, and the feasibility of their solutions. The stimulus deals with environmental problems that are *not* the result of government mismanagement. Since these are entirely different sets of problems, this choice is incorrect.

Answer choice (C): This choice concerns the feasibility of offering economic enticements, but the stimulus only concerns whether it is *necessary* to make enticements. Note: A necessary condition *can be impossible*; this would not prove that the condition was not necessary, it would merely prove that the sufficient condition could not occur. This choice does not address the gap in the stimulus and is therefore incorrect.

Answer choice (D): This choice is not a supporter assumption; it addresses the proportion of non-government-caused environmental problems that are major. This is not relevant to the discussion, and it does not provide any required link between the variables in the stimulus.

Answer choice (E): The argument in the stimulus does not concern whether changes in consumer habits are *sufficient* to solve the most serious problems, but rather whether major changes are *necessary* to solve those problems, so this answer choice does not reflect an assumption required by the argument. Furthermore, this choice does not address the leap in the stimulus from non-government-induced problems to serious problems in general.

Question #14: Must Be True—SN. The correct answer choice is (D)

This stimulus provides some conditional reasoning, with the conclusion presented in the first sentence: The economy is doing badly. This is based on the premise that two indicators (real estate and car sales) are performing poorly.

R.E.Slump
+ ⟶ Bad Economy likely
Low Car Sales

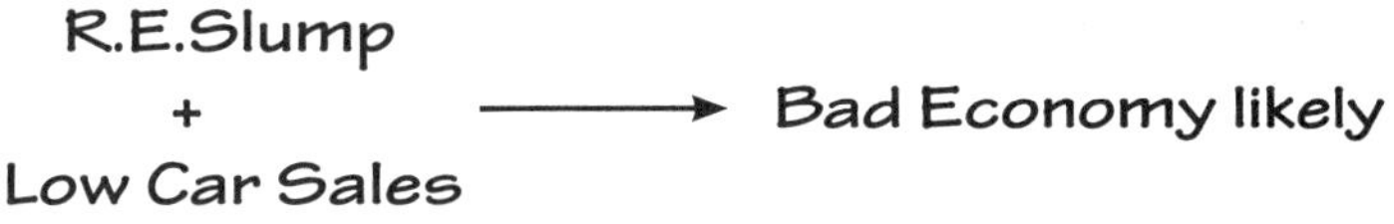

And the contrapositive:

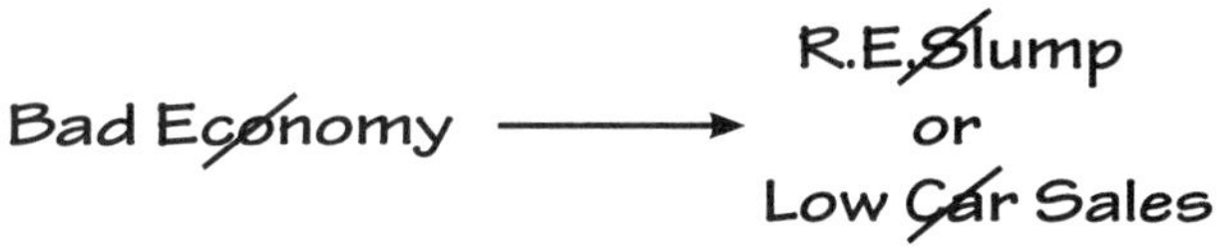

Bad E~~co~~nomy ⟶ R.E.~~S~~lump or Low ~~Ca~~r Sales

(Note that the author's logic requires that *both* indicators perform poorly in order to draw the conclusion that the economy is probably doing badly).

Answer choice (A): This choice is incorrect, because it suggests that low car sales *alone* are sufficient to indicate a bad economy. The stimulus suggests that either low car sales or a real estate slump alone is consistent with a good economy, which means a slump in either variable alone would be insufficient to establish the likelihood of a bad economy.

Answer choice (B): This answer choice characterizes the Bad Economy as the sufficient variable, but claims that success in the real estate or car sales market is *consistent* with a good economy, not that success in those markets *guarantee* a good economy. This choice is a Mistaken Reversal of the author's assertion that poor performance in real estate and car sales is likely to indicate a poor economy.

Answer choice (C): Healthy real estate or car sales performance is *consistent* with a good economy. This does not mean that a healthy economy is *likely,* only that it is possible, so this answer choice is incorrect.

Answer choice (D): This is the correct answer choice, as it reflects the logic from the contrapositive diagrammed above: A healthy economy ("Bad E~~co~~nomy" from the diagram) means that *at least one* of the two variables (real estate & car sales) is *not* faltering, which rules out at the possibility that *both* indicators are performing poorly.

Answer choice (E): This answer choice provides another example of a Mistaken Reversal. The stimulus tells us that poor performance in both real estate and car sales is sufficient to conclude that a bad economy is likely, which is much different from claiming that these factors are the necessary variables if we actually know that the economy is doing badly.

Question #15: Strengthen—CE. The correct answer choice is (D)

This Cause/Effect stimulus is much like many others on the LSAT; a causal relationship is presumed to exist where only a correlation has been shown. The stimulus explains that at the end of the Ice Age, the melting of ice depressurized the Earth's crust, causing it to crack. The author then concludes that the melting of ice likely helped to *cause* the earthquakes that took place in Sweden at the end of the Ice Age. As we know, there are several ways to weaken a Cause/Effect argument. Since we are asked to strengthen the argument, however, we should seek to better establish this causal connection.

Answer choice (A): Since this cracking would not necessarily cause any kind of large earthquakes, this choice would not help explain the earthquakes discussed in the stimulus.

Answer choice (B): The cracks in Northern Europe do not help establish the connection between the cracks and earthquakes, so this choice is incorrect.

Answer choice (C): Since we cannot assume that Northern Canada was significantly affected by melt-off from the Ice Age, and cannot assume that the crust in Canada cracked, this choice does not help establish a relationship between the cracks and earthquakes.

Answer choice (D): This is the correct answer choice. If cracks generally cause severe earthquakes in the immediate area, it seems more likely that they had something to do with the earthquakes in Sweden. Since this answer provides a causal connection between the cracks and the earthquakes, it is the correct choice.

Answer choice (E): By offering an alternative cause of earthquakes, this answer choice actually weakens the causal argument.

Question #16: Main Point. The correct answer choice is (E)

In this stimulus, the sociologist concludes that the supporters of political democracy can also support marketplace regulation. This conclusion, which comes at the end of the stimulus and is introduced with the word "hence," is based on the premise that there is a crucial distinction between the private consumer and the public citizen: Private consumers choose based on self-interest, argues the author, but the public citizen decides on the basis of beliefs about what is best for society.

In this case the question asks for the conclusion, which we should prephrase: supporters of political democracy can also support marketplace regulation.

Answer choice (A): This is perhaps an implication found in the stimulus, but it is not the conclusion, so this choice is incorrect.

Answer choice (B): The author's conclusion is that *regulated* markets are *compatible* with democratic sovereignty, not that *unregulated* markets are *incompatible*. This answer choice is basically a Mistaken Negation and is therefore incorrect.

Answer choice (C): This answer choice specifically reflects the belief of "some economists," as described in the stimulus, which is a position the author attacks. This choice is thus incorrect.

Answer choice (D): This is a premise used to support the conclusion, it is not the conclusion itself, so this answer choice is incorrect.

Answer choice (E): This is the correct answer choice. It is basically a rephrasing of the conclusion, found at the end of the stimulus.

Question #17: Must Be True. The correct answer choice is (C)

This stimulus consists of information with no explicit conclusion, but the numbers presented indicate a trend. It seems, at least anecdotally, that as the weight of a bird increases, the weight of its egg, relative to the size of the bird, decreases. This trend will likely be relevant, since we are asked which proposition is illustrated by the statements in the stimulus.

Answer choice (A): This choice might seem attractive, because the stimulus does discuss wide variation, but no volume-to-weight ratios are addressed.

Answer choice (B): The stimulus supports the idea that the ratio of egg-weight to body-weight increases as the bird gets smaller, but that does not mean the eggs themselves are larger in any absolute sense.

Answer choice (C): This is the correct answer choice, as it reflects a proposition illustrated by the stimulus. As the size of the adult bird increases, the ratio of egg-weight to body-weight decreases.

Answer choice (D): The stimulus itself does not allow us to make conclusions about the absolute sizes of the eggs, so we cannot make this comparison.

Answer choice (E): Since the stimulus never offered specific numbers to allow for comparison of bird size, we cannot conclude from the stimulus whether bird size or egg size has greater variation.

Question #18: Assumption. The correct answer choice is (D)

The argument concludes that, since vampire myths existed long before Bram Stoker's *Dracula*, the ability to become a bat is not an essential part of vampire myths.

The argument assumes some older vampire myths did not include bats as essential. Without this assumption, the observation that vampire myths existed before Bram Stoker's *Dracula* does not establish the conclusion. Since we are asked for a necessary assumption, we must address this gap, otherwise known as a *supporter assumption*.

Answer choice (A): This choice might be attractive, but we must not confuse "strictly nocturnal" with "turning into bats."

Answer choice (B): The corroboration of other sources on bats certainly does not lend credibility to the argument that bats are not essential parts of vampire myths, so this choice is wrong. Logically, this choice is meaningless, as it does not necessarily help establish anything about the European mythology, because the Central and South American myths could have arisen later.

Answer choice (C): The argument would not assume that vampire myths did not exist elsewhere, because it is possible that the existence of different vampire myths could help prove that bats are inessential.

Answer choice (D): This is the correct answer choice. At least one of the earlier myths must not portray vampires as able to turn into bats, if the advent of Bram Stoker's *Dracula* is to mean anything about whether bats are essential to the vampire myth. If all of the previous myths contained vampires with this ability, it would seem more likely that this ability actually is essential.

Answer choice (E): This fact might be helpful in determining where Stoker got his ideas, but it establishes nothing without knowing whether bats were used before him.

Question #19: Method of Reasoning—AP. The correct answer choice is (B)

The conclusion in this case is presented in the first sentence of the stimulus: It is unlikely that the world will ever be free of disease. This conclusion is based on the premise that most diseases are caused by microorganisms that quickly adapt to new medicines, while maintaining the ability to infect and kill humans.

The question asks us to identify the role of the first sentence, which is the conclusion of the argument.

Answer choice (A): Even though the first sentence is the conclusion, it is not supported by any premises about numerous microorganisms. "Prolific" means "productive," and in this context it simply refers to the ability of the microorganisms to adapt, survive, and continue infecting and killing humans. This choice is wrong.

Answer choice (B): This is the correct answer choice, because the first sentence is the conclusion, and it is supported by the premise that disease-causing microorganisms adapt well to medicines.

Answer choice (C): The claim in question is not a premise, so this choice is incorrect.

Answer choice (D): The first sentence in the stimulus is not a "generalization used to predict," so this choice is incorrect.

Answer choice (E): The claim in question is the conclusion, but the argument is only that disease-causing microorganisms *adapt well* to medicines, not that they are *immune*.

Question #20: Weaken—CE. The correct answer choice is (B)

The scientist's conclusion (which happens to follow the words "I conclude") is that there is a causal connection between the gene variant and thrill-seeking behavior. This is based on the premise that children who engage in impulsive behavior similar to adult thrill-seeking behavior tend to have the gene variant.

The scientist's argument is flawed for many reasons. First, there is no established causal link between the dopamine response (essentially the variant) and impulsive behavior. Second, it is not shown that impulsive behavior would have the same cause as thrill-seeking behavior.

Answer choice (A): The scientist makes the leap from impulsive children to thrill-seeking adults, so, oddly enough, impulsive adults are irrelevant to the argument.

Answer choice (B): This is the correct answer choice, as it weakens the argument with an attack on the data. If it is not possible to distinguish impulsive behavior from other types of behavior, then what sample are we studying? If this is the case, then the scientist's argument really has no basis.

Answer choice (C): There is no claim in the stimulus that the children were engaging in thrill-seeking behavior, so implying that children are misrepresented as thrill-seeking will not weaken the argument.

Answer choice (D): In the stimulus the author alludes to one possible cause of certain tendencies in children and of similar tendencies in adults. The fact that behavioral changes take place in "many" people between childhood and adulthood does not serve to weaken the argument.

Answer choice (E): It does not matter whether thrill-seeking correlates with other behaviors; this choice fails to attack the causal argument.

Question #21: Flaw in the Reasoning. The correct answer choice is (E)

The flawed reasoning in this stimulus can be broken down as follows:

Premise:	Most people who are not classical pianists don't recognize Schumann.
Premise:	Most classical pianists do recognize Schumann's work.
Premise:	Claudette does recognize Schumann's work.
Conclusion:	Claudette is "highly likely" to be a classical pianist.

The discussion concerns one test case (Claudette), and her placement in one of two groups, classical pianists or non classical pianists. Since we know nothing of the absolute or even relative sizes of these two groups, we have no way to assess the likelihood of Claudette's proper placement into one group or the other.
In order to determine the likelihood that Claudette is classical pianist, we would need to consider the population of people who recognize Schumann. Within this group are there more classical pianists or non-pianists? This would tell us more about the likelihood that Claudette is a classical pianist. The assumption in the stimulus appears to be that within this Schumann recognition group, there are more classical pianists than non-classical-pianists.

Answer choice (A): It is not a flaw to ignore this possibility. Familiarity with other works would not prove that Claudette is not a classical pianist, so this choice is incorrect.

Answer choice (B): Ignoring the possibility that people could recognize works without knowing of the composer has no effect on the argument, because the author never stated that Claudette knew the composer's name, only that she recognized the works.

Answer choice (C): The stimulus contains no assertions, implicit or explicit, about classical musicians' abilities with other musical instruments.

Answer choice (D): The term "classical" when describing a pianist is not vague.

Answer choice (E): This is the correct answer choice. In arriving at the conclusion that Claudette is highly likely to be a classical pianist, the author must assume that most who recognize Schumann are classical pianists, thus ignoring the possibility that most Schumann recognizers are actually not classical-pianists.

Question #22: Parallel Reasoning. The correct answer choice is (E)

Based on the premise that Dr. Grippen's and Dr. Heissmann's theories predict mutually exclusive outcomes, the author concludes that the planned experiment will confirm one theory at the expense of the other.

The reasoning is flawed, because it ignores the possibility that the experiment might disprove both theories. There is no reason to presume that one of the theories must be confirmed. Since we are asked to parallel the flaw, we must find a choice that similarly neglects the possibility of two negative evaluations.

Answer choice (A): This reasoning is fairly sound. If David and Jane often disagree, *at least one* of their methods is probably flawed. This choice does not parallel the reasoning in the stimulus, because *at least one* in this case means *either one or both.*

Answer choice (B): The reasoning in this choice is bad, but only because it neglects the possibility that both David and Jane agree on the description of the tree, but simply disagree over its name, which is not a similar flaw.

Answer choice (C): This choice is wrong, because it ignores that even if David is one tree better, a difference of one tree is really not enough to decide who is better at identifying trees. However, the two flaws are not analogous, so this choice is wrong.

Answer choice (D): The reasoning in this choice is sound. Examining the whole forest would establish whether David is correct to believe there are more beeches than elms in the forest, so this response contains no logical flaw and is incorrect.

Answer choice (E): This is the correct answer choice. Both David and Jane could be wrong, so Maria does not have to confirm either of these judgments, but the choice ignores that possibility. That is exactly the flaw in the stimulus. In this case, David and Jane are the scientists, and Maria is the experiment.

Question #23: Assumption. The correct answer choice is (B)

The conclusion in this case is presented at the end of the stimulus: Modern technology reduces the well-being of its users. This is based on the premise that the relief modern technology provides renders its users dependent on it, thus reducing self-sufficiency.

Since the columnist leaps from self-sufficiency to well-being, an implicit premise (or *assumption*) is that well-being and self-sufficiency are somehow related. Since we are asked to identify an essential assumption, we should seek this Supporter Assumption, which will fill a gap in the argument by linking these two variables.

Answer choice (A): This choice is neither supported nor required by the stimulus. The columnist argues that it is the lack of self-sufficiency that reduces well-being, not the lack of physical labor. Furthermore, the author argues that there is a *reduction* in *well-being*, which is not equivalent to saying that something is *essential* to a fulfilling life.

Answer choice (B): This is the correct answer choice. The argument assumes that self-sufficiency and well-being are related, and this answer choice reflects that relationship. Applying the Assumption Negation technique, if self-sufficiency did not contribute to well-being, then we wouldn't be able to conclude that modern technology reduces the well-being of its users.

Answer choice (C): Since the argument in the stimulus does not concern freedom, this answer choice can be confidently eliminated. Although "freedom" is aligned with the concept of "self-sufficiency," this choice does not provide the necessary link to well-being. This is not the supporter assumption we are seeking.

Answer choice (D): Since the columnist does not consider whether anything discussed is *justifiable*, but rather discusses only outcome, this choice is off-topic and incorrect.

Answer choice (E): This choice does not reflect an assumption required by the argument. The author claims that *modern* technology, not technology *in general*, reduces the well-being of its users. Applying the Assumption Negation technique, we can negate this answer choice to arrive at the following: "Technology doesn't necessarily inherently limit the well-being of its users." This negated version does not weaken the argument in the stimulus, so we know that this choice cannot be an assumption on which the author's argument relies.

Question #24: Method of Reasoning—AP. The correct answer choice is (E)

In this stimulus, the psychologist concludes that since dream content varies widely, dreams cannot be entirely explained as simply physiological phenomena. The psychologist makes this argument to counter the claim that dreams, as purely physical processes, reveal nothing about character or psychology.

The question asks us to identify the role of the claim that dream content varies enormously. This claim is a premise offered by the psychologist to support the conclusion. It is also worth noting that this claim attacks the other psychologists' conclusions.

Answer choice (A): The claim is not used to support any anti-Freudian conclusion. In fact, the author appears to be defending Freud, disputing those with anti-Freudian views.

Answer choice (B): This choice might be attractive, but it is wrong, because "explicit" means "definitively stated." The speaker implies that a fully satisfactory, or complete, explanation of dreams might allow for psychological considerations; the psychologist never explicitly states this conclusion, however, so this answer choice is incorrect.

Answer choice (C): The psychologist does not make the claim that neither line of reasoning offers a complete explanation, only that dreams cannot be completely understood in terms of physiological function.

Answer choice (D): The stimulus is not meant to illustrate the general difficulties of *completely* explaining dreaming, but rather to argue that dreams cannot be completely understood in terms of physiological function.

Answer choice (E): This is the correct answer choice. The claim is a premise which supports the psychologist's conclusion, and serves to undermine an opposing claim.

Question #25: Flaw in the Reasoning—CE. The correct answer choice is (E)

This stimulus seeks to explain why, after a brief stint in 1817, bicycles virtually disappeared until the 1860s. The premise offered is that the acceptance of a technology *requires* coherence with society's values, and based on this the author concludes that a change in values must have been the *cause* of the 43 year disappearance.

When we recognize this to be a Cause/Effect question we should immediately consider the various ways to weaken such an argument (in this case we know the supposed effect, and we are asked to identify a flaw, so we might start by considering possible alternative causes).

Answer choice (A): The argument does not presume that fads are *never* indicative of genuine acceptance, but instead points out that *this particular* fad was not initially indicative of genuine acceptance.

Answer choice (B): The argument does not fail to recognize that the reappearance of bicycles indicated a genuine acceptance; in fact, the author implies in the conclusion that there *has* been general acceptance.

Answer choice (C): Failure to provide support for one of the premises is not a flaw.

Answer choice (D): The question posed has direct relevance to the conclusion. It is a request for an explanation, which is provided by the conclusion (even though the underlying reasoning is flawed).

Answer choice (E): This is the correct answer choice, as it articulates the flaw in many causal arguments: The failure to consider possible alternative causes.

3

Chapter Three: PrepTest 45 Logical Reasoning Section II

Chapter Three: PrepTest 45 Logical Reasoning Section II

POWERSCORE

BY BARBRI

PrepTest 45
Logical Reasoning Section II

PREPTEST 45 LRII

SECTION II
Time—35 minutes
25 Questions

Directions: The questions in this section are based on the reasoning contained in brief statements or passages. For some questions, more than one of the choices could conceivably answer the question. However, you are to choose the best answer; that is, the response that most accurately and completely answers the question. You should not make assumptions that are by commonsense standards implausible, superfluous, or incompatible with the passage. After you have chosen the best answer, blacken the corresponding space on your answer sheet.

1. Mayor McKinney's policies have often been criticized on the grounds that they benefit only wealthy city residents, but that is not a fair evaluation. Some of McKinney's policies have clearly benefited the city's less affluent residents. McKinney actively supported last year's proposal to lower the city's high property taxes. Because of this tax decrease, more development is taking place in the city, helping to end the housing shortage and stabilize the rents in the city.

   Which one of the following most accurately expresses the main conclusion of the argument?

   (A) It is impossible to tell whether McKinney is more committed to the interests of the wealthy than to those of the poor.
   (B) McKinney's policies have often been criticized for benefiting only wealthy city residents.
   (C) The decrease in property taxes that McKinney supported caused more development to take place in the city.
   (D) The criticism that McKinney's policies benefit only the wealthy is unjustified.
   (E) McKinney's efforts helped end the housing shortage and stabilize the rents in the city.

2. A factory spokesperson argued that the factory should not be required to clean up the water in the nearby wetlands, maintaining that although wastewater from the factory polluted the wetlands over the past several years, the factory is not to blame for this, since the disposal of the factory's wastewater is handled entirely by an independent contractor.

   Which one of the following arguments most closely conforms to the principle underlying the reasoning in the spokesperson's argument?

   (A) A recent survey revealed that over two-thirds of the teachers in the district are permitted to teach classes on subjects in which they have received no formal training. Thus parents of students in the district should check the qualifications of their children's teachers.
   (B) I object to the policy of making parents responsible for the offenses of their older adolescent children. After all, these adolescents have minds of their own and freely choose to act as they do, often in ways that do not reflect the wishes of their parents.
   (C) The students are justified in their objection to the reading assignment. Many of the topics concern material that is not covered in class, and students should not be required to do such reading in order to do well in the course.
   (D) The most recent appointee to the prize committee should not be permitted to participate in the selection of this year's winner. Unlike each of the other committee members, the appointee has a relative in the contest.
   (E) Despite all the publicity, I am skeptical of the politician's claims of having just returned from the remote village. Just two days ago a reporter spoke with the villagers and said that not a single one reported seeing the politician in the past several months.

GO ON TO THE NEXT PAGE.

3. Nylon industry spokesperson: Even though cotton and nylon are used for similar purposes, some people have the mistaken notion that cotton is natural but nylon is not. However, nylon's main components come from petroleum and from the nitrogen in the atmosphere. Clearly the atmosphere is natural. And petroleum comes from oil, which in turn comes from ancient plants—a natural source.

   Which one of the following principles, if valid, most helps to justify the nylon industry spokesperson's reasoning?

   (A) A substance is unnatural only if the function it serves is unnatural.
   (B) A substance is no less natural than the processes used in its production.
   (C) A substance is no more natural than its least natural component.
   (D) One substance can be more natural than another if only one is wholly derived from natural substances.
   (E) A substance is natural if the origins of its main components are natural.

4. Computer manufacturers and retailers tell us that the complexity involved in connecting the various components of personal computers is not a widespread obstacle to their use, but this is wrong. Customers who install accessories to their personal computers have to take full responsibility for the setting of jumpers and switches to satisfy mysterious specifications. Many accessories require extra software that can cause other accessories to stop working; adding a modem, for instance, may disable a printer.

   Which one of the following, if true, most seriously weakens the argument?

   (A) Personal computer instruction manuals usually explain the purposes of the jumpers and switches.
   (B) Software for accessories can often be obtained for free.
   (C) Installing an accessory will become extremely easy in the foreseeable future.
   (D) A personal computer is usually sold as part of a package that includes accessories and free installation.
   (E) Computer manufacturers rarely take into account ease of installation when they are designing programs or accessories.

5. Rats fed high doses of the artificial sweetener saccharin develop silicate crystals that are toxic to cells lining the bladder. When the cells regenerate, some are cancerous and form tumors. Unlike rats, mice fed high doses of saccharin do not get bladder cancer.

   Which one of the following, if true, does the most to resolve the apparent discrepancy in the information above?

   (A) Urine proteins that react with saccharin to form silicate crystals are found in rats but not in mice.
   (B) Cells in the bladder regenerate more quickly in mice than they do in rats.
   (C) High doses of saccharin are much more likely to produce silicate crystals than lower doses are.
   (D) The silicate crystals are toxic only to the cells lining the bladder and not to other bladder cells.
   (E) High doses of other artificial sweeteners have been shown to produce silicate crystals in mice but not in rats.

6. Although we could replace the beautiful—but dilapidated—old bridge across Black River with a concrete skyway, we should instead replace it with a cable bridge even though this would be more expensive than building a concrete skyway. The extra cost is clearly justified by the importance of maintaining the beauty of our river crossing.

   Which one of the following is an assumption on which the argument depends?

   (A) It is no more costly to maintain a cable bridge than a concrete skyway.
   (B) A concrete skyway would not have any practical advantages over a cable bridge.
   (C) The beauty of the river crossing must be preserved.
   (D) If the new cable bridge is built, most people who see it will think the extra money well spent.
   (E) Building a cable bridge across Black River would produce a more aesthetically pleasing result than building a concrete skyway.

GO ON TO THE NEXT PAGE.

7. A typical gasoline-powered lawn mower emits about as much air-polluting material per hour of use as does an automobile. Collectively, such mowers contribute significantly to summer air pollution. Since electric mowers emit no air pollutants, people can help reduce air pollution by choosing electric mowers over gasoline ones whenever feasible.

Which one of the following, if true, provides the most support for the argument?

(A) Lawns help to clean the air, replacing pollutants with oxygen.
(B) Electric lawn mowers are more expensive to purchase and maintain than are gasoline mowers.
(C) Producing the power to run an electric mower for an hour causes less air pollution than does running an automobile for an hour.
(D) Most manufacturers of gasoline lawn mowers are trying to redesign their mowers to reduce the emission of air pollutants.
(E) Lawn mowers are used for fewer hours per year than are automobiles.

8. Ariel: Government art subsidies never benefit art, for art's role is to challenge society's values. A society's values, however, are expressed by its government, and artists cannot challenge the very institution upon which they depend.

Sasha: I agree that art should challenge society's values. However, by its very nature, a democratic government respects dissent and encourages challenges to its own values. Therefore, in a democratic society, government art subsidies ensure that artists can be fully committed to their work while expressing themselves freely.

The dialogue most supports the claim that Ariel and Sasha disagree with each other about whether

(A) art's role is to challenge society's values
(B) a society's values are expressed by its government
(C) artists can express themselves freely in a nondemocratic society
(D) art subsidies provided by a democratic government benefit art
(E) only governments that respect dissent ensure that art subsidies are fairly distributed

9. Public health expert: Until recently people believed that applications of biochemical research would eventually achieve complete victory over the microorganisms that cause human disease. However, current medical research shows that those microorganisms reproduce so rapidly that medicines developed for killing one variety will only spur the evolution of other varieties that are immune to those medicines. The most rational public health strategy, therefore, would place much more emphasis than at present on fully informing people about the transmission of diseases caused by microorganisms, with a view to minimizing the incidence of such diseases.

Of the following, which one most accurately expresses the conclusion drawn by the public health expert?

(A) A medicine that kills one variety of disease-causing microorganism can cause the evolution of a drug-resistant variety.
(B) A patient who contracts a disease caused by microorganisms cannot be effectively cured by present methods.
(C) There is good reason to make a particular change to public health policy.
(D) No one who is fully informed about the diseases caused by microorganisms will ever fall victim to those diseases.
(E) Some previous approaches to public health policy ignored the fact that disease-causing microorganisms reproduce at a rapid rate.

10. The enthusiastic acceptance of ascetic lifestyles evidenced in the surviving writings of monastic authors indicates that medieval societies were much less concerned with monetary gain than are contemporary Western cultures.

The reasoning in the argument is most vulnerable to criticism on the grounds that the argument

(A) employs the imprecise term "ascetic"
(B) generalizes from a sample that is likely to be unrepresentative
(C) applies contemporary standards inappropriately to medieval societies
(D) inserts personal opinions into what purports to be a factual debate
(E) advances premises that are inconsistent

GO ON TO THE NEXT PAGE.

11. Between 1976 and 1985, chemical wastes were dumped into Cod Bay. Today, 3 percent of the bay's bluefin cod population have deformed fins, and wary consumers have stopped buying the fish. In seeking financial reparations from companies that dumped the chemicals, representatives of Cod Bay's fishing industry have claimed that since the chemicals are known to cause genetic mutations, the deformity in the bluefin cod must have been caused by the presence of those chemicals in Cod Bay.

The answer to each of the following questions would be helpful in evaluating the representatives' claim EXCEPT:

(A) What is the incidence of deformed fins in bluefin cod that are not exposed to chemicals such as those dumped into Cod Bay?
(B) What was the incidence of deformed fins in bluefin cod in Cod Bay before the chemical dumping began?
(C) Has the consumption of the bluefin cod from Cod Bay that have deformed fins caused any health problems in the people who ate them?
(D) Are bluefin cod prone to any naturally occurring diseases that can cause fin deformities of the same kind as those displayed by the bluefin cod of Cod Bay?
(E) Are there gene-altering pollutants present in Cod Bay other than the chemical wastes that were dumped by the companies?

12. Columnist: If you received an unsigned letter, you would likely have some doubts about the truth of its contents. But news stories often include statements from anonymous sources, and these are usually quoted with the utmost respect. It makes sense to be skeptical of these sources, for, as in the case of the writer of an unsigned letter, their anonymity makes it possible for them to plant inaccurate or slanted statements without ever having to answer for them.

The columnist's argument proceeds by

(A) pointing out that a certain attitude would presumably be adopted in one situation, in order to support the claim that a similar attitude would be justified in an analogous situation
(B) drawing an analogy between an attitude commonly adopted in one situation and a different attitude commonly adopted in another situation, and establishing that the latter attitude is better justified than the former
(C) inferring that an attitude would be justified in all situations of a given type on the grounds that this attitude is justified in a hypothetical situation of that type
(D) calling into question a certain type of evidence by drawing an analogy between that evidence and other evidence that the argument shows is usually false
(E) calling into question the motives of those presenting certain information, and concluding for this reason that the information is likely to be false

13. Art theft from museums is on the rise. Most stolen art is sold to wealthy private collectors. Consequently, since thieves steal what their customers are most interested in buying, museums ought to focus more of their security on their most valuable pieces.

The argument depends on assuming which one of the following?

(A) Art thieves steal both valuable and not-so-valuable art.
(B) Art pieces that are not very valuable are not very much in demand by wealthy private collectors.
(C) Art thieves steal primarily from museums that are poorly secured.
(D) Most museums provide the same amount of security for valuable and not-so-valuable art.
(E) Wealthy private collectors sometimes sell their stolen art to other wealthy private collectors.

GO ON TO THE NEXT PAGE.

14. Insufficient rain can cause crops to falter and agricultural prices to rise. Records indicate that during a certain nation's recent crisis, faltering crops and rising agricultural prices prompted the government to take over food distribution in an effort to prevent starvation. Thus, the weather must have played an important role in bringing about the crisis.

The argument's reasoning is most vulnerable to criticism on the grounds that the argument

(A) concludes, merely from the fact that the period of insufficient rain occurred before the nation's crisis, that insufficient rain caused the nation's crisis
(B) fails to take into account the possibility that the scarcity was not severe enough to justify the government's taking over food distribution
(C) uses the term "crisis" equivocally in the reasoning, referring to both a political crisis and an economic crisis
(D) infers, merely from the fact that one event could have caused a second event, that the first event in fact caused the second
(E) takes for granted that any condition that is necessary for an increase in agricultural prices is also sufficient for such an increase

15. The cost of a semester's tuition at a certain university is based on the number of courses in which a student enrolls that semester. Although the cost per course at that university has not risen in four years, many of its students who could afford the tuition when they first enrolled now claim they can no longer afford it.

Each of the following, if true, helps to resolve the apparent discrepancy above EXCEPT:

(A) Faculty salaries at the university have risen slightly over the past four years.
(B) The number of courses per semester for which full-time students are required to enroll is higher this year than any time in the past.
(C) The cost of living in the vicinity of the university has risen over the last two years.
(D) The university awards new students a large number of scholarships that are renewed each year for the students who maintain high grade averages.
(E) The university has turned many of its part-time office jobs, for which students had generally been hired, into full-time, nonstudent positions.

16. People are not happy unless they feel that they are needed by others. Most people in modern society, however, can achieve a feeling of indispensability only within the sphere of family and friendship, because almost everyone knows that his or her job could be done by any one of thousands of others.

The statements above most strongly support which one of the following?

(A) People who realize that others could fill their occupational roles as ably as they do themselves cannot achieve any happiness in their lives.
(B) The nature of modern society actually undermines the importance of family life to an individual's happiness.
(C) Most people in modern society are happy in their private lives even if they are not happy in their jobs.
(D) A majority of people in modern society do not appreciate having the jobs that they do have.
(E) Fewer than a majority of people in modern society can find happiness outside the sphere of private interpersonal relationships.

17. Art critic: Criticism focuses on two issues: first, whether the value of an artwork is intrinsic to the work; and second, whether judgments about an artwork's quality are objective rather than merely matters of taste. These issues are related, for if an artwork's value is not intrinsic, then it must be extrinsic, and thus judgments about the quality of the work can only be a matter of taste.

The art critic's reasoning is most vulnerable to the criticism that it takes for granted that

(A) judgments about the quality of an artwork are always a matter of taste
(B) people sometimes agree about judgments that are only matters of taste
(C) judgments about extrinsic value cannot be objective
(D) judgments about intrinsic value are always objective
(E) an artwork's value is sometimes intrinsic to it

GO ON TO THE NEXT PAGE.

18. Decentralization enables divisions of a large institution to function autonomously. This always permits more realistic planning and strongly encourages innovation, since the people responsible for decision making are directly involved in implementing the policies they design. Decentralization also permits the central administration to focus on institution-wide issues without being overwhelmed by the details of daily operations.

The statements above most strongly support which one of the following?

(A) In large institutions whose divisions do not function autonomously, planning is not maximally realistic.
(B) Innovation is not always encouraged in large centralized institutions.
(C) For large institutions the advantages of decentralization outweigh its disadvantages.
(D) The central administrations of large institutions are usually partially responsible for most of the details of daily operations.
(E) The people directly involved in implementing, policies are always able to make innovative and realistic policy decisions.

19. According to some astronomers, Earth is struck by a meteorite large enough to cause an ice age on an average of once every 100 million years. The last such incident occurred nearly 100 million years ago, so we can expect that Earth will be struck by such a meteorite in the near future. This clearly warrants funding to determine whether there is a means to protect our planet from such meteorite strikes.

The reasoning in the argument is most subject to criticism on the grounds that the argument

(A) makes a bold prescription on the basis of evidence that establishes only a high probability for a disastrous event
(B) presumes, without providing justification, that the probability of a chance event's occurring is not affected by whether the event has occurred during a period in which it would be expected to occur
(C) moves from evidence about the average frequency of an event to a specific prediction about when the next such event will occur
(D) fails to specify the likelihood that, if such a meteorite should strike Earth, the meteorite would indeed cause an ice age
(E) presumes, without providing justification, that some feasible means can be found to deter large meteorite strikes

20. Polling data reveal that an overwhelming majority of nine-year-olds can correctly identify the logos of major cigarette brands. However, of those nine-year-olds who recognize such logos, less than 1 percent smoke. Therefore, there is little or no connection between recognition of cigarette brand logos and smoking.

Which one of the following uses flawed reasoning most similar to the flawed reasoning above?

(A) The concern about the long-term effect on dolphins of small quantities of mercury in the ocean is unfounded. During a three-month observation period, 1,000 dolphins were exposed to small quantities of mercury in seawater, with no effect on the animals.
(B) Many ten-year-olds dream of becoming actors. Yet it is not likely they will seriously consider becoming actors, because most parents discourage their children from pursuing such a highly competitive career.
(C) Most dentists recommend using fluoride to reduce the incidence of cavities, but few recommend giving up candy entirely; so, using fluoride is probably more effective in preventing cavities than is avoiding sweets.
(D) A large percentage of men exercise moderately throughout their lives, but the average life span of those who do so is not significantly greater than of those who get little or no exercise. So there is little or no correlation between moderate exercise and good health.
(E) Most people cannot name their legislative representatives. Nonetheless, this is insignificant, for when queried, most of them displayed an adequate command of current political issues.

GO ON TO THE NEXT PAGE.

21. Etiquette firmly opposes both obscene and malicious talk, but this does not imply that speech needs to be restricted by law. Etiquette does not necessarily even oppose the expression of offensive ideas. Rather, it dictates that there are situations in which the expression of potentially offensive, disturbing, or controversial ideas is inappropriate and that, where appropriate, the expression and discussion of such ideas is to be done in a civil manner.

Which one of the following judgments most closely corresponds to the principles of etiquette stated above?

(A) Neighbors should not be gruff or unfriendly to one another when they meet on the street.
(B) When prosecutors elicit testimony from a cooperative witness they should do so without intensive questioning.
(C) There should be restrictions on speech only if a large majority of the population finds the speech offensive and hateful.
(D) The journalists at a news conference should not ask a politician potentially embarrassing questions about a controversial policy issue.
(E) The moderator of a panel discussion of a divisive moral issue should not allow participants to engage in name-calling.

22. The only preexisting recordings that are transferred onto compact disc are those that record companies believe will sell well enough on compact disc to be profitable. So, most classic jazz recordings will not be transferred onto compact disc, because few classic jazz recordings are played on the radio.

The conclusion above follows logically if which one of the following is assumed?

(A) Few of the preexisting recordings that record companies believe can be profitably transferred to compact disc are classic jazz recordings.
(B) Few compact discs featuring classic jazz recordings are played on the radio.
(C) The only recordings that are played on the radio are ones that record companies believe can be profitably sold as compact discs.
(D) Most record companies are less interested in preserving classic jazz recordings than in making a profit.
(E) No recording that is not played on the radio is one that record companies believe would be profitable if transferred to compact disc.

23. Agricultural economist: Over the past several years, increases in worldwide grain production have virtually ceased. Further increases will be extremely difficult; most usable farmland is already being farmed with near-maximal efficiency. But worldwide demand for grain has been increasing steadily, due largely to continuing population growth. Hence, a severe worldwide grain shortage is likely.

Which one of the following most accurately describes the role played in the agricultural economist's argument by the claim that further increases in worldwide grain production will be extremely difficult?

(A) It is one of the two conclusions drawn by the agricultural economist, neither of which is used to provide support for the other.
(B) It is a description of a phenomenon, a causal explanation of which is the main conclusion of the argument.
(C) It is the only premise offered in support of the argument's main conclusion.
(D) It is a prediction for which the agricultural economist's first claim is offered as the primary justification.
(E) It is an intermediate conclusion that is presented as evidence for the argument's main conclusion.

GO ON TO THE NEXT PAGE.

24. Bardis: Extensive research shows that television advertisements affect the buying habits of consumers. Some people conclude from this that violent television imagery sometimes causes violent behavior. But the effectiveness of television advertisements could be a result of those televised images being specifically designed to alter buying habits, whereas television violence is not designed to cause violent behavior. Hence we can safely conclude that violent television imagery does not cause violence.

The reasoning in Bardis's argument is flawed because that argument

(A) relies on an illegitimate inference from the fact that advertisements can change behavior to the claim that advertisements can cause violent behavior
(B) fails to distinguish a type of behavior from a type of stimulus that may or may not affect behavior
(C) undermines its own position by questioning the persuasive power of television advertising
(D) concludes that a claim is false on the basis of one purported fault in an argument in favor of that claim
(E) fails to consider the possibility that the argument it disputes is intended to address a separate issue

25. Sarah: Our regulations for staff review are vague and thus difficult to interpret. For instance, the regulations state that a staff member who is performing unsatisfactorily will face dismissal, but they fail to define unsatisfactory performance. Thus, some staff may be dismissed merely because their personal views conflict with those of their supervisors.

Which one of the following generalizations, if applicable to Sarah's company, most helps to justify her reasoning?

(A) Performance that falls only somewhat below expectations results in disciplinary measures short of dismissal.
(B) Interpreting regulations is a prerogative that belongs solely to supervisors.
(C) A vague regulation can be used to make those subject to it answer for their performance.
(D) A vague regulation can be used to keep those subject to it in subordinate positions.
(E) Employees usually consider specific regulations to be fairer than vague regulations.

S T O P

IF YOU FINISH BEFORE TIME IS CALLED, YOU MAY CHECK YOUR WORK ON THIS SECTION ONLY.
DO NOT WORK ON ANY OTHER SECTION IN THE TEST.

PREPTEST 45 LOGICAL REASONING SECTION II

1. D	8. D	15. A	22. E
2. B	9. C	16. E	23. E
3. E	10. B	17. C	24. D
4. D	11. C	18. A	25. B
5. A	12. A	19. C	
6. E	13. B	20. A	
7. C	14. D	21. E	

PrepTest 45 Logical Reasoning Section II Explanations

Question #1: Main Point. The correct answer choice is (D)

The author opens this stimulus by presenting a criticism and quickly refuting it. The Mayor's policies have been criticized as benefiting only the wealthy residents of the city, but the author asserts that this criticism is unfair; this is the conclusion of the argument. In the remaining sentences the author offers supporting evidence for that conclusion, namely that McKinney's policies benefit all by fostering development and keeping housing costs in check.

In Main Point questions you may encounter one or more answer choices supported by the stimulus, but you are required to select the statement that best represents the author's conclusion.

Answer choice (A): The stimulus did not attempt to decide which group McKinney favors. We know that the critics believe that McKinney favors the wealthy, but the author's exact position is unknown (only that some of McKinney's policies favor the less affluent), and certainly the main point is not that it is impossible to tell which group McKinney favors.

Answer choice (B): This answer choice refers to the position of McKinney's critics, and that is a position that the author rebuts. This response is exactly opposite of what is required.

Answer choice (C): This is a premise of the argument, not the conclusion. The premise of an argument is never the correct answer in a Main Point question.

Answer choice (D): This is the correct answer choice. This answer paraphrases the author's stance in the first sentence. According to the argument, the criticisms are unfair, and thus unjustified.

Answer choice (E): This is a premise in the argument, and supports the idea that McKinney's policies have benefited the less affluent. This response is incorrect because the correct answer should reflect the conclusion of the argument.

Question #2: Must Be True—PR. The correct answer choice is (B)

The factory spokesperson quoted in this stimulus argues that the factory should not be required to clean up the pollution caused by its wastewater, because the real offender is the independent contractor who is in charge of the factory's wastewater disposal.

Although the argument contains flaws (for example, perhaps the factory is responsible for choosing a reliable contractor?), the question asks you to select a response based on the *same principle*, so you must seek the answer choice that best reflects the reasoning in the stimulus.

A principle is a broad rule that specifies what actions or judgments are correct in a certain situation, One way to state the principle in this problem would be, "we are not to blame since we didn't actually do it," or, perhaps more succinctly, as "let's pass the buck."

Answer choice (A): This response implies that parents have a responsibility or interest, which is an idea contrary to the principle in the stimulus.

Answer choice (B): This is the correct answer choice. Like the stimulus, this response is broadly based on the principle that people should not be held responsible for the independent actions of others (even if those others are somewhat under their control). Just as the factory could have selected a more responsible contractor or taken action to insist on proper disposal, a parent of an adolescent has had influence and can perhaps take actions to ensure proper behavior.

Answer choice (C): This response attempts to absolve students of a responsibility; however, it contains no separation between a responsible party and the students. The process of blaming someone else is a critical part of the principle presented in the stimulus, so this response is incorrect.

Answer choice (D): Does this answer choice fit the principle of, "we are not to blame since we didn't actually do it?" No, this response merely limits someone's activity.

Answer choice (E): This response is not at all related to the principle that one not be blamed for another's actions. Instead, this answer seems to better characterize a principle such as, "when there is evidence to the contrary, I will be skeptical."

Question #3: Strengthen—PR. The correct answer choice is (E)

Here, the nylon industry spokesperson argues that since nylon is made mainly from petroleum and nitrogen—both of which are derived from natural resources—nylon is in fact natural (the conclusion of the argument is alluded to in the phrase "some people have the mistaken notion that cotton is natural and nylon is not.").

The spokesperson uses the term "natural" rather loosely, as the author admits that only the "main" components that come from natural products (no mention is made of the processes to which these substances are subjected). However, the question asks you to strengthen that position, so you must find a response that helps proves that anything made mainly from "natural" sources can be called "natural." And remember, because this is a principle question the correct answer need not mention "nylon" or cotton" but can instead just generally encompass ideas that will assist the author's position, that when the very basic components of something are natural, that thing can be considered "natural" as well.

Answer choice (A): The stimulus did not discuss the *function* a substance serves, only its components. Thus this answer cannot assist in strengthening the argument.

In addition, note that this answer is in the form of a conditional statement:

Substance unnatural ⟶ Function it serves unnatural

Contrapositive:

Function it serves natural ⟶ Substance natural

However, you cannot reasonably conclude or know that every use of nylon is natural (and thus you cannot enact the sufficient condition), so this response does not strengthen the stimulus.

Answer choice (B): This choice might actually weaken the stimulus because this choice suggests that we might focus on how nylon is manufactured, and there may be processes applied to create nylon that are not natural.

Answer choice (C): This response could either strengthen or weaken the argument, so it is incorrect. On the weaken side, the stimulus allowed for the possibility that nylon might have non-natural ingredients ("main components"). If the substance can be considered no more natural than its least natural ingredients, that could make nylon non-natural.

Answer choice (D): The stimulus never concerned which substance was "more natural," only whether nylon was "natural." Thus, this response addresses a different issue than the one in the stimulus, and it cannot strengthen the reasoning.

Answer choice (E): This is the correct answer choice. The answer is in the form of the following conditional relationship:

Origins of main components natural ⟶ Substance natural

Since the main components of nylon are of natural origins, according to this relationship we can then conclude that nylon is natural. Thus, if this principle is valid (and we are told it is by the question stem), then the argument is strengthened.

Question #4: Weaken—CE. The correct answer choice is (D)

The author of this stimulus uses a variation of the classic "Some people claim" argument structure. In this case, computer manufacturers and retailers claim that the complexity involved in connecting the components of personal computers is not a barrier to their use. As is often the case, the author denies that claim, concluding that "this is wrong." The remainder of the stimulus is comprised of two premises that provide support for the author's conclusion that complexity is a widespread obstacle to the use of computers.

You are asked to weaken the argument, which means that we want to refute the idea that complexity is a barrier. The correct answer choice will likely give some reason to believe that the associated complexity is not prohibitive.

Answer choice (A): This response attracted many test takers, since they assumed that it would make it less likely that the addition of accessories was difficult. However, explaining the *purpose* of a switch or jumper does not necessarily clarify the proper settings, and this response does not address the problems with accompanying software. Additionally, this answer does not attack the idea in the stimulus that customers "have to take full responsibility for the settings of jumpers and switches."

Answer choice (B): The cost of the software for accessories has nothing to do with the issue of difficulty of proper installation, so this response is incorrect.

Answer choice (C): Since the argument concerns the present, this response, which concerns the future, is off-topic and incorrect.

Answer choice (D): This is the correct answer choice. If personal computers are sold as a package including accessories and free installation, the difficulties described in the stimulus become irrelevant as an expert, not the consumer, will resolve the problems. In the case of installation, cost is relevant, because a costly installation might inspire many consumers to do it themselves, thus making the claims about difficulty more compelling. In this response, the suggestion that installation is free counters the idea that consumers would need, or want, to install components on their own.

Answer choice (E): This response serves to strengthen the argument by showing that manufacturers do not knowingly or intentionally try to make it easier to install accessories.

If you selected this choice, you may have misread the stimulus and incorrectly identified the manufacturer's position as the conclusion, or misunderstood the question as asking you to help the author attack the manufacturers.

Question #5: Resolve the Paradox. The correct answer choice is (A)

This stimulus contains a fact set that presents a paradox, so you should have expected a Resolve question. To resolve the discrepancy, you must understand the contrast:

1. Rats fed high doses of saccharine get bladder cancer.

2. Mice fed high doses of saccharine don't.

Even though it is difficult to predict the exact solution to most Resolve questions, it is safe to say that the rats and mice must be different from each other in some important way (other than species).

Answer choice (A): This is the correct answer choice. This answer resolves the paradox by offering an explanation that accounts for the differing outcomes. Since the toxic crystals seem to be part of the process that leads to cancer in rats, their absence in mice might explain why mice do not get bladder cancer from saccharine.

Answer choice (B): This response mentions an important difference between rats and mice, but does not resolve the paradox. First of all, it is unclear what the effect of the different regeneration rates would be. It is entirely possible that a faster regeneration rate would make an animal more prone to cancer, and that would actually make the paradox worse.

Second, on a more esoteric note, some test takers who chose this response might have assumed that it implied the cancer could come about because certain areas of the bladder are damaged for too long in rats, or at least for much longer than in mice. Unfortunately, this response neither suggests that the rat's regeneration rates are insufficient nor suggests that the mice have a much greater regeneration rate.

Answer choice (C): This attempted explanation might be consistent with the information we have regarding rats, but we have no information on crystal formation in mice. Thus, this answer cannot explain the differing cancer rates.

Answer choice (D): This information might explain that the silicate crystals have a limited possible effect; however, it does not explain why mice wouldn't experience an effect from the crystals, similar to rats.

Answer choice (E): This answer points out a difference between rats and mice, and it suggests that certain sweeteners have different effects on the two animals. However, you are trying to explain why the high doses of saccharin have one effect in rats and a different effect in mice. This answer does nothing to help explain that difference because it does not mention saccharin, and nothing can be inferred from the actions of the other sweeteners.

Question #6: Assumption. The correct answer choice is (E)

This argument can be broken down as follows:

Premise:	We could replace the beautiful dilapidated old bridge across Black River with a concrete skyway,
Conclusion:	We *should* instead replace it with a cable bridge
Premise:	This would be more expensive than building a concrete skyway.
Premise:	...But the extra cost is clearly justified by the importance of maintaining the beauty of our river crossing.

Since you are asked to identify an assumption on which the argument depends, you must look for any leaps in the reasoning (Supporters), or any ideas that threaten the stimulus that must be rejected (Defenders).

As in any Assumption question, consider the conclusion: we should replace the old bridge with a cable bridge. Why is that the case? The author states that we must do so despite the expense in order to maintain the beauty of the river crossing (this reasoning is extremely questionable because it fails to consider that a properly designed concrete skyway might be just as beautiful as a cable bridge). You might immediately note that connection, and realize that the author has assumed that the cable bridge will be more attractive. Using that prephrase, they are then able to effectively dispose of this question by accelerating through this problem and selecting (E).

If you did not see that connection after reading the stimulus, do not forget to use the Assumption Negation Technique, which can help confirm that you have selected the correct answer.

Answer choice (A): The author does not see cost as a major issue, so the author is not committed to the idea that the cable bridge is not more costly to maintain.

If you are unconvinced, negate the answer, and consider how the author would respond to the negation. Even if the cable bridge were more expensive to maintain, the author of this argument might still insist that the beauty is worth the cost, so this response is not critical to the argument.

Answer choice (B): The argument cannot depend on an assumption that is contradictory to the argument's premises (cost advantage is most certainly a practical advantage), so this response is definitely wrong. Furthermore, even allowing for some leeway with this response, the author might not care about practical concerns.

Answer choice (C): This is the most attractive incorrect answer. However, "beauty" in this stimulus is only tied to a concept the author wishes to maintain, and the author is not tied to a specific level of beauty. For example, preservation implies a reasonably equal level of beauty, and technically the author's argument allows for the possibility that preservation of the site's current level of beauty is not essential. The author could accept some lower standard of beauty, and therefore still choose to advocate a more beautiful bridge.

From an Assumption Negation Technique standpoint, the correct negation of this answer is: "The beauty of the river crossing does not necessarily need to be preserved." In response to this negation, the author could note that while it doesn't need to be preserved, there are still benefits to having some level of beauty present, and that therefore the cable bridge is still the preferred choice.

Answer choice (D): This answer choice trades on how people would react to the cable bridge, but popular opinion is not a good method of proof or disproof on the LSAT. Even if most people believed the money poorly spent, the money could still be well spent. Also, people could simply have no particular opinion at all, and that would not damage the argument. In the realm of argumentation, opinions mean little and prove less. Search for an answer with a basis in fact.

Answer choice (E): This is the correct answer choice. If you are uncertain as to whether this answer is correct, use the Assumption Negation Technique. If the cable bridge is *not* more beautiful than the concrete bridge, how is the author's argument affected? Because beauty was a driving factor in advocating a cable bridge, the negation of this answer choice would severely weaken the author's argument, and hence this answer is correct.

Mechanistically, notice that "beauty" appears in one of the premises and nowhere else, and "cable bridge" appears in the conclusion but nowhere else. Not surprisingly, these ideas are linked in this assumption of the argument.

Question #7: Strengthen. The correct answer choice is (C)

The argument presented in this stimulus can be summarized as follows: because electric mowers produce no air pollution, but gas-powered mowers produce significant air pollution, people can help reduce air pollution by using electric instead of gas-powered mowers.

Because you are asked to strengthen the argument, you should look for a choice that supports the idea that adopting an electric-powered mower is a good idea. This will likely be presented either as some other benefit associated with the use of an electric mower, or further some down side to the use of the traditional gas-powered mower.

Answer choice (A): This response is irrelevant because the stimulus is about lawn mowers, not lawns. And, of course, we cannot assume that cutting the lawn with one mower rather than another would change the effect of mowing on the grasses' ability to clean the air.

Answer choice (B): The cost of the product does not affect whether people *should* adopt it, only whether they ultimately will. Thus, this answer choice cannot help the argument prove that "people can help reduce air pollution by choosing electric mowers."

Answer choice (C): This is the correct answer choice. The power for an electric mower has to come from somewhere, and this choice establishes that producing the power for an electric mower causes less pollution than for a gas-powered mower. This information makes the argument much more believable since it establishes that there is not a "hidden" pollution cost somewhere along the line of electrical power production.

Answer choice (D): This response only serves to suggest that using electric-powered mowers might not have much effect, since the gas-powered mowers are improving. If anything, this answer may weaken the argument by suggesting that in the future gas-powered mowers may be more emission efficient.

Answer choice (E): The stimulus compared gas mowers to electric mowers, and the reference to automobiles is only intended to imply that gas mowers produce pollution at a significant rate. In short, whether or not lawn mowers produce as much pollution as automobiles is irrelevant, because the issue is how gas mowers' pollution production compares with that of electric mowers.

Question #8: Point at Issue—CE. The correct answer choice is (D)

Ariel's conclusion is that government subsidies never benefit art. Sasha's conclusion is that democratic government subsidies can benefit art by allowing artists to be fully devoted and artistically free.

Since this two-speaker stimulus is followed by a Point at Issue question, you should focus on understanding the general nature of the disagreement before heading to the answer choices. Do not worry too much about the details of the premises because you can always refer back to the stimulus if you need to confirm the particulars of the statements made by each speaker. If you understand the basic disagreement (over the question of whether government subsidies can benefit art) that will likely be sufficient.

Remember, all answer choices in a Point at Issue question must pass the Agree/Disagree Test.

Answer choice (A): Both Ariel and Sasha agree that the role of art is to challenge values, so this response is incorrect.

Answer choice (B): Ariel would agree with this answer choice. Sasha's exact position on this statement is unknown, and you cannot infer from her statement that "a democratic government... encourages challenges to its own values" that those values are not the same as society's values.

Answer choice (C): One easy way to eliminate this answer is to realize that Sasha never commented on nondemocractic societies, just on a democratic one. Thus, since her position on this statement would be unknown, this answer choice is immediately incorrect.

Answer choice (D): This is the correct answer choice. Ariel would disagree with this statement, because she states that government subsidy never benefits art. Sasha would agree with this statement, because her entire argument is structured to support the idea that democratic governments are able to benefit art through subsidy.

Answer choice (E): The issue of fair distribution is never mentioned by either speaker, so this answer can be eliminated immediately.

In addition, this answer is quasi-Mistaken Reversal of Sasha's argument, because this response states:

Art subsidies fairly distributed ⟶ *Government respects dissent*

However, Sasha's argument implies that a respect of dissent is a sufficient condition, not necessary, for art subsidy distribution. Thus, Sasha's stance on this choice is again unknown.

Question #9: Main Point. The correct answer choice is (C)

The argument presented by the public health expert here can be summarized as follows:

We used to believe that we could eventually defeat the microorganisms that cause disease.

But current research suggests that microorganisms evolve too fast. Thus, we should instead try to focus on informing people in order to minimize disease transmission.

Your task in this problem is to find the answer choice that best matches the conclusion.

Answer choice (A): This is a premise of the argument, not the conclusion. In Main Point questions a premise is never the correct answer.

Answer choice (B): This is unsupported by the argument. Microorganisms are evolving, and cannot, in general, be eradicated, but that does not mean that a specific patient cannot be cured of a specific disease.

Answer choice (C): This is the correct answer choice. In the last sentence the expert believes that there should be a change of strategy: since current research suggests that microorganisms evolve too fast to be eliminated, we should shift our focus to informing people about transmission in order to minimize disease.

Answer choice (D): The expert referred specifically to "*minimizing* the incidence of such diseases," so there is no reason to believe that he or she concludes that educating people about transmission will *eliminate* the diseases.

Answer choice (E): Some chose this answer because it sounds more specific than answer choice (C). However, there are two reasons this answer is incorrect. First, the conclusion of the argument goes beyond the possible flaws of previous approaches to advocate a new approach. So, even if this statement were true, it is not the main point. Second, when current medical research reveals new information about a situation, it would be improper to say that previous beliefs "ignored" that evidence.

Question #10: Flaw in the Reasoning. The correct answer choice is (B)

The conclusion of this author's argument is that medieval societies were much less concerned about money than are today's Western cultures. The premise in support of that conclusion is that the writings of medieval monks showed that they enthusiastically embraced an austere lifestyle. Remember, always try to personalize arguments when you read them. Does this premise convince you that the conclusion is true? To get a true sense of our society today would we refer solely to the writings of the clergy? Probably not.

Since the question stem asks you to identify the flaw, simply accelerate through the answers and find the choice that best captures a weakness in the author's argument.

Answer choice (A): This answer falls under the category of flaw known as the Uncertain use of a Term. Ascetic, which Webster's defines as "a person who dedicates his or her life to a pursuit of contemplative ideals and practices extreme self-denial or self-mortification for religious reasons," is not an imprecise term as it is used here, and you should never assume a term on the LSAT is flawed simply because you lack familiarity.

Furthermore, every time the LSAT has contained a flaw based on usage, the term has been a very common one with which most reasonably aware persons would be acquainted (which is not to say it is always easy to pick out). This is because the LSAT is supposed to test your reasoning skills, and knowledge of abstruse vocabulary is *not* a reasoning skill. Ascetic, as you know, is *not* a common term and plenty of people may have no idea what it means.

Answer choice (B): This is the correct answer choice. Medieval monks present a certain view of life in medieval society, but their writings would certainly not capture all aspects of life. So, to claim that on the basis of their writings that there was an enthusiastic acceptance of ascetic lifestyles is to generalize from a sample that does not represent the views of all of society.

Notice that understanding the meaning of "ascetic" is entirely irrelevant to recognizing that monks probably do not represent common attitudes. The LSAT test-writers do in fact hope that some students get hung up on "ascetic," but you should focus on the broad method of reasoning.

Answer choice (C): Be careful when reading this answer choice. Some students think this answer says, "*Compares* contemporary standards..." and since there was a discussion of the medieval and contemporary societies, they incorrectly select this answer. Remember, any correct Flaw in the Reasoning answer choice must pass the Fact Test, so test each part of the answer to see whether it occurred. First, were contemporary standards applied? No. A comparison was made, but no standard from contemporary society was applied. Thus, this answer cannot be correct.

Answer choice (D): The stimulus makes no reference to personal opinion.

Answer choice (E): The premise is not inconsistent with itself, and the premise and conclusion are not inconsistent because they concern different time periods. This answer would fall into the category of flaw known as the Internal Contradiction.

Question #11: Evaluate the ArgumentX—CE. The correct answer choice is (C)

The author of this argument opens with the presentation of two premises: in the past chemical wastes were dumped into Cod Bay, and today 3 percent of the bluefin cod have deformed fins, which has led consumers to stop buying the cod. The Cod Bay fishing representatives claim that since the chemicals that were dumped are known to cause genetic mutations, those chemicals must have then caused the deformities in the bluefin cod. Thus, they believe the companies that dumped the chemicals should be financially liable for, presumptively, the fishing industry's loss in sales of bluefin cod.

The problem with the fishermen's argument, of course, is that we cannot conclude that the chemicals caused genetic mutations based solely on the chemicals' ability to do so.

The question stem is an unusual Evaluate the Argument Except question, where the four incorrect answers help evaluate the validity of the argument and the one correct answer does not help evaluate the validity of the argument. Remember to use the Variance Test when trying to confirm the correct answer or eliminate wrong answers.

Answer choice (A): This answer helps in evaluating the argument because it would help determine if the 3 percent deformity rate is normal or unusual. If the incidence of fin-deformity in non-exposed cod is always about 3%, or is close, there is no reason to believe that the chemicals caused the deformity. Therefore, even if consumers are wary of the fish because of its deformities, the chemical companies are not necessarily responsible. On the other hand, if the incidence of fin-deformity is normally zero, the assertion that chemical dumping caused the problem is more plausible.

Remember that with answers requiring percentages, the Variance Test suggests that you use 0 and 100. If the answer to the question in this answer is 0, the representatives' claim is strengthened; if the answer to the question in this answer is 100, the representatives' claim is severely weakened. Thus, this answer passes the Variance Test, and in an Except question we know the answer is incorrect.

Answer choice (B): This response is in the same vein as answer choice (A). Using the Variance Test, if the answer to the question in this answer is 0, the representatives' claim is strengthened; if the answer to the question in this answer is 100, the representatives' claim is severely weakened. Thus, this answer passes the Variance Test, and in an Except question the answer is incorrect.

Answer choice (C): This is the correct answer choice. Remember, this is an Except question, so this answer does not help in evaluating the representatives' claim.

In short, the argument is about what caused the deformed fins and who is liable for the losses incurred from lost sales. This answer deals with an after-the-issue fact, and so it does not bear on the representatives' claim.

Using the Variance Test, try "yes" and "no" responses to the question posed in this answer choice. If the answer to the question in this answer is Yes, the representatives' claim is unaffected; if the answer to the question in this answer is No, the representatives' claim is unaffected. Thus, this answer fails the Variance Test, and in an Except question we know the answer is correct.

Answer choice (D): If bluefin cod in general are susceptible to deformity-causing illnesses, it is possible that disease, rather than the chemicals, is the cause of the deformities in the Cod Bay bluefin. This response raises the possibility of an alternate cause, which is critical, so this response is incorrect.

Using the Variance Test, if the answer to the question in this answer is No, the representatives' claim is strengthened; if the answer to the question in this answer is Yes, the representatives' claim is weakened. Thus, this answer passes the Variance Test, and in an Except question the answer is incorrect.

Answer choice (E): Read this answer closely: "Are there gene-altering pollutants present...*other than* the chemical wastes that were dumped?" This answer is asking whether there could be some other type of pollutant besides the dumped chemicals. If so, that would call into question whether the dumped chemicals really did cause the deformities. Thus, this choice, like answer choice (D) raises the possibility that there is an alternate cause for the deformities.

Using the Variance Test, if the answer to the question in this answer is No, the representatives' claim is strengthened; if the answer to the question in this answer is Yes, the representatives' claim is weakened. Thus, this answer passes the Variance Test, and in an Except question the answer is incorrect.

Question #12: Method of Reasoning. The correct answer choice is (A)

Here the columnist notes that although both unsigned letters and certain news sources are anonymous, the news sources are usually accepted without question. However, because in both cases a person may be able to make incorrect statements with impunity, the columnist concludes that it makes sense to be skeptical of anonymous news sources.

The question stem asks you to identify the method of reasoning, so you should seek an answer that describes the path taken by the author, who points out that certain factors should lead to skepticism regardless of context. The author reaches this conclusion by pointing out the analagous anonymity in two different contexts, and arguing that the same attitude should be taken in response to each.

Answer choice (A): This is the correct answer choice. A comparison between two like things is an analogy, so any answer using the word "analogy" would be an initial Contender. Let's break down this answer choice and make sure it passes the Fact Test:

> "pointing out that a certain attitude would presumably be adopted in one situation..."

The "certain attitude" is skepticism, and the "one situation" is skepticism toward an unsigned letter.

> "...in order to support the claim that a similar attitude would be justified in an analogous situation"

The "similar attitude" is again skepticism, and the "analogous situation" is anonymous news sources. Thus, each element of the answer does occur, and this does correctly describe the reasoning used by the author.

Note that the validity of the analogy is irrelevant, because you are not asked to describe the flaw in the reasoning.

Answer choice (B): This response may seem attractive because it also references an "analogy." However, the answer is wrong for two reasons. Perhaps the easiest flaw to focus on is the fact that this choice claims that the "latter attitude is more justified than the former," but the argument claimed that the skepticism toward the letter—the former attitude presented—was the more justified. Thus, this answer has the relationship backward, and that alone is enough to eliminate this choice.

Furthermore, the analogy was between the sources, not the attitudes.

Answer choice (C): This argument involved an analogy between different things that actually occur, and not a generalization from a hypothetical situation, so this choice is incorrect.

There is also a problem with the phrase "all situations of a given type," because the "given type" would refer to anonymous items, yet there has only been a discussion of two types of anonymous items (and therefore not "all situations").

Answer choice (D): This response may also seem attractive because it references an "analogy." But, the argument does not show that any evidence is "usually false," only that a person would likely have some doubts and should be skeptical.

Answer choice (E): The argument does not conclude that the evidence is "likely to be false," only that a person would likely have some doubts and should be skeptical.

Question #13: Assumption. The correct answer choice is (B)

The author of this stimulus points out that art theft is on the rise, and that most stolen art is sold to wealthy collectors. The author then argues that since thieves steal what their customers are most interested in buying, security should focus on protecting museums' most valuable pieces.

If you are having trouble identifying the conclusion, note the use of the conclusion/premise indicator form "Consequently, since…" The conclusion is "museums ought to focus more of their security on their most valuable pieces."

The conclusion of the argument introduces a new idea: "most valuable pieces." Where does the basis for this new idea come from? There is no concrete statement about the value of the pieces, so obviously the author makes a leap to arrive at this concept, and in an Assumption question it is likely that the correct answer will address this new idea (notably, only answer choices (A), (B), and (D) address the value of art, and this means that answer choices (C) and (E) are unlikely to be correct). The premise just prior to the conclusion also includes a new idea: "what their customers are most interested in buying." This new idea will also likely be addressed in the correct answer, and notably only answer choice (B) addresses this idea. Thus, just based on an analysis of the pieces of this argument, answer choice (B) jumps out as the most likely correct answer because it connects the "new ideas" in the premise and conclusion. Remember, to excel on the LSAT you must understand how the test makers operate and take advantage of the patterns they use.

Answer choice (A): This response would serve to undermine the argument, so this choice is wrong.

Answer choice (B): This is the correct answer choice. This Supporter answer establishes a connection between value of the art and what the collectors want, and that fills the gap in the author's argument.

Note the proper negation of this answer: "Art pieces that are not very valuable *are* very much in demand by wealthy private collectors." As this negation would undermine the author's argument, we know from the Assumption Negation Technique that this is the correct answer.

Answer choice (C): This response is irrelevant because the stimulus does not concern adding security, but refocusing it. In any case, the general need for security is neither essential nor helpful in establishing that a refocusing of security is a good plan.

Answer choice (D): This was the most popular incorrect answer. The author's argument does not depend on the idea that most museums equally protect all their art, just that the most valuable art in some museums is not maximally protected.

Consider the negation of this answer: "Most museums provide *different* amounts of security for valuable and not-so-valuable art." Does this statement undermine the argument? No, because even if the security currently focuses more on valuable items than on non-valuable items, the author could claim it is a good idea to focus *even more* on those items. Since the negation of this answer choice does not undermine the author's argument, we know from the Assumption Negation Technique that this is an incorrect answer.

Answer choice (E): What wealthy private collectors do with their art after they buy it is beyond the scope of this argument, and so this choice is wrong.

Question #14: Flaw in the Reasoning—CE. The correct answer choice is (D)

This stimulus begins by presenting a statement indicating that insufficient rain *can* cause crops to falter and prices to rise. Then the author proceeds to state that in a recent crisis a nation experienced rising prices and faltering crops (which led to government intervention). Finally, the author draws a causal conclusion indicating that weather *must* have played a role in causing the crisis.

The abstract form of this argument is, "A can cause B. B occurred, so A must have caused B." As with all causal conclusions, this one is suspect because there is the possibility that other causes led to the effect, or that there is no causal relationship at all. There is also another error in the argument because the stimulus only states that insufficient rain is *possibly* a cause for faltering crops and rising prices. The conclusion is that, in this case, weather *must* have played a role, or was the cause, even though the premises neither state that weather has to be the cause, nor give any reason to believe that some other factor (insects, perhaps) could not cause crop failure as well.

Since you are asked to identify a flaw, and the stimulus features causal reasoning, remember to look for answer choices that use the word *cause* or *effect*, because it is very difficult to describe a causal flaw without using at least one of those words, or a synonym. In this case, only answer choices (A) and (D) contain those words, and you should seek and attack those answer choices.

Answer choice (A): The stimulus seeks to *conclude* that insufficient rain occurred, and does not start from the *premise* that insufficient rain occurs. This response, which confuses the conclusion with a premise, is incorrect.

Answer choice (B): Since the argument is not about whether the government was justified in its efforts to prevent starvation, this answer choice is off-topic. Furthermore, the severity of the crisis is not clearly related to the cause of the crisis.

Answer choice (C): This answer describes a flaw known as the Uncertain Use of a Term. However, "crisis" is not used differently in two separate contexts. Each use of the term refers very clearly to the crisis involving faltering crops and rising prices. This response attempts to respond to a political dimension that may exist in the test taker's mind, but certainly does not exist in the stimulus, and this choice is wrong.

Answer choice (D): This is the correct answer choice. The argument infers that because insufficient rain is a possible cause, it is in this case the definite cause, and that unsupported shift from possibility to certainty is a flaw.

Answer choice (E): This answer describes an error of conditional reasoning, not an error of causal reasoning.

Question #15: Resolve the ParadoxX—#%. The correct answer choice is (A)

The author of this stimulus presents an apparent paradox, so you should note the apparently contrasting elements:

1. Tuition per class has not risen over a four-year period.

2. Within that period, many students who once could afford tuition no longer can.

There are many ways to resolve this paradox. First of all, the stimulus leaves you a clue when it refers to tuition per class. Perhaps the students are taking more classes now, which would make their tuition rise even though tuition per class is constant. Second, there are many other factors—including income, scholarships, and living costs—that play into whether a student can afford even a constant tuition.

Since the question is a Resolve EXCEPT question, you should eliminate the four choices that resolve the paradox, and select the choice that does not resolve the paradox.

Answer choice (A): This is the correct answer choice. This answer addresses teacher salaries, and teacher salaries do not affect the ability of students to afford tuition when the tuition per class is unchanged.

Answer choice (B): This choice resolves the paradox by pointing out that full-time students are required to enroll in more classes, and thus they pay more money this year (remember, the stimulus referenced *per-class* tuition as being constant).

Answer choice (C): This choice resolves the paradox by establishing that living costs are rising, which would mean that the students have less money to spend on tuition.

Answer choice (D): This response resolves the paradox in very sly fashion. Even though it does not establish that a significant number of students fail to keep their scholarships, it does suggest that a great number of the students would initially be able to afford tuition because of the scholarships, and the possibility of losing that scholarship reduces one's ability to afford tuition.

Answer choice (E): This choice resolves the paradox by suggesting that many students no longer have work-study jobs available. Those students who needed the part-time office jobs might find employment elsewhere, but cutting the students out of the university jobs would have some effect on student income, and therefore their ability to afford tuition. For instance, the university town could be small and unable to support the students as part-time employees, working in-town could present conflicts with classes, or non-university jobs might tend to pay much less.

Question #16: Must Be True—FL. The correct answer choice is (E)

This stimulus is a fact set that does not contain a paradox, so you can expect a Must Be True question, or, less likely, a Cannot Be True question. In this instance, you are presented with a Must Be True question. In such a situation, it is important to be acquainted with the facts and any immediate conclusions that you can legitimately draw.

The first premise is that people are not happy unless they feel needed by others, and the second premise is that most people can feel needed only within the sphere of family and friends. Given the presence of the formal logic terms "unless" and "most," you should realize that this stimulus contains a formal logic relationship:

Happy ⟶ Feel Needed ⟶(M) Within Sphere of Friends and Family

However, this relationship does not yield a traditional inference, leaving some test takers at a loss. In a situation like this, move on to the answer choices and use them to help gain perspective on the problem.

Answer choice (A): This choice tries to trade on the last phrase of the stimulus, which suggests that almost everyone knows they can be replaced. However, this answer ignores the possibility of obtaining happiness within the sphere of family and friends, and so it is incorrect.

Answer choice (B): If anything, the stimulus implies that family life is very important to an individual's happiness, and so this answer choice moves in the opposite direction of what is needed.

Answer choice (C): There is no reason in the stimulus to suppose that most people actually find happiness. The stimulus concerned only how people might achieve happiness, not whether they have actually found it.

Answer choice (D): There was no indication that people do not appreciate having their jobs. It is illogical to conclude that the fact that others could do the job would cause people to appreciate their jobs less. In fact, the knowledge that someone else could do your job might actually cause you to value your job more.

Answer choice (E): This is the correct answer choice. Based on the weakness of the previous four answers (with the possible exception of (C)), this may have been an easy answer to select, especially since this answer seems to link several of the key ideas from the stimulus. Regardless, let's examine the logic of this answer and find the support in the stimulus. We know the following:

1. Everyone who is Happy is in the Feel Needed group

2. More than half of the Feel Needed group is in the Within the Sphere of Friends and Family group

Thus, looking solely at the Feel Needed group, since most of them are in the Sphere group, we know that less than half of the Feel Needed group could be Happy but at the same time not in the Sphere group. Thus, we can conclude that less than a majority of people can be Happy but at the same time not be Within Sphere of Friends and Family group.

Since this is a tricky concept, here is a numerical illustration based on a group of 100 people:

1. Suppose that 51 people are Happy. Accordingly, all 51 Happy people also Feel Needed.

2. Using the maximally beneficial circumstance for this answer, then, of the Feel Needed group we could say that 51 are Happy, and 49 are not Happy.

3. Using the maximally beneficial circumstance for this answer, at least 51 people in the Feel Needed group are in the Sphere group and at most 49 people are not in the Sphere group.

Conclusion 1: At least 2 of the people in the Sphere group are Happy, so a majority of the people cannot be Happy without some of them also being in the Sphere group.

So, a majority of people cannot be Happy without some of them being in the Sphere group, and less than a majority of people are Happy without being in the Sphere group (Even if you play with the numbers, you will find that the statement in this answer choice is supported).

Notice also, this is a conclusion about the *majority of all people*, which is warranted, rather than about the *majority of happy people*, which would be unwarranted.

Question #17: Flaw in the Reasoning. The correct answer choice is (C)

When you read through this stimulus, you may have noted that the author assumes that extrinsic value must be a matter of taste, and cannot be objective. If you recognize the presence of that assumption, this question is easy.

However, if you do not see that leap, this stimulus is best addressed by understanding the conditions in the critic's argument. The critic claims that the issues of value and judgment are related, and offers a conditional statement in the first part of the last sentence:

Value Not Intrinsic ⟶ Value Extrinsic

The critic then concludes that if an artwork's value is extrinsic, then judgments about the quality of the work can only be a matter of taste. The critic is incorrectly confusing objectivity with intrinsic qualities, and assuming that any extrinsic value cannot be objective.

Answer choice (A): The critic attempts to say that judgments are merely taste in a certain instance, so the critic does not take for granted that the judgments are *always* a matter of taste.

Answer choice (B): The critic only believes that in certain situations judgments can only be a matter of taste, not that people sometimes *agree about judgments* that are only matters of taste.

Answer choice (C): This is the correct answer choice. As discussed, this is exactly the premise that the critic assumes to draw his conclusion.

Answer choice (D): This answer is attractive because it connects judgments to objectivity. However, despite having some of the terms we expect to see in the correct answer, this is actually a Mistaken Negation of the correct answer (and thus a Mistaken Negation of the actual assumption in the argument). The correct answer can be diagrammed as:

Judgment about extrinsic value ⟶ ~~Objective~~

This answer can be diagrammed as:

Judgment about intrinsic value ⟶ Objective

Although it is easy to see why this was an attractive answer choice, the critic did not take this relationship for granted in the argument.

Answer choice (E): The author does seem to take this statement for granted, but that is not a flaw in the argument, because the argument concerns linking extrinsic value to judgment based on taste.

Question #18: Must Be True—SN. The correct answer choice is (A)

This stimulus describes the various benefits of decentralization to large organizations:

> Decentralization allows for autonomy, which *always* permits more realistic planning and encourages innovation.
>
> Decentralization allows the central administration to focus on the big picture rather than details.

Since you are asked to find the most strongly supported statement, you should simply look for a response that follows from the information in the stimulus.

Answer choice (A): This is the correct answer choice. Most students are probably turned off by the certainty of this answer choice, but such language is supported by the stimulus. Since, in large organizations, autonomy *always* allows more realistic planning, planning in a large organization without autonomous divisions *cannot* be as realistic as possible.

Remember, extreme answers are not necessarily wrong in Must Be True questions. They are only incorrect if the language of the stimulus is not extreme.

Answer choice (B): This response may be attractive, but is incorrect. The autonomy involved in decentralization encourages innovation, but that does not mean that centralized organizations discourage innovation. This answer choice is similar to a Mistaken Negation, and must be eliminated.

Answer choice (C): The stimulus listed some benefits of decentralization, but never weighed them against any drawbacks, so you cannot conclude from the stimulus anything certain about the value of decentralization relative to centralization, so this choice is wrong.

Answer choice (D): This was the most popular incorrect answer choice. Although the stimulus indicates that the central administrations of large institutions are partially responsible for *some* of the details of daily operations, we do not know that the central administrations of large institutions are partially responsible for *most* of the details of daily operations.

Answer choice (E): The stimulus stated that autonomy always *permits* more realistic planning, and *strongly encourages* innovation, but those statements do not mean that thc people implementing the policies are *always* able to achieve those ends. This difference in certainty makes this answer choice incorrect.

Furthermore, the stimulus discussed people who make decisions and are involved in implementation, but this choice only mentions people who are involved in implementation. Implementation was an *essential* part of improving decision making, but you should not make the mistake of assuming that anyone involved in implementation is also involved in decision-making, because that would be a Mistaken Reversal.

Question #19: Flaw in the Reasoning—#%. The correct answer choice is (C)

This argument has a complex structure, featuring two premises and a sub-conclusion that is then used to support the main conclusion of the argument:

Premise:	According to some astronomers, Earth is struck by a meteorite large enough to cause an ice age on an average of once every 100 million years.
Premise:	The last such incident occurred nearly 100 million years ago,
Sub-conclusion:	so we can expect that Earth will be struck by such a meteorite in the near future.
Main Conclusion:	This clearly warrants funding to determine whether there is a means to protect our planet from such meteorite strikes.

Do the supporting statements prove the main conclusion? Again, personalize the argument—does it make sense that if the earth has been struck "on an average of once every 100 million years" that suddenly we are in imminent danger? Of course not. The problem is that historical averages are only averages, and you cannot predict that a meteorite strike is overdue or likely based on such averages. The reasoning in the argument is made even weaker when you consider the scale of time involved.

Even if the historical pattern holds on average, a million or two million year variation would be a very small deviation compared to 100 million years, so it makes absolutely no sense to conclude that there will definitely be a meteorite strike in the "near future." And, of course, if there is no certainty that earth will be struck in the near future, how can funding be "clearly warranted?"

Answer choice (A): This choice was commonly selected, but there is no justification for this answer. The first section of the answer—"makes a bold prescription"—does occur in the reasoning. However, the second part—"on the basis of evidence that establishes only a high probability for a disastrous event"—does not occur because the stimulus does not establish a high probability for a disastrous event.

Of course, even if you saw the stimulus as establishing a high probability for disaster, wouldn't that high probability of disaster actually be a good justification for a "bold prescription?" Probably so, and thus it is hard to see how this choice would actually describe a flaw even if everything described within it had occurred.

Answer choice (B): The argument presumes precisely the opposite of this choice because the author believes that the probability of a chance event—the meteorite—is affected by whether or not it has happened recently. In the stimulus, the author makes clear that she believes that there is a greater likelihood of a meteorite strike today because there has not been a meteorite strike recently.

Furthermore, this choice describes reasoning that is often sound, as opposed to unsound, reasoning. Typically, a chance event is not affected by preceding events or whether there has been a recent occurrence of that event, and that is what is described in this answer. The reasoning in the stimulus, on the other hand, implies that for chance events, the past affects the future. Believing the stimulus is similar to a gambler believing that since he has thrown snake-eyes on average every third roll, it will keep happening every third roll. Historical averages, without some other supporting data, are prone to misrepresentation and misinterpretation, and should not be assumed to repeat.

Answer choice (C): This is the correct answer choice. Both parts of the answer occur, and what is described is a flaw:

> "moves from evidence about the average frequency of an event"—this section describes the fact that a large meteorite strikes earth on an average of once every 100 million years.
>
> "to a specific prediction about when the next such event will occur"—this section describes the sub-conclusion that "we can expect that Earth will be struck by such a meteorite in the near future."

An average cannot be used to make a specific prediction, and therein lies the flaw.

Answer choice (D): This choice could be relevant to whether investing in preventing a strike makes good public policy; however, it does not address the main flaw in the argument. Furthermore, even if the likelihood of an ice age resulting from a strike is very low, there could be other effects such as the destruction of cities that would suggest meteorite strike prevention as valuable, so the issue of ice ages is not critical.

Answer choice (E): The argument does not make any presumption that preventing large strikes is feasible, it only suggests that we begin investigations into protecting Earth.

Question #20: Parallel Flaw—CE. The correct answer choice is (A)

The author of this stimulus claims that because most nine-year-olds correctly identify the logos of major cigarette brands but very few nine-year-olds smoke, there is little connection between logo recognition and smoking. Abstractly, the argument attempts to show that a possible cause (logo recognition) does not have an expected effect (smoking).

The question stem asks you to identify the answer choice with the most similar flawed reasoning. Keeping in mind the different tests for Parallel Reasoning questions, consider the following when selecting an answer:

Match the Method of Reasoning: The argument asserts that a cause and effect relationship does not exist, so the correct answer choice must feature a similar type of relationship.

Match the Conclusion: The conclusion is fairly strong—"there is little or no connection between two items." The correct answer must feature a similar idea.

Match the Premises: There are two premises, one of which addresses a poll (a survey or a study would be similar ideas) and the other about results from that poll which indicate that a possible cause is not having an effect.

Match the Validity of the Reasoning: In this case the question stem tells you that the correct answer must contain flawed reasoning.

Obviously, the poll proves little, because it refers to juveniles who cannot purchase their own cigarettes, and ignores the potential effect that may occur by the time the child is old enough to plausibly pursue obtaining cigarettes. Since you are asked to identify the choice that contains similar reasoning, you should look for a response that refers to a group that has not yet had ample opportunity to develop a response to a particular cause.

Answer choice (A): This is the correct answer choice. Similar to the stimulus, a causal relationship is denied on the basis of a study. The conclusion, although worded differently, has the same meaning as that in the stimulus.

Specifically, three months is definitely not enough time to infer anything about the long-term effect of mercury poisoning, so this answer choice similarly does not cover enough time to rule out a cause-effect relationship.

Answer choice (B): This choice introduces two potential causes—dreams and parental influence—and asserts that one is more important to establishing an effect. The stimulus only involves ruling out a single cause and does not posit another, so this response is incorrect. The intent of this conclusion also differs from that in the stimulus.

Answer choice (C): This choice involves deciding which strategy—using fluoride or avoiding sweets—would have the greatest effect. However, the stimulus does not evaluate strategies or the importance of multiple causal factors, so this choice is wrong.

Answer choice (D): This answer choice was, by far, the most popular wrong answer choice *on this LSAT*. Most likely the cause of this popularity is that the wording of the conclusion is virtually identical to that in the stimulus. So, the problem with this answer lies elsewhere.

One serious problem is that this answer switches terms from the premise to the conclusion. One of the premises is about "average life span," but the conclusion is about "good health," and those two concepts are not the same. The stimulus, on the other hand, used the same terms from premise to conclusion.

Another problem is that this answer relates the group to an average ("average life span") whereas the stimulus related the group to a specific, definable result ("smoking"). This difference, while minor, helps indicate that this answer is problematic.

Answer choice (E): This quite possibly reasonable argument assumes that command of the issues, not knowledge of representatives' names, is a more important factor. Since the assumption is not entirely unwarranted, it is difficult to say that this choice is fatally flawed, though it certainly would be somewhat more strongly reasoned with the addition of another premise. In any case, the stimulus did not involve a comparison of factors, so this choice is dissimilar and incorrect.

Question #21: Must Be True—PR. The correct answer choice is (E)

In a nutshell, the author of this stimulus engages in an explanation of etiquette's relation to offensive speech. The argument states that etiquette need not involve the restriction of speech by law, but that it does demand that the expression of potentially offensive ideas be done in appropriate forums in a civil manner.

Since you are asked to apply the principle in the stimulus, you should search for an answer that conforms to these restrictions:

1. Etiquette opposes obscene and malicious speech.

2. Etiquette allows for civil discussion of possibly offensive ideas in the proper forum.

Answer choice (A): This answer choice very likely reflects some aspect of etiquette, but this particular aspect is not discussed in the stimulus. The correct response will involve potentially offensive ideas or language.

Answer choice (B): There is no reason to suppose that the stimulus refers to this sort of etiquette. The ideas expressed in a court room are not necessarily offensive. This choice is incorrect.

Answer choice (C): The stimulus does not give reason to believe there should be any legal restrictions on free speech, and you should not conclude that etiquette is governed by "majority rule." In fact, considering what etiquette is, and what common opinion is, you should realize that it is unwarranted to equate etiquette to popular opinion.

Answer choice (D): A news conference is precisely the forum in which a politician ought to be asked relevant questions of any sort, as long as the questioning is civil, so this choice contains a recommendation that is possibly contrary to the principles in the stimulus. Further, assuming the questions are posed in a civil manner, a question by itself is not necessarily offensive or embarrassing even though the underlying topic may be offensive, and thus this answer does not necessarily correspond to the principles discussed.

Answer choice (E): This is the correct answer choice. The principle of etiquette in the stimulus allows us to oppose obscene, malicious, or uncivil speech. Name-calling is probably malicious, and certainly uncivil. Since this response establishes the context as a panel on a "divisive moral issue," the ideas expressed may be potentially offensive and definitely controversial, bringing in the criteria of civil expression in that proper forum, so the moderator would be correct in disallowing name-calling under the principles in the stimulus.

Question #22: Justify the Conclusion—FL. The correct answer choice is (E)

Here the author states that only recordings projected to sell profitably will be transferred to compact disc, and concludes that most classic jazz recordings will not be transferred, because few such recordings are played on the radio.

Mechanistically speaking, there are two elements in the stimulus that are not duplicated elsewhere. The first is the idea of profitability, and the second is the idea of being played on the radio. As the mechanistic approach to Justify questions dictates that new or rogue elements typically appear in the correct answer, you should seek an answer that contains *both* of these elements. A scan of the answers indicates that answer choices (A), (B), and (D) include, in each case, just one of the two elements. These answers are thus less likely to be correct. Answer choices (C) and (E) contain both elements, and are much more likely to be correct. Not surprisingly, one is the right answer, and below we discuss why (C) is incorrect and (E) is correct. Note that, if you are pressed for time, you could simply guess between (C) and (E) since working through the formal logic aspect of this problem is time-consuming for most students.

In the interests of thoroughness, to separate answer choices (C) and (E) we must analyze the formal logic relationship present in the stimulus, so let's take a moment to deconstruct the structure of the author's argument:

> Remember that in a Justify question the premises do not, by themselves, prove the conclusion. So, you must first isolate the premises and then analyze the conclusion separately. In this problem, the first sentence is a premise and the last clause is a premise; the conclusion is in the middle, prefaced by "So."

To designate the terms in the stimulus, we will use the following notation:

TCD = Transferred onto Compact Disc
P = Profitably sell on compact disc
CJ = Classic Jazz
PR = Played on Radio

Using these symbols, reduce the stimulus to its diagrammatic components:

First premise:

TCD ———→ P

Contrapositive of the first premise:

$$\not{P} \longrightarrow T\not{C}D$$

Second premise:

$$CJ \xrightarrow{M} \not{P}\not{R}$$

Conclusion:

$$CJ \xrightarrow{M} T\not{C}D$$

The justifying statement, $\not{P}\not{R} \longrightarrow \not{P}$, would link the second statement to the first contrapositive to create the following chain:

$$CJ \xrightarrow{M} \not{P}\not{R} \longrightarrow \not{P} \longrightarrow T\not{C}D$$

Resulting in the following conclusion, which is identical to the one in the stimulus:

$$CJ \xrightarrow{M} T\not{C}D$$

Since you are asked to justify the conclusion by making it follow logically, you will need to supply the sufficient assumption, $\not{P}\not{R} \longrightarrow \not{P}$, or its contrapositive.

Answer choice (A): From a mechanistic perspective we already know this answer is insufficient to produce the conclusion in the argument.

Specifically, even if very few of the profitably transferable recordings are jazz recordings, all the jazz recordings could be included, since *all recordings* is a much larger group than *all jazz recordings*. Thus, there would be no justification for the conclusion that most classic jazz recordings will not be transferred onto compact disc.

Answer choice (B): Again, mechanistically, we know this answer does not have the correct components to produce the conclusion in the argument.

This choice somewhat reiterates the notion that few classic jazz recordings are played on the radio. Since compact disc transferals of jazz recordings will not in a sense outnumber originals, this statement tells us nothing that was not already inferred from the premises, and cannot justify the stimulus.

Answer choice (C): From our mechanistic analysis, we know this is one of the two leading Contenders. From a formal logic standpoint, this answer is close, but it is actually a Mistaken Negation of what is required to justify the conclusion.

This answer choice associates PR with P, and can be diagrammed as follows:

$$PR \longrightarrow P$$

This choice is a Mistaken Negation of the statement sufficient to justify the conclusion, which is:

$$\not{PR} \longrightarrow \not{P}$$

In this answer choice, the word "only" has a dramatic effect on the conditional relationship presented, and ultimately causes this answer to be incorrect. In addition, you should be aware that the test makers know that some students have learned to look just for modifiers, so the test makers have used a confusing grammatical structure that places "only" and its modified phrase "profit" on opposite ends of the sentence. Always remember that LSAT problems require careful, detailed reading.

Answer choice (D): Mechanistically, we know this answer is insufficient to produce the conclusion in the argument. This choice might offer an explanation for the companies' behaviors; however, it is neither a useful nor a sufficient assumption. The stimulus has already stated that only expectably profitable recordings are transferred, and the companies' motives do not matter.

Answer choice (E): This is the correct answer choice. The wording, however, is challenging and intentionally designed to confuse. Let's look at the language in the answer choice closely:

> "No recording that is not played on the radio is one that record companies believe would be profitable if transferred to compact disc."

The "No recording" refers to "one that record companies believe would be profitable if transferred to compact disc." The remaining section—"that is not played on the radio"—is the sufficient condition. Had the test makers been more benevolent, they could have rewritten this answer in the following simplified manner:

"If a recording is not played on the radio, then record companies do not believe that recording would be profitable in compact disc format."

The correct diagram for this answer choice is:

$$\cancel{PR} \longrightarrow \cancel{P}$$

As explained in the discussion of the stimulus, this is the statement that justifies the conclusion.

Question #23: Method of Reasoning—AP. The correct answer choice is (E)

As with all Method-Argument Part questions, you must be able to identify the logical components of the argument presented by the author:

Premise:	Over the past several years, increases in worldwide grain production have virtually ceased.
Sub-conclusion:	Further increases will be extremely difficult to achieve;
Premise:	most usable farmland is already being farmed with near-maximal efficiency.
Premise:	But worldwide demand for grain has been increasing steadily, due largely to continuing population growth.
Main Conclusion:	Hence, a severe worldwide grain shortage is likely.

The agricultural economist concludes that a worldwide grain-shortage is likely, and supports that by claiming that, while demand for grain is increasing, it will be difficult to significantly increase production of grain.

Note that in a question of this type you do not need to spend a long time thinking about the validity of the argument. Yes, the stimulus is flawed in that it does not consider the likelihood of advanced technologies or the like, but since the question simply asks you to identify the role played by one of the statements, you only need to know the structure of the argument. In this case, the role is that of sub-conclusion; that is, the claim follows from a premise and is then used to support the main conclusion.

Answer choice (A): This is a classic Half Right, Half Wrong answer. The first part of this answer—"It is one of the two conclusions drawn by the agricultural economist"—is an accurate description of the statement in question. However, since the claim is then used to support the main conclusion, the remainder of this answer incorrectly describes the statement.

Answer choice (B): This choice might have been attractive, but fails to grasp the correct causal flow, so this choice is wrong. The argument does attempt to justify the claim that future increases would be difficult by mentioning that farmland is almost maximally used already; however, the difficulty is offered as a cause of shortage, so the *main conclusion* uses difficulty as a cause instead of trying to explain what causes difficulty.

Answer choice (C): The claim is a premise, but it is certainly not the only premise.

Answer choice (D): The claim that future increases will be difficult to achieve is actually unsupported by the first sentence, so this response is incorrect. The economist's intent was to show that the situation has been present for some time, not to justify the idea that the situation would continue into the future. In any case, this response totally fails to identify the claim as a premise supporting the main conclusion.

Answer choice (E): This is the correct answer choice. In the second sentence, the claim is supported by the information that most available farmland is already being farmed with near-maximal efficiency, so the claim is a conclusion. The claim is also used to support the main conclusion, so all parts of this answer choice are verified.

PREPTEST 45 LR EXPLANATIONS

Question #24: Flaw in the Reasoning—CE. The correct answer choice is (D)

Here, Bardis presents evidence concerning the effects of television imagery on viewers. Apparently, research has proven that television advertisements affect consumers. On the basis of this evidence, some people have further concluded that violent television imagery sometimes causes violent behavior. Bardis disputes this notion by pointing out that the television ads might be effective because they are designed for that purpose whereas the violent imagery is not designed to cause violence. On the strength of this premise, Bardis concludes that television violence does not cause actual violence.

When examining the conclusion, note the absolute nature of the language. Does the premise prove beyond a shadow of a doubt that violent television imagery does not cause violence? Considering this issue will assist you in identifying the flaw in the reasoning.

Answer choice (A): Bardis never claims that advertisements can cause violent behavior, so this choice fails the Fact Test.

Answer choice (B): This was the most popular incorrect answer choice, primarily because it addresses cause and effect and it is clear that the stimulus contains causal reasoning. However, the flaw described in this answer choice is not the same as the flaw in the argument.

This response claims that Bardis confuses a "behavior" with a "stimulus," which is equivalent to confusing an effect with a cause. Since Bardis actually clearly defines his posited cause and effect, and there is no confusion between the two, this answer is incorrect.

Answer choice (C): The argument does not undermine itself, and does not question the persuasive power of advertising. It merely presumes that images have to be intended for a purpose to accomplish that purpose (this is illogical but it does not call into question the power of advertising).

Answer choice (D): This is the correct answer choice. The choice describes a classic error in the use of evidence, specifically one where some evidence against a position is taken to prove that the position is false. Bardis has raised a valid point against the people concluding that television violence causes violent behavior, namely that television violence is not designed to achieve this end where as television advertising is designed to achieve a specific end. However, that one point does not justify concluding that violent television imagery *never* causes violence.

For the record, the claim in "concluding that a claim is false" refers to the belief that television violence sometimes causes violent behavior. The "one purported fault" refers to the evidence that television violence is not designed to produce violence.

Answer choice (E): It is difficult to see how "causing violence" could be a separate issue from "causing violence." There is no key term that is confused, and the argument, while somewhat weak, does not get off-target, and the aim is always to define whether television violence causes actual violence.

Question #25: Strengthen—PR. The correct answer choice is (B)

In this stimulus, Sarah points out that the regulations for staff review are vague and difficult to interpret. She offers the example of regulations that state that unsatisfactory performance will be met with dismissal, but those same regulations do not define unsatisfactory performance. She concludes that some staffers may be dismissed simply because their personal views are different from their supervisors' views.

Sarah's reasoning is flawed because she ignores the likelihood that other employee contracts and guidelines define required performance quite well, and that the regulations are merely broad so as to avoid restatements or possible conflicts when future policy changes are made. Furthermore, she cynically assumes that supervisors will equate personal views with job performance and use their positions of power to blatantly exceed the review guidelines.

Regardless of the flaws in Sarah's argument, you are asked to find a principle that will strengthen Sarah's conclusion, which is that "some staff may be dismissed merely because their personal views conflict with those of their supervisors."

Answer choice (A): This principle does not serve to strengthen the claim that supervisors will or can act in a capricious manner, so this answer does not strengthen the conclusion.

If anything, this choice might actually serve to weaken the stimulus. If performance that falls slightly below standards is not met with dismissal, that might establish that supervisors have some leeway. But, it also establishes that supervisors have some tendency toward leniency. If supervisors are lenient, how does that help establish that they will terminate employees for personal differences?

Answer choice (B): This is the correct answer choice. If supervisors have the sole prerogative to interpret the regulations, that means that there are no other documents or guidelines that could restrict the supervisors from making the interpretation they wish to make. Accordingly, the supervisors would then have the power to dismiss employees for whatever reason they saw fit, and that fact helps strengthen the stimulus.

Answer choice (C): Sarah suggests that the regulations could be used to inappropriately punish people for having certain personal views, but she does not establish that supervisors could take that kind of action. This response helps support the idea that employees are accountable for their performance, and that is contrary to the idea (or at worst, neutral) that they would be punished for their personal views.

Answer choice (D): The argument attempted to show that some staff could be *dismissed* for their personal views. This answer only shows that employees can be kept in control or withheld from promotion. As those two issues are not the same, this answer does not assist in establishing Sarah's reasoning.

An answer such as this one can be attractive because it paints the company in a negative light. However, the task in this question is not to simply show that the company has poor policies, but rather that the policy in place can lead to the termination of an employee over their personal views. Always keep in mind precisely what you are supposed to strengthen in a question like this one.

Answer choice (E): Whether or not *employees* consider specific regulations to be fairer is not central to the issue at hand, which concerns how *supervisors* act.

4

Chapter Four: PrepTest 47 Logical Reasoning Section II

Chapter Four: PrepTest 47 Logical Reasoning Section II

PrepTest 47
Logical Reasoning Section II

SECTION III
Time—35 minutes
26 Questions

Directions: The questions in this section are based on the reasoning contained in brief statements or passages. For some questions, more than one of the choices could conceivably answer the question. However, you are to choose the best answer; that is, the response that most accurately and completely answers the question. You should not make assumptions that are by commonsense standards implausible, superfluous, or incompatible with the passage. After you have chosen the best answer, blacken the corresponding space on your answer sheet.

1. Although fiber-optic telephone cable is more expensive to manufacture than copper telephone cable, a telephone network using fiber-optic cable is less expensive overall than a telephone network using copper cable. This is because copper cable requires frequent amplification of complex electrical signals to carry them for long distances, whereas the pulses of light that are transmitted along fiber-optic cable can travel much farther before amplification is needed.

   The above statements, if true, most strongly support which one of the following?

   (A) The material from which fiber-optic cable is manufactured is more expensive than the copper from which copper cable is made.
   (B) The increase in the number of transmissions of complex signals through telephone cables is straining those telephone networks that still use copper cable.
   (C) Fiber-optic cable can carry many more signals simultaneously than copper cable can.
   (D) Signals transmitted through fiber-optic cable travel at the same speed as signals transmitted through copper cable.
   (E) The cost associated with frequent amplification of signals traveling through copper cable exceeds the extra manufacturing cost of fiber-optic cable.

2. Being near woodlands, the natural habitat of bees, promotes the health of crops that depend on pollination. Bees, the most common pollinators, visit flowers far from woodlands less often than they visit flowers close to woodlands.

   Which one of the following, if true, most strengthens the argument?

   (A) The likelihood that a plant is pollinated increases as the number of visits from pollinators increases.
   (B) Many bees live in habitats other than woodlands.
   (C) Woodlands are not the natural habitat of all pollinators.
   (D) Some pollinators visit flowers far from their habitats more often than they visit flowers close to their habitats.
   (E) Many crops that are not near woodlands depend on pollination.

3. According to the rules of the university's housing lottery, the only students guaranteed dormitory rooms are fourth-year students. In addition, any fourth-year student on the dean's list can choose a dormitory room before anyone who is not a fourth-year student.

   Which one of the following inferences is most strongly supported by the rules described above?

   (A) Benizer is a fourth-year student who is not on the dean's list, so she is not guaranteed a dormitory room.
   (B) Ivan and Naomi are both fourth-year students but only Naomi is on the dean's list. Therefore, Ivan can choose a dormitory room before Naomi.
   (C) Halle, a third-year student, is on the dean's list. Thus, she is guaranteed a dormitory room.
   (D) Gerald and Katrina are both on the dean's list but only Gerald is a fourth-year student. Thus, Gerald can choose a dormitory room before Katrina.
   (E) Anissa is a fourth-year student who is on the dean's list. Thus, since Jehan is a second-year student who is also on the dean's list, he can choose a dormitory room before Anissa.

GO ON TO THE NEXT PAGE.

4. To the editor:

For generations, magnificent racehorses have been bred in our area. Our most valuable product, however, has been generations of children raised with the character that makes them winners in the contests of life. Gambling is wrong, and children raised in an atmosphere where the goal is to get something for nothing will not develop good character. Those who favor developing good character in children over gambling on horses should vote against allowing our first racetrack to be built.

L.E.

Which one of the following, if true, most weakens L.E.'s argument?

(A) If good character is developed in children early, the children continue to have good character in different environments.
(B) In other areas with gambling, parents are able to raise children of good character.
(C) In most areas with horse racing, the percentage of adults who gamble increases gradually from year to year.
(D) Children whose parents gamble do not necessarily gamble when they become adults.
(E) Where voters have had the opportunity to vote on horse racing, they have consistently approved it.

5. Azadeh: The recent increase in the amount of organically produced food indicates that consumers are taking a greater interest in the environment. Thus, there is new hope for a healthier planet.

Ben: No, Azadeh, if you interviewed people who buy organic produce, you'd see that they're actually as selfish as everyone else, since they're motivated only by worries about their own health.

Azadeh's and Ben's statements provide the most support for holding that they disagree about whether

(A) it is likely that a healthy planet can be maintained if most people continue in their present eating habits
(B) people can become healthier by increasing their consumption of organic foods
(C) people ought to be more concerned about the environment than they currently are
(D) the rise in organic food production shows people to have a greater concern for the environment than they had before
(E) people can be persuaded to have a greater concern for the environment than they now have

6. Citizen: The primary factor determining a dog's disposition is not its breed, but its home environment. A bad owner can undo generations of careful breeding. Legislation focusing on specific breeds of dogs would not address the effects of human behavior in raising and training animals. As a result, such breed-specific legislation could never effectively protect the public from vicious dogs. Moreover, in my view, the current laws are perfectly adequate.

Which one of the following most accurately expresses the conclusion drawn by the citizen?

(A) The public would not be effectively protected from violent dogs by breed-specific legislation.
(B) A good home environment is more important than breeding to a dog's disposition.
(C) The home environment of dogs would not be regulated by breed-specific legislation.
(D) Irresponsible dog owners are capable of producing dogs with bad dispositions regardless of generations of careful breeding.
(E) The vicious-dog laws that are currently in effect do not address the effects of human behavior in raising and training dogs.

7. Legislator: To keep our food safe, we must prohibit the use of any food additives that have been found to cause cancer.

Commentator: An absolute prohibition is excessive. Today's tests can detect a single molecule of potentially cancer-causing substances, but we know that consuming significantly larger amounts of such a chemical does not increase one's risk of getting cancer. Thus, we should instead set a maximum acceptable level for each problematic chemical, somewhat below the level at which the substance has been shown to lead to cancer but above zero.

Of the following, which one, if true, is the logically strongest counter the legislator can make to the commentator's argument?

(A) The level at which a given food additive has been shown to lead to cancer in children is generally about half the level at which it leads to cancer in adults.
(B) Consuming small amounts of several different cancer-causing chemicals can lead to cancer even if consuming such an amount of any one cancer-causing chemical would not.
(C) The law would prohibit only the deliberate addition of cancer-causing chemicals and would not require the removal of naturally occurring cancer-causing substances.
(D) For some food additives, the level at which the substance has been shown to lead to cancer is lower than the level at which the additive provides any benefit.
(E) All food additives have substitutes that can be used in their place.

GO ON TO THE NEXT PAGE.

8. Consumer advocate: There is ample evidence that the model of car one drives greatly affects the chances that one's car will be stolen. The model of car stolen most often in our country last year, for example, was also the model stolen most often in the preceding year.

The consumer advocate's reasoning is most vulnerable to criticism on the grounds that it

(A) fails to address adequately the possibility that the model of car that was stolen most often last year was the most common model of car in the consumer advocate's country
(B) fails to address adequately the possibility that the age of a car also greatly affects its chances of being stolen
(C) fails to address adequately the possibility that the car model that was stolen most often last year was stolen as often as it was because it has a very high resale value
(D) presumes, without providing justification, that someone considering whether or not to steal a particular car considers only what model the car is
(E) presumes, without providing justification, that the likelihood of a car's being stolen should override other considerations in deciding which car one should drive

9. Laird: Pure research provides us with new technologies that contribute to saving lives. Even more worthwhile than this, however, is its role in expanding our knowledge and providing new, unexplored ideas.

Kim: Your priorities are mistaken. Saving lives is what counts most of all. Without pure research, medicine would not be as advanced as it is.

Laird and Kim disagree on whether pure research

(A) derives its significance in part from its providing new technologies
(B) expands the boundaries of our knowledge of medicine
(C) should have the saving of human lives as an important goal
(D) has its most valuable achievements in medical applications
(E) has any value apart from its role in providing new technologies to save lives

10. Naturalist: To be dependable, the accounting framework used by national economists to advise the government must take into account all of our nation's assets; but the current accounting framework used by our national economists assigns no value to government-owned natural resources, which are clearly assets.

The naturalist's statements, if true, most strongly support which one of the following?

(A) Economists' indifference toward the destruction of natural resources will lead policymakers to make poor decisions.
(B) Naturalists and economists disagree about whether natural resources have value.
(C) The accounting framework used by national economists is not reliable.
(D) Natural resources are a vital economic asset for every nation.
(E) Changes in the environment have a value that is not represented in any accounting framework.

11. Carrots are known to be one of the best sources of naturally occurring vitamin A. However, although farmers in Canada and the United States report increasing demand for carrots over the last decade, the number of people diagnosed with vitamin A deficiency in these countries has also increased in that time.

Each of the following, if true of Canada and the United States over the last decade, helps to resolve the apparent discrepancy described above EXCEPT:

(A) The population has significantly increased in every age group.
(B) The purchase of peeled and chopped carrots has become very popular, though carrots are known to lose their vitamins quickly once peeled.
(C) Certain cuisines that have become popular use many more vegetable ingredients, including carrots, than most cuisines that were previously popular.
(D) Carrot consumption has increased only among those demographic groups that have historically had low vitamin A deficiency rates.
(E) Weather conditions have caused a decrease in the availability of carrots.

GO ON TO THE NEXT PAGE.

12. Critics have argued that because Freudianism holds that people have unconscious desires that can defeat their attempts to follow rational life plans, it is incompatible with the predominantly rationalistic spirit of Western philosophical and psychological thought. But it is a central tenet of Freudianism that through psychoanalysis one can become conscious of one's previously unconscious desires, enabling one to avoid being defeated by them. Therefore, _______.

    Which one of the following most logically completes the argument?

    (A) Freudianism does not run counter to the rationalistic mainstream of Western philosophical and psychological thought
    (B) Freudianism holds that people can always achieve happiness through psychoanalysis
    (C) Freudianism may be the beginning of a new trend in Western philosophical and psychological thought
    (D) psychoanalysis provides one with a rational life plan
    (E) Freudianism reflects the predominantly rationalistic spirit of Western philosophical and psychological thought more than any other psychological theory

13. Writer: In the diplomat's or lawyer's world, a misinterpreted statement can result in an international incident or an undeserved prison term. Thus, legal and diplomatic language is stilted and utterly without literary merit, since by design it prevents misinterpretation, which in these areas can have severe consequences.

    The writer's argument requires assuming which one of the following?

    (A) Language that has literary value is more likely to be misunderstood than language without literary value.
    (B) Literary documents are generally less important than legal or diplomatic documents.
    (C) Lawyers and diplomats are much less likely to be misunderstood than are novelists.
    (D) The issues that are of interest to lawyers and diplomats are of little interest to others.
    (E) People express themselves more cautiously when something important is at stake.

14. Overexposure to certain wavelengths of strong sunlight is the main cause of melanoma, a virulent form of skin cancer. For this reason, doctors now urge everyone to put adequate sunblock on skin exposed to strong sunlight. Adequate sunblock, according to doctors, is any preparation that prevents sunburn even if the person is exposed to strong sunlight for a significant length of time.

    Which one of the following, if true, most weakens the recommendation that people wear adequate sunblock?

    (A) There is no evidence that there are wavelengths of sunlight that lead to both sunburn and melanoma.
    (B) There are people who have allergic reactions to certain chemicals found in many sunblocks.
    (C) Many sunblocks need repeated applications to remain effective for a significant length of time.
    (D) Toxins contained in certain chemical compounds also cause melanoma.
    (E) Sunburns appear immediately after exposure to the sun but melanoma appears years after repeated exposures.

15. In a study, parents were asked to rate each television program that their children watched. The programs were rated for violent content on a scale of one to five, with "one" indicating no violence and "five" indicating a great deal. The number of times their children were disciplined in school was also recorded. Children who watched programs with an average violence rating of three or higher were 50 percent more likely to have been disciplined than other children.

    Each of the following, if true, helps to explain the statistical relationship described above EXCEPT:

    (A) Children who are excited by violent action programs on television tend to become bored with schoolwork and to express their boredom in an unacceptable fashion.
    (B) When parents watch violent programs on television with their children, those children become more likely to regard antisocial behavior as legitimate.
    (C) Parents who rated their children's television viewing low on violence had become desensitized to the violence on television by watching too much of it.
    (D) Children learn from violent programs on television to disrespect society's prohibitions of violence and, as a result, are more likely than other children to disrespect the school disciplinary codes.
    (E) Parents who do not allow their children to watch programs with a high level of violence are more likely than other parents to be careful about other aspects of their children's behavior.

GO ON TO THE NEXT PAGE.

16. In the last election, 89 percent of reporters voted for the incumbent. The content of news programs reveals that reporters allowed the personal biases reflected in this voting pattern to affect their news coverage: 54 percent of coverage concerning the challenger was negative, compared with only 30 percent of that concerning the incumbent.

The argument is logically most vulnerable to criticism on the grounds that it

(A) presumes, without providing justification, that both candidates received equal amounts of coverage overall
(B) ignores the possibility that there was more negative news worthy of reporting concerning the challenger than there was concerning the incumbent
(C) presumes, without providing justification, that allowing biases to influence reporting is always detrimental to the resulting news coverage
(D) ignores the possibility that the electorate's voting behavior is not significantly affected by the content of coverage of candidates
(E) ignores the possibility that reporters generally fear losing access to incumbents more than they fear losing access to challengers

17. Art critic: Abstract paintings are nonrepresentational, and so the only measure of their worth is their interplay of color, texture, and form. But for a painting to spur the viewer to political action, instances of social injustice must be not only represented, but also clearly comprehensible as such. Therefore, abstract painting can never be a politically significant art form.

Which one of the following is an assumption that is required by the art critic's argument?

(A) Abstract painting cannot stimulate people to act.
(B) Unless people view representations of social injustice, their political activity is insignificant.
(C) Only art that prompts people to counter social injustice is significant art.
(D) Paintings that fail to move a viewer to political action cannot be politically significant.
(E) The interplay of color, texture, and form is not a measure of the worth of representational paintings.

18. North Americans who travel to Europe for the first time should include significant time in Italy on their itinerary. To develop an appreciation of a continent that goes beyond the mere accumulation of impressions, one needs to acquire a thorough knowledge of at least one country, and North Americans seem to find it easier to get to know Italy than other European countries.

Which one of the following best illustrates the principle illustrated by the argument above?

(A) A person who wants to learn to play the piano should study classical music, because though it is more difficult to play than is popular music, mastery of its techniques enables one to quickly master popular pieces.
(B) To overcome a fear of water that prevents one from swimming, one should paddle about in shallow water with a trusted friend who is a good swimmer.
(C) Edith Wharton is the most accessible of the classical U.S. writers. So in order to provide a superb introduction to U.S. literature, a class should emphasize her work while also studying the works of others.
(D) One can appreciate Taiko-drumming only if one understands how physically demanding it is. Thus, one should see Taiko-drumming and not just hear it in order to appreciate it fully.
(E) One should travel through North America by train rather than by automobile, because train travel imparts the same sense of open space as does automobile travel, while also affording one the full leisure to attend to the scenery.

GO ON TO THE NEXT PAGE.

19. Although high cholesterol levels have been associated with the development of heart disease, many people with high cholesterol never develop heart disease, while many without high cholesterol do. Recently, above average concentrations of the blood particle lipoprotein(a) were found in the blood of many people whose heart disease was not attributable to other causes. Dietary changes that affect cholesterol levels have no effect on lipoprotein(a) levels. Hence, there is no reason for anyone to make dietary changes for the sake of preventing heart disease.

    Which one of the following most accurately describes a flaw in the argument?

    (A) It fails to consider the possibility that lipoprotein(a) raises cholesterol levels.
    (B) It provides no evidence for a link between lipoprotein(a) and heart disease.
    (C) It presents but ignores evidence that, for some people, high cholesterol contributes to heart disease.
    (D) It fails to consider the possibility that poor diets cause some people to develop health problems other than heart disease.
    (E) It offers no explanation for why some people with high cholesterol levels never develop heart disease.

20. Philosopher: It is absurd to argue that people are morally obligated to act in a certain way simply because not acting in that way would be unnatural. An unnatural action is either a violation of the laws of nature or a statistical anomaly. There is no possibility of acting as one cannot, nor does the mere fact that something is not usually done provide any good reason not to do it.

    Which one of the following most accurately describes a technique used in the philosopher's argument?

    (A) undermining a concept by showing that its acceptance would violate a law of nature
    (B) stating the definition of a key term of the argument
    (C) using statistical findings to dispute a claim
    (D) undermining a claim by showing that the claim is self-contradictory
    (E) using empirical evidence to support one definition of a key term of the argument over another

21. Clearly, fitness consultants who smoke cigarettes cannot help their clients become healthier. If they do not care about their own health, they cannot really care for their clients' health, and if they do not care for their clients' health, they cannot help them to become healthier.

    The conclusion follows logically if which one of the following is assumed?

    (A) Anyone who does not care for his or her own health cannot help others become healthier.
    (B) Anyone who cares about the health of others can help others become healthier.
    (C) Anyone who does not care for the health of others cannot help them become healthier.
    (D) Anyone who does not smoke cares about the health of others.
    (E) Anyone who cares about his or her own health does not smoke.

GO ON TO THE NEXT PAGE.

22. If one does not have enough information to make a well-informed decision, one should not make a decision solely on the basis of the information one does possess. Instead, one should continue to seek information until a well-informed decision can be made.

Of the following, which one most closely conforms to the principle stated above?

(A) Economists should not believe the predictions of an economic model simply because it is based on information about the current economy. Many conflicting models are based on such information, and they cannot all be accurate.
(B) When deciding which career to pursue, one needs to consider carefully all of the information one has. One should not choose a career solely on the basis of financial compensation; instead, one should consider other factors such as how likely one is to succeed at the career and how much one would enjoy it.
(C) Though a researcher may know a great deal about a topic, she or he should not assume that all information relevant to the research is already in her or his possession. A good researcher always looks for further relevant information.
(D) When one wants to buy a reliable car, one should not choose which car to buy just on the inadequate basis of one's personal experience with cars. Rather, one should study various models' reliability histories that summarize many owners' experiences.
(E) When there is not enough information available to determine the meaning of a line of poetry, one should not form an opinion based on the insufficient information. Instead, one should simply acknowledge that it is impossible to determine what the line means.

23. Television network executive: Some scientists have expressed concern about the numerous highly popular television programs that emphasize paranormal incidents, warning that these programs will encourage superstition and thereby impede the public's scientific understanding. But these predictions are baseless. Throughout recorded history, dramatists have relied on ghosts and spirits to enliven their stories, and yet the scientific understanding of the populace has steadily advanced.

The television network executive's argument is most vulnerable to criticism on which one of the following grounds?

(A) It fails to consider that one phenomenon can steadily advance even when it is being impeded by another phenomenon.
(B) It takes for granted that if a correlation has been observed between two phenomena, they must be causally connected.
(C) It fails to consider that the occurrence of one phenomenon can indirectly affect the pervasiveness of another even if the former does not impede the latter.
(D) It fails to consider that just because one phenomenon is known to affect another, the latter does not also affect the former.
(E) It takes for granted that the contention that one phenomenon causes another must be baseless if the latter phenomenon has persisted despite steady increases in the pervasiveness of the former.

24. Police commissioner: Last year our city experienced a 15 percent decrease in the rate of violent crime. At the beginning of that year a new mandatory sentencing law was enacted, which requires that all violent criminals serve time in prison. Since no other major policy changes were made last year, the drop in the crime rate must have been due to the new mandatory sentencing law.

Which one of the following, if true, most seriously weakens the police commissioner's argument?

(A) Studies of many other cities have shown a correlation between improving economic conditions and decreased crime rates.
(B) Prior to the enactment of the mandatory sentencing law, judges in the city had for many years already imposed unusually harsh penalties for some crimes.
(C) Last year, the city's overall crime rate decreased by only 5 percent.
(D) At the beginning of last year, the police department's definition of "violent crime" was broadened to include 2 crimes not previously classified as "violent."
(E) The city enacted a policy 2 years ago requiring that 100 new police officers be hired in each of the 3 subsequent years.

GO ON TO THE NEXT PAGE.

25. A corporation created a new division. To staff it, applicants were rigorously screened and interviewed. Those selected were among the most effective, efficient, and creative workers that the corporation had ever hired. Thus, the new division must have been among the most effective, efficient, and creative divisions the corporation had ever created.

The flawed pattern of reasoning in which one of the following is most similar to that in the argument above?

(A) In order to obtain the best players for its country's Olympic team, a committee reviewed the performance of its country's teams. After reviewing statistics and reading reports, the committee chose one player from each of the six best teams, thus assuring that the six best players in the country had been chosen.
(B) Several salespeople were given incentives to recruit the largest number of new customers in one month. To monitor the incentive program, the boss interviewed one of the salespeople and found that the salesperson had already exceeded the minimum goals of the program. Thus the incentive program was indeed effective.
(C) A law firm decided to add a department devoted to family law. To obtain the best employees it could, the firm studied the credentials and composition of several other firms well known to have successful staffs working in family law. Eventually, the firm hired a staff of new lawyers and support personnel having training and aptitudes as much like those of the studied firms as possible. Thus the law firm must have created one of the best family-law departments.
(D) To put together this year's two All-Star Teams, the best players in the league were selected. Half of them were put on Team One, and half were put on Team Two. Since each player on the two teams was one of the best players in the league this year, it follows that the two All-Star Teams are the two best teams this year.
(E) Various schools chose teams of students to compete in a debate tournament. Each school's team presented a position and rebutted the others' positions. After the initial scores were in, the ten top teams competed against each other. Since one team eventually emerged with the highest average score, it was clearly the best team.

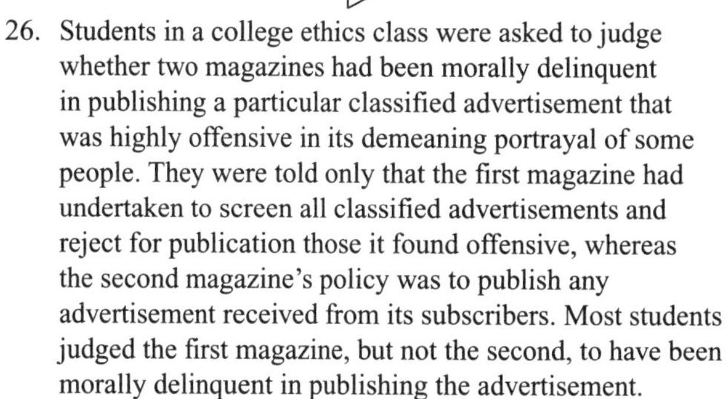

26. Students in a college ethics class were asked to judge whether two magazines had been morally delinquent in publishing a particular classified advertisement that was highly offensive in its demeaning portrayal of some people. They were told only that the first magazine had undertaken to screen all classified advertisements and reject for publication those it found offensive, whereas the second magazine's policy was to publish any advertisement received from its subscribers. Most students judged the first magazine, but not the second, to have been morally delinquent in publishing the advertisement.

Which one of the following principles, if established, provides the strongest justification for the judgment that the first magazine and not the second was morally delinquent?

(A) It is wrong to publish messages that could cause direct or indirect harm to innocent people.
(B) Anyone regularly transmitting messages to the public has a moral responsibility to monitor the content of those messages.
(C) If two similar agents commit two similar actions, those agents should be held to the same standard of accountability.
(D) Failure to uphold a moral standard is not necessarily a moral failing except for those who have specifically committed themselves to upholding that standard.
(E) A magazine should not be considered at fault for publishing a classified advertisement if that advertisement would not be offensive to any of the magazine's subscribers.

S T O P

IF YOU FINISH BEFORE TIME IS CALLED, YOU MAY CHECK YOUR WORK ON THIS SECTION ONLY.
DO NOT WORK ON ANY OTHER SECTION IN THE TEST.

PREPTEST 47 LOGICAL REASONING SECTION II

1. E	8. A	15. C	22. D
2. A	9. D	16. B	23. A
3. D	10. C	17. D	24. E
4. B	11. C	18. C	25. D
5. D	12. A	19. C	26. D
6. A	13. A	20. B	
7. B	14. A	21. E	

PrepTest 47 Logical Reasoning Section II Explanations

Question #1: Must Be True. The correct answer choice is (E)

This stimulus presents a comparison between the costs associated with fiber-optic cable and those associated with copper telephone cable. The fiber optic kind is more expensive to manufacture, yet it is the more cost-effective choice. The reason provided is that copper cable requires frequent amplification to carry complex electrical signals over long distances. The fiber optic option, on the other hand, carries pulses of light, which can travel much farther before amplification is needed.

In sum, the fiber optic cables cost more to make, but they are more cost effective because they require less signal amplification. Clearly, if fiber optic cable is more cost effective overall, the cost savings on amplification must be more than enough to compensate for the extra manufacturing costs. The question stem which follows is a Must Be True, which means that the correct answer choice must pass the Fact Test, and can be confirmed by the information from the stimulus alone.

Answer choice (A): Just because fiber-optic cable is more expensive to manufacture than copper cable does not necessarily mean that the *material* from which it is made is more expensive than copper. It is possible, for example, that the added cost of making fiber-optic cable is due to the equipment needed to make it, or to the complexity of the manufacturing process itself.

Answer choice (B): Although the stimulus provides that copper requires more amplification to travel the same distance, the author provides no evidence that telephone networks that still use copper cable are somehow strained. Remember: you cannot bring in information from outside the stimulus to answer the questions, even if such information is true in the "real" world. All of the information necessary to answer the question resides in the stimulus.

Answer choice (C): The author does not compare the number of signals that can be carried at once, by fiber-optic vs. copper cable. As with Answer choice (B), be careful not to bring in outside information when answering a Must Be True question. The correct answer choice must be confirmed by the information presented in the stimulus.

Answer choice (D): Because the relative speed of transmission of fiber-optic vs. copper cable is never discussed in the stimulus, this answer choice is incorrect.

Answer choice (E): This is the correct answer choice. Even if this choice had not been prephrased, we could confirm it as the right answer with the Fact Test: It must be true that the cost savings with fiber optic cable outweigh the extra costs associated with its manufacture.

Question #2: Strengthen. The correct answer choice is (A)

Crops that require pollination tend to be healthier when they are near woodlands, the natural habitat of bees, which are the main sources of pollination. Bees tend to visit plants near woodlands more often than they visit plants that are far from woodlands. Although the author is not explicit, it seems that the bees' more frequent visits to plants near woodlands promote the health of plants that need pollination.

The question stem requires you to find the answer choice that lends strength to the assertion that proximity to woodlands promotes the health of pollination-dependent plants.

Once you understand the logical structure of the argument, ask yourself if there is a missing link between the premise(s) and the conclusion. Observant test-takers will notice that the conclusion contains a new element—promoting the health of crops—which finds no support elsewhere in the stimulus. In other words, the author gives us no explicit reason to believe that the frequency of visits from pollinators is correlated with the crop's health.

Remember: Strengthen questions require you to choose the answer that most strengthens the argument. If true, the statement in Answer choice (A) improves the logical validity of the argument, but it does not prove the conclusion as true.

Answer choice (A): This is the correct answer choice. If true, the statement in Answer choice (A) improves the logical validity of the argument, but it does not prove the conclusion as true.

Answer choice (B): If many bees live in habitats other than woodlands, it is even more puzzling why crops are better off being near woodlands. This answer choice might weaken the argument, but it certainly does not strengthen it, so it is therefore incorrect.

Answer choice (C): The correct answer choice will strengthen the conclusion that it is good for pollination plants to be near woodlands. This choice provides that some pollinators live elsewhere. This does not strengthen the author's assertion—if anything it weakens it.

Answer choice (D): The use of the word "some" makes this information fairly weak: Basically, there is at least one pollinator that visits far-away flowers more often those nearby. This is fairly limited information, but it clearly does not strengthen the author's conclusion. In fact, it weakens the argument that crops benefit from proximity to pollinators.

Answer choice (E): If many crops that are not near woodlands depend on pollination, perhaps being far from the bees' natural habitat need not be a death sentence. Either way, since we have no indication as to whether these crops would be healthier if they were closer to the woodlands, it is impossible to evaluate the effect of this statement on the conclusion of the argument.

Question #3: Must Be True—PR. The correct answer choice is (D)

This stimulus provides two basic rules of a university housing lottery:

1. The only students guaranteed dorm rooms are fourth-year students.
2. Fourth year students on the dean's list can choose a dorm room before any non-fourth year.

The stimulus is followed by a Must Be True question stem, so we will be able to confirm the correct answer choice with the facts from the stimulus. Since the author provides only two rules, the correct answer choice will be the only one which breaks neither rule.

Answer choice (A): Whether Benizer is on the dean's list or not does not affect her chances of securing a dorm room. According to the first rule of the lottery, those who are guaranteed a dorm room need only be fourth-year students, regardless of whether they made the dean's list. Since Benizer satisfied the necessary condition in the question, it is possible (though not certain) that she would get a dorm room.

Answer choice (B): According to the second rule of the lottery, since Naomi is a fourth-year student who is on the dean's list, she will get a priority in choosing a dorm room over anyone who is not a fourth-year student. Given that Ivan *is* a fourth-year student, the rule is silent as to whether she can choose a room before him or not. Either way, since Ivan is not on the dean's list, there is no reason to suspect that he can choose a room before her either.

Answer choice (C): Even though Halle is on the dean's list, she is not a fourth-year student. Therefore, by the contrapositive property of the first rule, Halle will not be guaranteed a dorm room.

Answer choice (D): This is the correct answer choice. Since both Gerald and Katrina are on the dean's list but only Gerald is a fourth-year student, the second rule of the lottery guarantees that he can choose a dorm room before Katrina. Only this answer choice contains an inference that conforms to the rules that govern the housing lottery and is therefore the correct answer choice.

Answer choice (E): According to the second rule of the lottery, Anissa—a fourth-year student on the dean's list—will get priority over Jehan, who is a second-year student. This answer choice is the polar opposite of the correct one.

Question #4: Weaken—CE. The correct answer choice is (B)

To summarize the argument presented here, the letter to the editor warns against the building of a racetrack, because children raised in an atmosphere of gambling do not develop good character. The causal relationship asserted by the author can be diagrammed as follows:

C — E

Gambling ⟶ Children cannot develop good character

The answer to this question can certainly be prephrased, because a causal argument can be weakened in five ways. We should look for the answer choice which provides one of the following scenarios:

1. The hypothesized cause is present but the claimed effect is absent.
2. The supposed cause is absent, but the effect is present.
3. An alternative cause leads to the effect.
4. The supposed "cause" is actually the effect, and vice-versa.
5. A valid attack on a weakness in supporting data.

Answer choice (A): This answer choice does not adequately weaken the argument. Perhaps the children raised without gambling in the past were able to develop good character early, and will therefore not be affected by the introduction of a new racetrack. However, the author still has a point in arguing that the racetrack will be detrimental to future generations of children who will not develop good character at all.

Answer choice (B): This is the correct answer choice. If parents are able to raise children of good character despite the gambling around them, then perhaps gambling is not always a problem. By offering a counterexample in which the cause is present, but the effect is not, this answer choice weakens the causal relationship in the argument.

Answer choice (C): How the percentage of adults who gamble in areas with horse racing changes from year to year is irrelevant to examining the effect of gambling on children. Perhaps if that percentage increases from year to year, the author has a point in arguing that children should not be exposed to gambling. This answer choice certainly does not weaken the argument; if anything, it might support it.

Answer choice (D): Whether children raised by gambling parents might copy that behavior when they grow up is irrelevant to the author's conclusion. The author argues that gambling adversely affects the *character* of children, not their future propensity to gamble. In other words, even if children don't end up gambling when they become adults, their character may still have been affected by the environment in which they were raised. This is a classic Shell Game answer, used to attack a conclusion that is similar to, but slightly different from, the one presented in the stimulus.

Answer choice (E): Voter's approval of horse racing is immaterial to the question of whether horse racing will affect the character of children. This answer choice is incorrect.

Question #5: Point at Issue—CE. The correct answer choice is (D)

This dialogue deals with the increase in the production of organic produce and what has caused it. Azadeh's argument is that there is a new hope for a healthier planet, because the increase in the amount of organically produced food indicates that consumers are taking a greater interest in the environment. Ben, however, disagrees, stating that the increase in organic produce is motivated only by people's concerns about their own health. Clearly, the disagreement here is about whether the increase in organic food production is caused by environmental or health concerns:

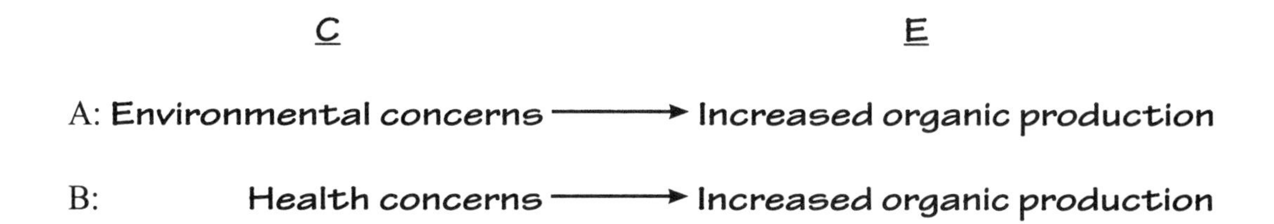

The dialogue is followed by a Point at Issue question, so we should probably look for the answer choice that concerns the motivation behind increased organic production.

In evaluating the five answer choices, remember that you can quickly apply the Agree/Disagree test to your contenders: the correct answer must produce responses where one speaker would say "I agree, the statement is correct" and the other speaker would say, "I disagree, the statement is incorrect." If those two responses are not produced, then the answer is incorrect.

Answer choice (A): Ben never mentions what it might take to maintain a healthier planet. This answer choice fails the Agree/Disagree Test and is therefore incorrect.

Answer choice (B): Azadeh never mentions health, so her opinion on this answer choice cannot be known. Without this information, this choice cannot be the correct answer.

Answer choice (C): Ben does not address whether people should be more concerned about the environment, so this answer choice also fails the Agree/Disagree Test. The disagreement here is not ethical but factual in nature: Azadeh and Ben disagree over what the cause for the increased organic production is, not over how people *ought* to behave.

Answer choice (D): This is the correct answer choice. This answer deals with the main point of contention between the two speakers—the question of what has motivated increased organic production. Azadeh would agree with the statement in this answer, and say that the increase does indicate a greater concern for the environment, while Ben would disagree, believing the increase to be motivated only by health concerns.

Answer choice (E): Ben never mentions whether he believes people can be persuaded to have a greater concern for the environment, so this answer fails the Agree/Disagree Test.

Question #6: Main Point. The correct answer choice is (A)

This citizen opens the statement with one simple premise: the primary factor determining a dog's disposition is its environment, not its breed. Legislation that focuses on specific breeds misses this point, and fails to consider the role of the human who raises and trains the dog. Thus, the author concludes, such legislation—that which focuses only on breed—cannot provide the public effective protection from vicious dogs. In closing, the author asserts the belief that current laws are adequate anyway.

Following the stimulus is a Main Point question, so the right answer choice will likely reflect the author's primary conclusion that breed-specific legislation could never protect the public from vicious dogs.

Answer choice (A): This is the correct answer choice, as it restates the conclusion of the argument.

Answer choice (B): This choice might be enticing, because it is factually accurate according to the stimulus, but keep in mind that this is a Main Point question, so this choice is incorrect.

Answer choice (C): While this answer choices also presents an accurate statement, they are both premises upon which the main conclusion is based, not the main point.

Remember: Main Point questions often contain incorrect answers that repeat premises of the argument: they are attractive because they are "true" based on what you have read, but do not summarize the author's main point.

Answer choice (D): While this answer choice is supported by the second sentence in the stimulus, it is a premise rather than the main point.

Answer choice (E): This answer is not supported by the information presented in the stimulus. If the current laws are adequate (last sentence of the stimulus), and the author's main concern is the effects of human behavior in raising and training dogs, then the vicious-dog laws that are currently in effect probably do address such effects.

Question #7: Weaken. The correct answer choice is (B)

In this dialogue, the legislator suggests prohibiting all substances that have been found to cause cancer. The commentator objects to the absolute ban on carcinogenic food additives claiming some cancer causing substances are safe in limited quantities, and concludes that setting a maximum acceptable level for each problematic chemical would be enough.

The question requires us to find the strongest counter to the commentator's argument—that is, the choice that will show the commentator's solution is not necessarily advisable. We might look for the choice that points to some other detriment associated with carcinogens, even in smaller amounts as suggested.

Answer choice (A): Just because the level at which a given food additive can cause cancer in children is only half the level at which it leads to cancer in adults, this does not hurt the commentator's argument. The commentator points to the extreme example of a single molecule, and the argument is that it might be safe to consume *some* such additives—an amount that is greater than zero. Such a small amount could still fall significantly below the children's cancer causing level as well, so this choice fails to weaken the commentator's argument.

Answer choice (B): This is the correct answer choice. If small amounts of several carcinogens would be enough to cause cancer, then any amount in a given food might be too much.

Answer choice (C): Since the distinction between naturally-occurring and deliberately-added carcinogenic substances is not discussed in either argument, the legislator has no reason to suspect that commentator's proposition would target only the deliberately-added chemicals.

Answer choice (D): At issue is not whether the benefit provided by some food additives can outweigh the increased risk of cancer, but whether the acceptable level of such additives should be set at zero. For the legislator to engage in any sort of cost-benefit analysis would entirely miss the point.

Answer choice (E): Just because all food additives have substitutes that can be used in their place does not help determine whether the commentator's objection is a valid one. Why use a substitute if the cancer-causing additive is never used in quantities that are large enough to cause harm? This answer choice does not weaken the commentator's conclusion and is therefore incorrect.

Question #8: Flaw in the Reasoning—#%, CE. The correct answer choice is (A)

The consumer advocate points out the fact that the same model was the most commonly stolen car for the last two years. Based on this premise, the advocate asserts that most often for two consecutive years indicates that the choice of car one drives can affect the chances of one's car being stolen. The advocate clearly believes that driving a model of car that is popular among car thieves causes one to be more likely a victim of car theft.

Perhaps this makes intuitive sense: if the Honda Accord consistently ranks as the most frequently stolen car model in the U.S., wouldn't driving an Accord make you more vulnerable to theft?

Not necessarily: to properly evaluate the scenario, we might also want information about how common that model is in general. For example, what if the Accord were also one of the most commonly driven car models in the U.S.? Then the statistics presented could simply be explained by that model's popularity, rather than its attractiveness to thieves.

Answer choice (A): This is the correct answer choice. If the model that was most often stolen over the last two years also happens to be the most popular car in the country, then that would provide an explanation for its popularity among thieves. Rather than leading to more thefts, the model is simply overrepresented in the general car population.

Answer choice (B): Because the author does not claim that the car model is the *only* factor affecting its chances of being stolen, it is unnecessary to consider other potentially relevant factors.

Answer choice (C): The author does not need to address the possibility that the most commonly stolen car might be popular because of its high resale value. That fact is consistent with the author's argument that driving such a car might affect the chances of one's car being stolen.

Answer choice (D): The author does not assume that the car model is the only relevant consideration for a thief. As with Answer choice (B), because the author does not claim that the car model is the *only* factor affecting its chances of being stolen, it is unnecessary to consider other factors that might play some role.

Answer choice (E): The author does not claim that the likelihood of one's car being stolen overrides any other considerations for a buyer. Even if there are other relevant factors to consider when buying a car, the conclusion still holds.

Question #9: Point at Issue. The correct answer choice is (D)

In this dialogue the speakers discuss the value of pure research as applied in different contexts. Laird says that technology's ability to save lives is great, but that the most worthwhile goal of pure research is to expand our knowledge. Kim disagrees, arguing that saving lives counts more. Essentially, the two speakers disagree over what is the most important goal of pure research: whether it is its role in expanding our knowledge (Laird), or its role in providing new technologies that save lives (Kim).

In evaluating the five answer choices, remember to apply the Agree/Disagree test to your contenders: The correct answer will produce responses where one speaker would say "I agree, the statement is correct" and the other speaker would say, "I disagree, the statement is incorrect." If those two responses are not produced, then we should consider the other answer choices.

Answer choice (A): While Laird would agree that pure research derives its significance *in part* from its providing new technologies, there is no evidence that Kim would disagree with that statement. Because her argument does not mention new technologies, this answer choice fails the Agree/Disagree test.

Answer choice (B): Both Laird and Kim would agree that pure research expands the boundaries of our knowledge of medicine. Laird explicitly states that in the second sentence of his argument, while Kim implies that pure research is necessary for the advancement of medicine ("without pure research, medicine would not be as advanced as it is"). Because this is a point of agreement, this answer choice is incorrect.

Answer choice (C): Both Laird and Kim would agree that saving lives is an important goal of pure research: Laird explicitly refers to saving lives as "worthwhile." They would disagree over whether saving lives is the *most* important goal of pure research, not whether it is an important goal. Because this is a point of agreement, this answer choice is incorrect.

Answer choice (D): This is the correct answer choice. Laird would disagree with the statement that pure research has its most valuable achievements in medical applications: for him, its role in expanding our knowledge trumps the importance of new technologies in saving lives. Kim, on the other hand, believes that saving lives (i.e. a medical application of pure research) counts most. Because this answer choice passes the Agree/Disagree test, it is the correct answer.

Answer choice (E): Both speakers would agree that the value of pure research extends beyond the provision of new technologies to save lives. Laird clearly states that in the second sentence of his argument. Kim's conclusion ("saving lives is what counts *most of all*," emphasis added) concedes that other factors matter too, just not as much.

Question #10: Must Be True. The correct answer choice is (C)

The naturalist quoted in this stimulus asserts that in order for an accounting system to be dependable, the framework used by national economists to advise the government must take into account all of the nations assets:

reliable framework ⟶ account for all national assets

Despite this, the current framework used assigns no value to government-owned resources, which means that not all of the nations assets are being accounted for. Although the author's opinion regarding the reliability of the current accounting framework should be fairly obvious, it is not stated outright. Regardless, if any reliable system will consider all national assets, then the currently used framework is not reliable. This is represented in the contrapositive of the conditional statement above. If a reliable accounting framework requires that all national assets are accounted for, then a system which fails to account for all national assets is not reliable:

does not account for all national assets ⟶ not reliable

When a stimulus that contains Conditional Reasoning is combined with a Must Be True question stem, immediately look for the contrapositive in the answer choices. Avoid Mistaken Reversal and Mistaken Negations.

Answer choice (A): The prospect for policy makers to make poor decisions is never discussed by the naturalist, so this choice fails the Fact Test.

Answer choice (B): The author does not discuss the perspective of the economists in this context, but there is no reason to believe that they would see no value in natural resources.

Answer choice (C): This is the correct answer choice, and the one whose conditional relationship is diagrammed in the discussion above: if an accounting system does not account for all national assets, then it is not a reliable framework.

Answer choice (D): This answer choice is too strong; the author does not discuss how important natural resources are to every nation. Since this information cannot be determined based on the information from the stimulus, this choice fails the Fact Test and cannot be correct.

Answer choice (E): The naturalist only asserts that a reliable framework must consider all of a nation's assets. There is no way to know whether changes in the environment might be represented in some accounting frameworks. Since this choice is unsupported by the stimulus, it must be ruled out as a contender for this Must Be True question.

Question #11: Resolve the ParadoxX. The correct answer choice is (C)

The author of this stimulus presents the apparent discrepancy between the growing demand for carrots, an important source of vitamin A, and the increasing number of vitamin A deficiencies during that same time (during the past decade). The stimulus is followed by a ResolveX question, which means that among the five answer choices, the four incorrect ones will provide a resolution to the paradox, and the one correct choice will not.

Answer choice (A): If the population has grown over the past decade, that provides an alternate explanation for the growing demand for carrots and for the increasing number of vitamin A deficiencies. Perhaps the market cannot keep up with demand, and as a result members of the growing population might not be able to get enough vitamin A. Because this answer choice resolves the paradox in the stimulus, it is not the correct answer to this ResolveX question.

Answer choice (B): If most of the carrots consumed are in peeled or chopped form, they would provide fewer vitamins, which would explain why the increase in consumption did not help people ward off vitamin A deficiency. Because this answer choice resolves the paradox in the stimulus, it is incorrect.

Answer choice (C): This is the correct answer choice. Even though the popularity of new cuisines that use a lot of carrots might help explain the growing demand, it does not help to explain why the number of vitamin A deficiencies has increased. Since this answer choice explains only one side of the paradox, it fails to resolve the discrepancy described in the stimulus and is therefore the correct answer choice to this ResolveX question.

Answer choice (D): If those who already consumed plenty of vitamin A (and thus had low vitamin A deficiency rates) were the same people who increased their carrot consumption, this would explain why the benefits of increased consumption of vitamin A have not been spread across the population. Because this answer choice resolves the paradox in the stimulus, it is incorrect.

Answer choice (E): If weather conditions have made carrots less readily available, this would explain why an increase in the demand for carrots might not have any effect at all. It wouldn't matter if everyone wanted carrots—as they became scarcer, we might expect deficiencies to increase, regardless of the increasing, but unmet, demand. Because this answer choice does help to explain the apparent inconsistency in the stimulus, it is incorrect.

Question #12: Main Point—FIB. The correct answer choice is (A)

This stimulus ends with a fill-in-the-blank, which generally means on the LSAT that we are dealing with a Main Point question. The conclusion indicator at the start of the last sentence ("therefore") should help you recognize that you are being asked for the conclusion of the argument.

Whenever the author begins an argument by outlining someone else's position ("critics have argued that..."), you should anticipate the author's direct disagreement with that position. In this case, the Freudian belief that people's unconscious desires can defeat their rational life plans is criticized by some as incompatible with the rationalistic spirit of Western philosophical and psychological thought. However, the author points out, Freudianism also holds that awareness of previously unconscious desires can allow a person to avoid being defeated by them. The blank which follows will likely go on to point out that the critics are therefore wrong in their claims of incompatibility.

Answer choice (A): This is the correct answer choice. As prephrased above, the main point of the stimulus is that there is not necessarily an incompatibility between Freudianism and Western philosophical and psychological thought because answer choice (A) contains a statement that is the exact opposite of the critics' position, it must be the author's main conclusion and is therefore the correct answer choice.

Answer choice (B): The stimulus contains no evidence that Freudianism holds such a position, and even if it did, that wouldn't be the author's main point.

Answer choice (C): The stimulus contains no evidence that Freudianism may be the beginning of a new trend in Western philosophical thought. Remember—Main Point questions require an answer that is provable by the information contained in the stimulus. Answers introducing new ideas cannot, therefore, be correct.

Answer choice (D): It is one thing for the author to believe that psychoanalysis is not incompatible with the rationalistic spirit of Western philosophical and psychological thought, and an entirely different thing to claim that psychoanalysis provides one with a rational life plan. Given the author's disagreement with the critics, she might believe that a Freudian approach does not necessarily defeat our attempts to follow rational life plans. However, this would merely be a subsidiary conclusion of the argument, which, as a whole, is driven towards discrediting the claim that psychoanalysis is incompatible with Western thought.

Answer choice (E): This answer choice goes too far. The author never claimed that Freudianism reflects the rationalistic spirit of Western philosophical thought, let alone claimed that it does a better job than any other psychological theory.

Question #13: Assumption. The correct answer choice is (A)

In the world of the lawyer or the diplomat, this stimulus provides, misinterpretation can lead to an international incident or wrongful prison sentences. Therefore, the author asserts, legal and diplomatic language has no literary merit, because such language is designed to avoid potentially costly misinterpretation:

Premise: Legal/Diplomatic language ⟶ Prevent misinterpretation

Conclusion: Legal/Diplomatic language ⟶ No literary merit

You might note that the conclusion makes a significant logical leap: the author clearly believes that a language designed to prevent misinterpretation cannot have literary merit.

Answer choice (A): This is the correct answer choice. You can always verify by using the Assumption Negation technique: what if language that has literary value is no more likely to be misunderstood than language without literary value? If the chances of misunderstanding either type of language were the same, then it would be illogical to conclude that legal language has no literary merit just because it is designed to prevent misinterpretation. Because the logical opposite of this answer weakens the conclusion of the argument, it contains a valid assumption.

Answer choice (B): The relative importance of literary vs. legal documents is not discussed in the stimulus, and therefore the conclusion cannot rely on it. This answer choice is incorrect.

Answer choice (C): Given that legal and diplomatic language seeks to prevent misinterpretation, lawyers and diplomats may well be less likely to be misunderstood than novelists. However, because this is not a Must Be True question and the implications that stem from the author's position are not essential to her conclusion, this answer choice is incorrect.

Answer choice (D): It is entirely irrelevant whether the issues that are of interest to lawyers are of any interest to other parties. Even if they were, the author's conclusion would still stand.

Answer choice (E): The idea of caution is only marginally relevant to the lawyers' imperative to prevent misinterpretation. Perhaps lawyers and diplomats are indeed more cautious than are other professionals, given the nature of their work. Nonetheless, the author's argument does not depend on it: imagine if people did not express themselves more cautiously even when something important was at stake? It is still possible that legal and diplomatic language is without literary merit because those who use it seek to prevent misinterpretation. Whether they do so with caution or not is irrelevant to the conclusion, which is why this answer choice is incorrect.

Question #14: Weaken. The correct answer choice is (A)

Because melanoma is caused by overexposure to certain wavelengths of strong sunlight, and adequate sunblock prevents sunburn, doctors recommend the use of sunblock (any preparation which prevents sunburn even where there is significant exposure to bright sunlight). You might have noticed the inconsistency between the two causal relationships: melanoma and sunburn are two different phenomena, but the suggested preventative approach is the same for both. Since the stimulus is followed by a Weaken question, we might look for the answer that points out this distinction.

Answer choice (A): This is the correct answer choice. If it is possible that the wavelengths of sunlight that lead to sunburn are different from those that lead to melanoma, then using the same approach for the prevention of both might not be effective.

Answer choice (B): The doctors never suggested that sunblock is entirely safe to use: they only urged everyone to use it in order to decrease their risk of melanoma, a virulent form of skin cancer. As long as the benefits of using sunblock outweigh the costs (such as the risk of developing allergic reactions to the chemicals found in it), the doctors' recommendation still holds.

Answer choice (C): Doctors never implied that it only takes a single layer of sunblock to protect against sunburn: they recommended that everyone wear *adequate* sunblock, defined as "any preparation that prevents sunburn" (whatever it takes). The point that many types of sunblock need repeated applications in order to remain effective does not challenge this recommendation; it merely clarifies its meaning.

Answer choice (D): The recommendation that people wear adequate sunblock was not based on the presumption that overexposure to sunlight is the *only* possible cause of melanoma. What if toxins can also cause melanoma? Doctors never suggested that the use of sunblock would entirely eliminate the risk of developing the skin cancer—only that it would prevent one particular cause of that cancer.

Answer choice (E): Just because melanoma, unlike sunburn, takes years to develop does not mean we should suddenly stop using sunblock. In fact, if repeated exposure to sun were shown to cause both sunburn and, eventually, melanoma, perhaps the use of sunblock is justified. This answer choice does not refute the doctors' recommendation and is therefore incorrect.

Question #15: Resolve the ParadoxX. The correct answer choice is (C)

Here the author describes a study in which parents rated the violence level of the television shows watched by their children. Using a scale of one to five, the parents rated the violence at a level of three or higher. The study also tracked the number of times each child was disciplined in school. The kids whose television shows ranked three or higher were 50% more likely to have been disciplined.

While not technically a paradox, the stimulus describes this correlation between children's exposure to violence on television and their likelihood of being disciplined in school. Since the question stem is a ResolveX, the four incorrect answer choices will successfully explain the correlation, while the correct answer choice will fail to do so.

Answer choice (A): If watching violence on TV leads to boredom with schoolwork, then it makes sense that children who watch violent programs are more frequently disciplined in school. Because this answer choice establishes a causal link between witnessing violence on TV and being disciplined in school, the statistical relationship described in the stimulus is thereby explained and the answer choice is incorrect.

Answer choice (B): If parents who watch violent programs with their children end up legitimizing antisocial behavior, it isn't surprising that their children are more frequently disciplined in school. Because this answer choice establishes a causal link between watching violence on TV and being disciplined in school, it explains the statistical relationship described in the stimulus and is therefore incorrect.

Answer choice (C): This is the correct answer choice. The statistical relationship described in the stimulus has to do with how *children*, not parents, react to violence on TV. The desensitization of the parents is inconsequential and fails to explain the correlation presented in the stimulus.

Answer choice (D): If children mimic what they learn from watching violent programs on TV, little wonder they are more likely to be disciplined in school. Because this answer choice establishes a causal link between witnessing violence on TV and being disciplined in school, the statistical relationship described in the stimulus is thereby explained and the answer choice is incorrect.

Answer choice (E): While this answer choice presents a correlation that seems irrelevant at first, we need to examine its implications a bit more closely. If parents who do not allow their children to watch violence on TV are also careful about other aspects of their children's behavior, it is reasonable to suspect that such children are better behaved and less likely to be disciplined than other children. By comparison, children who watch more violence on TV would be *more* likely to be disciplined.

Because this answer choice establishes a causal link between *not* witnessing violence on TV and *not* being disciplined in school, the statistical relationship is thereby explained and the answer choice is incorrect.

Question #16: Flaw in the Reasoning—CE, #%. The correct answer choice is (B)

In this stimulus the author presents information about media coverage of an election in which 89% of reporters were in favor of the incumbent. The author argues that reporters allowed their personal biases toward the incumbent to affect their news coverage, since 54 percent of the coverage concerning the challenger was negative, compared with only 30 percent of that concerning the incumbent. The causal relationship that underlies this argument can be diagrammed as follows:

C   E

Personal bias toward incumbent ⟶ Higher rate of negative coverage of challenger

As with many flawed causal arguments, the problem here is that the author has noted a correlation and mistakenly concluded that a causal relationship must exist. The correct answer choice will likely provide an alternative explanation for the relatively greater percentage of negative media coverage of the challenger.

Answer choice (A): There is no presumption that the candidates received the same amount of coverage. In fact, the actual amount of coverage is not mentioned at all. Rather, the author focuses on the negative *portion* of coverage for each candidate. Because the author compares what proportion of the coverage concerning each candidate was negative and not the actual *amount* of negative coverage devoted to them, it wouldn't matter if either candidate received more coverage overall.

Answer choice (B): This is the correct answer choice. The author of the stimulus wrongly presumes that bias can be the only cause for the different rates of negative coverage. This choice provides an alternative cause; if there was simply more negative news to cover with regard to the challenger, this would provide a reasonable explanation for the different rates of negative media coverage.

Answer choice (C): The author does not presume that allowing biases to influence reporting is always detrimental to the resulting news coverage, only that it was detrimental in this particular instance. This answer choice is incorrect.

Answer choice (D): The author never blamed the media for affecting voting behavior (besides, we have no idea who ultimately won the election, so voting behavior is entirely outside the scope of the stimulus). The argument only proposes that the content of coverage reflects the media's personal bias toward the incumbent.

Answer choice (E): If reporters fear losing access to incumbents more than they fear losing access to challengers, this makes the author's accusation of bias even more credible, thus strengthening her argument.

Question #17: Assumption. The correct answer choice is (D)

The art critic quoted in this stimulus concludes that abstract paintings can never be a politically significant form of art, because they are not comprehensibly representational and therefore do not spur the viewer to political action. This argument is based on conditional reasoning, so it may be worth your time to quickly diagram it:

AP = abstract paintings
R = representational
SPA = spur political action
PSA = politically significant art form

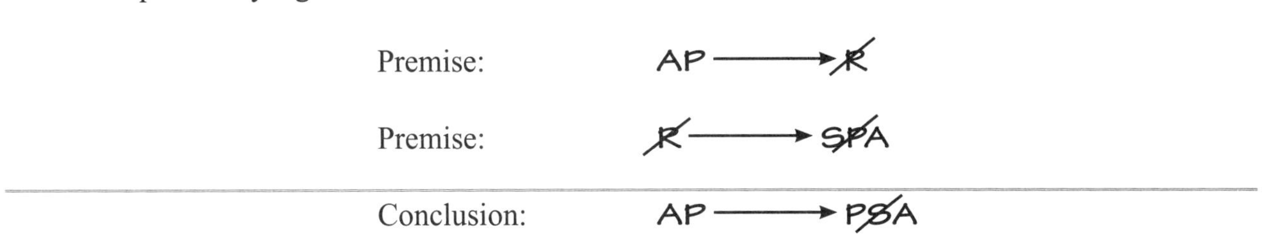

The two premises, when taken together, only lend support to the idea that abstract paintings cannot spur the viewer to political action (~~SPA~~) That does not, however, justify the claim that they are not a politically significant art form. In fact, nowhere else in this argument does the author talk about what constitutes a "politically significant art form." Because this is the new, rogue element in the conclusion, the proper Supporter Assumption must connect it to the premise set. A quick scan through all five answer choices reveals that only answer choice (D) deals with the idea of what a politically significant art form is—and that, of course, is the correct answer. If a painting does not spur to political action, it is not a politically significant art form (~~SPA~~ ⟶ ~~PSA~~).

Answer choice (A): The argument does not rely on the idea that abstract paintings cannot stimulate people to act—the premise is that they do not stimulate political action. Try the Assumption Negation technique: even if abstract paintings *could* stimulate people to act, they may still be unable to stimulate political action.

Answer choice (B): The significance of people's political activity is irrelevant to this argument.

Answer choice (C): Because this answer choice links political action to artistic significance, it may seem attractive at first. However, significant art need not be restricted to art that prompts people to counter social injustice. What if other art forms were equally (or more) significant? This would not change the conclusion, which is about politically significant art forms, not significant art forms in general. Had the author concluded that abstract paintings can never be significant art, this would have been a fine answer.

Beware of Shell Game answers—they occur when an idea or concept is raised in the stimulus and then a very similar idea appears in the answer choice, but the idea is changed just enough to be incorrect but still attractive. In Assumption questions, the Shell Game is usually used to support a conclusion that is similar to, but slightly different from, the one presented in the stimulus.

Answer choice (D): This is the correct answer choice. The author relies on the assumption that paintings that fail to move a viewer to political action cannot be politically significant. You can always double-check your answer by using the Assumption Negation technique: what if paintings that fail to move the viewer to political action can still be politically significant (for other reasons)? If that were so, the conclusion would be seriously undermined.

Answer choice (E): Even if the worth of representational paintings could be measured by analyzing the interplay of color, texture and form, representational paintings are not the focus of this argument: abstract paintings are. Furthermore, measuring the worth of any painting is an irrelevant consideration in this argument.

Question #18: Parallel Reasoning—PR. The correct answer choice is (C)

This stimulus describes how North Americans who travel to Europe for the first time should develop an appreciation of continent by including significant time in Italy on the itinerary (since it's easier to get to know Italy than other European countries).

The question stem asks you to identify an answer choice that illustrates that principle. The first step, then, might be to produce an abstraction of the principle in the argument. The basic idea in this case is that the best way to learn about a new field is to emphasize an aspect that is most easily accessible.

Answer choice (A): This answer choice counters the principle underlying the argument in the stimulus: the author recommended that we start with what's most accessible, not with what's most difficult to master.

Answer choice (B): The first part of this answer choice is attractive, since paddling about in shallow water is arguably easier than swimming in the deep ocean. However, the suggestion that we trust a friend who is a good swimmer has no parallel in the stimulus: for instance, had the author recommended that we hire a local guide to show us around, this answer choice would have conformed more closely to the principle in the stimulus.

Answer choice (C): This is the correct answer choice. Like the stimulus, the author of this answer recommends an easily accessible starting point for learning. Since Wharton is the most accessible writer, people should emphasize her work when first learning about the broad topic of US literature.

Answer choice (D): This answer choice does not parallel the principle underlying the stimulus because it indicates that one needs to experience something in order to appreciate it. This is markedly different from the principle contained in the stimulus.

Answer choice (E): This answer choice promotes a principle wherein two ways of accomplishing the same goal are compared and contrasted, and the recommended option has all the benefits of the rejected alternative while also affording additional benefits as well. This is markedly different from the principle contained in the stimulus.

Also, you should note that this answer choice is about traveling in North America, which is close enough to the subject matter of the stimulus (North Americans traveling in Europe) to make you worry. Any answer choice which addresses a similar subject as the stimulus should be a red flag. Such answer choices are occasionally correct, but they are usually traps for hurried or careless students.

Question #19: Flaw in the Reasoning—CE. The correct answer choice is (C)

The author begins this stimulus with the point that high cholesterol levels and heart disease have been associated, but not everyone who has one has the other. A recent study found elevated levels of lipoprotein(a) in many whose heart disease was not attributable to any other causes. Because diet has no effect on the levels of lipoprotein(a), the author concludes, there is no reason for *anyone* to make dietary changes for the sake of preventing heart disease.

The author has based a very bold and questionable conclusion on limited information. Although diet does not directly change lipoprotein levels, there could be any number of reasons that dietary changes might bolster the body's defenses. Changes in diet, after all, can have many different effects, including changing cholesterol levels (although there is not a *perfect* correlation between high cholesterol levels and heart disease, the stimulus begins with the point that high cholesterol levels and heart disease *have* been associated). Because we have reason to believe that not all cases of heart disease are attributable to lipoprotein(a), dietary changes that lower our cholesterol levels can still be an effective means of preventing heart disease.

Answer choice (A): Even if lipoprotein(a) raises cholesterol levels, those levels cannot be high enough to cause heart disease, because—as the description of the recent study points out—the heart disease in those with high lipoprotein(a) levels was not attributable to any other causes, including high cholesterol.

Answer choice (B): Actually, it does—the recent study clearly suggests a link between lipoprotein(a) and heart disease, considering the heart disease in those with high lipoprotein(a) levels was not attributable to any other causes. Perhaps the evidence is not conclusive, but it's still there.

Answer choice (C): This is the correct answer choice. The author opens the passage with the fact that high cholesterol and heart disease have been associated. While some people do have one without the other, meaning that there is not a *perfect* correlation between the two conditions, this does not change the fact that the two are associated.

Answer choice (D): Since the argument is only concerned with whether or not people should make dietary changes *for the sake of preventing heart disease*, it need not consider the possibility that poor diets can cause other health problems.

Answer choice (E): Granted, the author offers no explanation as to why some people with high cholesterol levels never develop heart disease. Her conclusion, however, is not contingent on explaining why the correlation between the two is imperfect. Perhaps those with high cholesterol levels who never develop heart disease have really low levels of lipoprotein(a)?

Question #20: Method of Reasoning. The correct answer choice is (B)

The philosopher quoted in this passage concludes that moral obligations to act in a certain way cannot be derived from the premise that it would be unnatural not to do so. For instance, it would be absurd to argue that everyone should be a vegetarian just because eating meat might be "unnatural." To defend her claim, the philosopher defines "unnatural" actions in the following way:

Unnatural action ⟶ Violation of laws of nature or Statistical anomaly

Because the laws of nature cannot be violated ("there is no possibility of acting as one cannot"), the only unnatural actions would be statistical anomalies. However, a statistical anomaly cannot be grounds for creating moral obligations. Therefore, moral obligations cannot be based on the finding that certain actions are unnatural.

Answer choice (A): The philosopher implies that the laws of nature cannot be violated, and accepting the idea of "unnatural" actions is not what violates the laws of nature. This answer choice is incorrect.

Answer choice (B): This is the correct answer choice. The key term in this argument is "unnatural action." By describing unnatural actions as either violations of the laws of nature or statistical anomalies, the philosopher seeks to demonstrate that unnatural actions cannot be legitimate grounds for moral obligations.

Answer choice (C): The philosopher is not using any statistical findings; she merely states that statistical anomalies cannot be grounds for moral obligations. This answer choice is incorrect.

Answer choice (D): This is by far the most commonly chosen incorrect answer, since the philosopher does undermine the claim that people can be morally obligated to act in a certain way. However, she does not show that this claim is self-contradictory (for instance, she never implied that "unnatural" actions are somehow "moral," or that "moral obligations" are always "unnatural"). This answer choice is incorrect.

Answer choice (E): The philosopher does not use any empirical evidence to support a claim, let alone distinguish between two definitions of a key term: the key term here ("unnatural action") has only one definition, which is comprised of two necessary conditions ("violation of laws of nature" or "statistical anomaly"). The author has not chosen to adopt one condition over another.

Question #21: Justify the Conclusion—SN. The correct answer choice is (E)

The conclusion here is that fitness consultants who smoke cannot help their clients become healthier. This is based on the following conditional chain: if someone does not care about their own health, they cannot care for their clients' health, and if they do not care for their clients' health, they cannot help their clients become healthier.

The missing link in this chain is the connection between someone caring for his/her own health, and that person smoking cigarettes (note that smoking is only mentioned in the conclusion; this is a key indicator that it must be connected back to other stimulus information in order to prove the conclusion is correct). To prove this conclusion, we must explicitly show that someone who smokes does not care about his or her own health, which would allow you to follow the chain and conclude that they cannot help their clients become healthier. Conditionally, this information can be diagrammed as follows:

COH = care about own health
CCH = care about clients' health
HCH = help clients become healthier

Premise 1: $C\not{O}H \longrightarrow C\not{C}H$

Premise 2: $C\not{C}H \longrightarrow H\not{C}H$

Justify Formula: $\text{Smoke} \longrightarrow C\not{O}H$

Conclusion: $\text{Smoke} \longrightarrow C\not{O}H \longrightarrow C\not{C}H \longrightarrow H\not{C}H$

Answer choice (A): This answer choice does not address smoking cigarettes so it cannot be correct. However, since it represents an additive inference from the two premises ($C\not{O}H \longrightarrow H\not{C}H$), it can be a trap for careless students who misunderstood the nature of the question stem.

Answer choice (B): This answer choice does not address smoking cigarettes so it cannot be correct. It is analogous to a Mistaken Negation of the second premise.

Answer choice (C): This answer choice does not address smoking cigarettes so it cannot be correct. It is a more general description of the second premise of the argument.

Answer choice (D): This answer choice is about people who do not smoke, so it does not address the new information in the conclusion (people who do smoke). Further, we need the chain to connect smoking with caring for one's own health, which this answer does not do.

Answer choice (E): This is the correct answer choice. If you take its contrapositive, you find that anyone who smokes does not care about his or her own health, so they cannot care about their clients' health, and as a result cannot help their clients become healthier (the conclusion is proven true). Since the contrapositive to a conditional statement is logically equivalent to it, either one would justify the conclusion of the argument.

Question #22: Must Be True—PR. The correct answer choice is (D)

Here the author's message is basically that decisions should be well-informed. The author warns against making decisions on the basis of incomplete information, and recommends that we continue gathering information until a well-informed decision can be made.

The question stem asks you to identify an answer that conforms to that principle. The correct choice will likely either have someone gathering information until a well-informed decision can be made, or avoiding making a decision without sufficient information.

Answer choice (A): Because at least some of the economic models based on current information are inaccurate, the author warns against making decisions on the basis of information that does not guarantee uniformly accurate predictions. This is markedly different from the principle presented in the stimulus.

Answer choice (B): Here, the author recommends that we consider all of the *available* information before deciding which career to pursue. This is slightly different from the principle presented in the stimulus, which recommended that we continue gathering *new* information until the point at which a well-informed decision can be made.

Answer choice (C): The stimulus warns against making decisions on the basis of incomplete information, while this answer choice warns against assuming that we already know everything about a topic. Furthermore, this choice recommends that researchers *always* look for further relevant information, which is somewhat different from the suggestion to delay acting until a well-informed decision can be made.

Answer choice (D): **This is the correct answer choice**. If our information about the reliability of a given car is inadequate, the author recommends that we gather more information before choosing which car to buy. Because this advice matches the principle advanced in the stimulus, it is the correct answer choice.

Answer choice (E): The first part of this answer choice is deceptively similar to the principle we are asked to apply: both warn against forming an opinion based on incomplete information. However, unlike the author of the stimulus, answer choice (E) does not recommend that we continue gathering information until a well-informed decision can be made; instead, it concedes that it is impossible to make a decision.

Question #23: Flaw in the Reasoning. The correct answer choice is (A)

The television network executive takes issue with those who claim that TV programs depicting paranormal incidents impede scientific understanding by increasing superstition. The executive says that such claims are baseless. This conclusion is based on a single premise: the paranormal has been used by dramatists throughout history, and yet scientific knowledge has advanced regardless.

There are several potential problems with this argument. First, the strength of the executive's analogy between TV programs and dramas depends on the extent of their similarity. Second, just because scientific understanding has advanced does not mean that it hasn't also been impeded by the dramatists' use of the paranormal. Without ghosts or spirits, perhaps our scientific knowledge would have advanced even more substantially.

Answer choice (A): This is the correct answer choice. As discussed above, the author fails to consider the possibility that scientific knowledge can advance even though it has been impeded.

Answer choice (B): Although errors in causality are quite common on the test, the executive is neither observing a correlation between two phenomena, nor implying that they are causally connected. On the contrary: she observes that depictions of the paranormal do not impede scientific understanding, thus rejecting the causal connection between them.

Answer choice (C): The objection that depictions of the paranormal might indirectly affect scientific understanding does nothing to the executive's argument, which is about whether such depictions *impede* our scientific understanding. Since this answer choice concedes that the former (i.e. depictions of the paranormal) does not impede the latter (i.e. scientific understanding), it fails to describe a problem in the executive's logic.

Answer choice (D): The possibility that scientific knowledge might somehow affect depictions of the paranormal reverses the causality between the two. Because the executive never claimed that the two are causally related (quite on the contrary—she rejects such causation in order to defend her programs), the possibility of a reverse cause-and-effect does nothing to the argument. If anything, this answer choice describes a flaw in the scientists' method of reasoning, not the executive's.

Answer choice (E): To avoid being deceived by the description given in this answer choice, compare it to the stimulus: the executive's argument assumes that depictions of the paranormal cannot impede the public's scientific understanding if the latter (i.e. scientific understanding) has persisted despite steady increases in the pervasiveness of the former (i.e. depictions of the paranormal). Because the stimulus contains no evidence suggesting that depictions of the paranormal have become more pervasive, this answer choice fails to describe an error in the executive's reasoning.

Question #24: Weaken—CE. The correct answer choice is (E)

Noting a 15% decrease in last year's violent crime rate, and the fact that a new mandatory sentencing law enacted last year, the police commissioner claims that the mandatory sentencing law must have been effective.

The police commissioner attributes the drop in their city's crime rate to the new mandatory sentencing laws because no other policy changes were made that year:

<u>C</u>		<u>E</u>
New mandatory sentencing law	⟶	Drop in crime rate

As we have seen, there are several ways to attack a causal conclusion, with an alternative explanation of the evidence presented. In this case, since we know that there was a drop in the city's crime rate last year, one possibility is that the right answer choice might suggest an alternative cause for the noted effect—last year's decrease in the crime rate.

Answer choice (A): This seems like an attractive choice at first: indeed, if many other cities have shown a correlation between improving economic conditions and decreased crime rates, perhaps we have an alternate cause for the decrease in the rate of violent crime in this particular city. However, there is no evidence that the commissioner's city is anything like the other cities that participated in the study; as we know, the term "many" is rather vague.

Answer choice (B): If judges had imposed harsh penalties for some crimes before the new law was enacted, could this be the reason for the decrease in violent crime rate last year? Perhaps, but why didn't the rate drop sooner? If it did, perhaps the penalties do represent a viable alternate cause and the commissioner's conclusion is weakened. On the other hand, if the crime rate began dropping only after the new mandatory sentencing law was enacted, the commissioner's conclusion would be strengthened. Given that we have no information about how the penalties affected the crime rate before the imposition of the new law, this answer choice cannot conclusively weaken the causal relationship in this stimulus.

Answer choice (C): The decrease in the city's overall crime rate is irrelevant to an argument that seeks to explain only the decrease in the violent crime rate.

Answer choice (D): This is a commonly chosen incorrect answer, since changing the way we define "violent crime" can potentially affect how much "violent crime" is registered in the city. Unfortunately, this answer choice strengthens the argument: if the definition was broadened, we would expect the city to register *more* violent crimes. Given that the city experienced a decrease in the rate of violent crimes despite the broadening of their definition, it seems even more likely that the newly enacted sentencing law had an effect.

Answer choice (E): This is the correct answer choice If the city enacted a policy 2 years ago requiring that 100 new police officers be hired in each of 3 subsequent years, then last year was the first year in which the city hired 100 new police officers. It is still true that no other major policy changes were made last year, but a policy change made *two* years ago only went into *effect* last year. Since this choice provides an alternate explanation for the decrease in the violent crime rate, the commissioner's argument is weakened.

Question #25: Parallel Flaw. The correct answer choice is (D)

Following a certain corporation's rigorous screening and interview process, a new division was created. Because the applicants selected to staff the new division were among the most effective, efficient, and creative workers that the corporation had ever hired, the author concludes that the new division must also have been among the most effective, efficient, and creative divisions the corporation had ever created. Clearly, this is an error of composition (part-to-whole): the author assumes that just because something is true of each of the parts, it is true of the whole as well. This need not be the case: what if each new employee is extremely creative and efficient, but they don't work well together as a team?

To answer the Parallel Flaw question, you need to examine the argumentative structure of each answer choice and select the one that commits a similar error of composition.

Answer choice (A): Here, the committee chose one player from each of the six best teams, thus assuring that the six best players had been chosen. The committee does not claim that they assembled the best Olympic team possible, only that *each* of the six players is the best in the country.

Observant test-takers will notice that the logical fallacy behind this conclusion is one of division, not composition: the author mistakenly assumes that just because the six teams from which the players were chosen were the best in the country, the players themselves were also the best in the country. An error of division occurs when the author attributes a characteristic of the whole (the teams) to a part of that whole (the players). Because this is the reverse of the error committed in the stimulus, answer choice (A) is incorrect.

Answer choice (B): The author concludes that the incentive program was effective because it proved effective in one isolated case (the interviewed salesperson). The logical fallacy behind this conclusion is one of overgeneralization: taking a small number of instances and treating those instances as if they support a broad, sweeping conclusion. While erroneous, this argument is markedly different from the argument in the stimulus, which attributed a characteristic of *each* part of the group to the group as a whole.

Answer choice (C): Here, the law firm studied the staffing of other, successful firms and then tried to replicate their credentials in hiring its own staff of attorneys. The decision process is markedly different from the one described in the stimulus, which involved no attempt at imitating other, successful divisions.

Some students might be tempted to choose this answer because, like the argument in the stimulus, it is about hiring personnel. Remember: any answer choice which addresses a similar subject as the stimulus should be a red flag. Such answer choices are rarely correct.

Answer choice (D): This is the correct answer choice. Since each of the players on the two teams was among the best in the league, the two teams must also have been the two best teams of the year. The author commits the same error of composition, attributing a characteristic of each individual part of the group (the players) to the group as a whole (the two teams).

NB! Do not be misled by the fact that the players were split into two teams: the logical fallacy (part-to-whole) is still exactly the same as the one in the stimulus.

Answer choice (E): This answer choice describes a tournament, in which victorious teams compete against each other until one team emerges with the highest average score. This selection process is logically sound, and has no parallel in the stimulus.

Question #26: Strengthen—PR. The correct answer choice is (D)

This stimulus deals with a college ethics class and how its members perceive moral delinquency with regard to a highly offensive classified advertisement placed in two different magazines, one of which had undertaken to screen all of its advertisements, and the other of which provided no monitoring whatsoever. The ethics class perceived only the first of the two magazines to be morally delinquent.

The question stem asks for a principle that would support this judgment. It seems that because the first magazine had undertaken the task of screening all ads and rejecting the ones it deemed offensive, whereas the second one never promised anything of the sort, students may have felt that the first magazine had defined itself as a monitor, creating an expectation of monitoring. With the second magazine, there was apparently no such expectation, so the students perceived no moral delinquency.

Answer choice (A): This principle imposes moral liability whenever harm was done. Based on it, both magazines should have been judged morally delinquent, since they both published the offensive advertisement.

Answer choice (B): This principle imposes moral liability whenever someone regularly transmits messages to the public. Because both magazines are in this business, both should have been judged morally delinquent.

Answer choice (C): Because the two magazines did commit similar actions but only one of them was deemed morally delinquent, this principle does not justify exonerating the second magazine from responsibility.

Answer choice (D): This is the correct answer choice. The failure of a magazine to uphold some kind of moral standard is only a failing (or a mark of moral delinquency) if a commitment has been made to uphold such a standard. This would explain why the students only found the actions of the first magazine objectionable, and didn't seem to mind the fact that the second magazine had run the very same ad.

Answer choice (E): Because the advertisement was offensive to subscribers from both magazines, this principle would not apply in either case.

5

Chapter Five: PrepTest 58 Logical Reasoning Section I

Chapter Five: PrepTest 58 Logical Reasoning Section I

POWERSCORE
BY BARBRI

PrepTest 58

Logical Reasoning Section I

PREPTEST 58 LRI

SECTION IV
Time—35 minutes
26 Questions

Directions: The questions in this section are based on the reasoning contained in brief statements or passages. For some questions, more than one of the choices could conceivably answer the question. However, you are to choose the best answer; that is, the response that most accurately and completely answers the question. You should not make assumptions that are by commonsense standards implausible, superfluous, or incompatible with the passage. After you have chosen the best answer, blacken the corresponding space on your answer sheet.

1. Commentator: Although the present freshwater supply is adequate for today's patterns of water use, the human population will increase substantially over the next few decades, drastically increasing the need for freshwater. Hence, restrictions on water use will be necessary to meet the freshwater needs of humankind in the not-too-distant future.

Which one of the following is an assumption required by the argument?

(A) Humans will adapt to restrictions on the use of water without resorting to wasteful use of other natural resources.
(B) The total supply of freshwater has not diminished in recent years.
(C) The freshwater supply will not increase sufficiently to meet the increased needs of humankind.
(D) No attempt to synthesize water will have an appreciable effect on the quantity of freshwater available.
(E) No water conservation measure previously attempted yielded an increase in the supply of freshwater available for human use.

2. Psychologist: The best way to recall a certain word or name that one is having trouble remembering is to occupy one's mind with other things, since often the more we strive to remember a certain word or name that we can't think of, the less likely it becomes that the word will come to mind.

The principle that underlies the psychologist's argument underlies which one of the following arguments?

(A) Often, the best way to achieve happiness is to pursue other things besides wealth and fame, for there are wealthy and famous people who are not particularly happy, which suggests that true happiness does not consist in wealth and fame.
(B) The best way to succeed in writing a long document is not to think about how much is left to write but only about the current paragraph, since on many occasions thinking about what remains to be done will be so discouraging that the writer will be tempted to abandon the project.
(C) The best way to overcome a serious mistake is to continue on confidently as though all is well. After all, one can overcome a serious mistake by succeeding in new challenges, and dwelling on one's errors usually distracts one's mind from new challenges.
(D) The best way to fall asleep quickly is to engage in some mental diversion like counting sheep, because frequently the more one concentrates on falling asleep the lower the chance of falling asleep quickly.
(E) The best way to cope with sorrow or grief is to turn one's attention to those who are experiencing even greater hardship, for in many circumstances this will make our own troubles seem bearable by comparison.

GO ON TO THE NEXT PAGE.

3. Letter to the editor: The Planning Department budget increased from $100,000 in 2001 to $524,000 for this year. However, this does not justify your conclusion in yesterday's editorial that the department now spends five times as much money as it did in 2001 to perform the same duties.

   Which one of the following, if true, most helps to support the claim made in the letter regarding the justification of the editorial's conclusion?

   (A) Departments other than the Planning Department have had much larger budget increases since 2001.
   (B) Since 2001, the Planning Department has dramatically reduced its spending on overtime pay.
   (C) In some years between 2001 and this year, the Planning Department budget did not increase.
   (D) The budget figures used in the original editorial were adjusted for inflation.
   (E) A restructuring act, passed in 2003, broadened the duties of the Planning Department.

4. At mock trials in which jury instructions were given in technical legal jargon, jury verdicts tended to mirror the judge's own opinions. Jurors had become aware of the judge's nonverbal behavior: facial expressions, body movements, tone of voice. Jurors who viewed the same case but were given instruction in clear, nontechnical language, however, were comparatively more likely to return verdicts at odds with the judge's opinion.

   Which one of the following is best illustrated by the example described above?

   (A) Technical language tends to be more precise than nontechnical language.
   (B) A person's influence is proportional to that person's perceived status.
   (C) Nonverbal behavior is not an effective means of communication.
   (D) Real trials are better suited for experimentation than are mock trials.
   (E) The way in which a judge instructs a jury can influence the jury's verdict.

5. Doctor: While a few alternative medicines have dangerous side effects, some, such as many herbs, have been proven safe to consume. Thus, though there is little firm evidence of medicinal effect, advocates of these herbs as remedies for serious illnesses should always be allowed to prescribe them, since their patients will not be harmed, and might be helped, by the use of these products.

   Which one of the following, if true, most seriously weakens the doctor's argument?

   (A) Many practitioners and patients neglect more effective conventional medicines in favor of herbal remedies.
   (B) Many herbal remedies are marketed with claims of proven effectiveness when in fact their effectiveness is unproven.
   (C) Some patients may have allergic reactions to certain medicines that have been tolerated by other patients.
   (D) The vast majority of purveyors of alternative medicines are driven as much by the profit motive as by a regard for their patients' health.
   (E) Any pain relief or other benefits of many herbs have been proven to derive entirely from patients' belief in the remedy, rather than from its biochemical properties.

6. When a nation is on the brink of financial crisis, its government does not violate free-market principles if, in order to prevent economic collapse, it limits the extent to which foreign investors and lenders can withdraw their money. After all, the right to free speech does not include the right to shout "Fire!" in a crowded theatre, and the harm done as investors and lenders rush madly to get their money out before everyone else does can be just as real as the harm resulting from a stampede in a theatre.

   The argument does which one of the following?

   (A) tries to show that a set of principles is limited in a specific way by using an analogy to a similar principle that is limited in a similar way
   (B) infers a claim by arguing that the truth of that claim would best explain observed facts
   (C) presents numerous experimental results as evidence for a general principle
   (D) attempts to demonstrate that an explanation of a phenomenon is flawed by showing that it fails to explain a particular instance of that phenomenon
   (E) applies an empirical generalization to reach a conclusion about a particular case

GO ON TO THE NEXT PAGE.

7. Although many political candidates object to being made the target of advertising designed to cast them in an adverse light, such advertising actually benefits its targets because most elections have been won by candidates who were the targets of that kind of advertising.

The pattern of flawed reasoning in the argument most closely parallels that in which one of the following?

(A) Although many people dislike physical exercise, they should exercise because it is a good way to improve their overall health.
(B) Although many actors dislike harsh reviews of their work, such reviews actually help their careers because most of the really prestigious acting awards have gone to actors who have had performances of theirs reviewed harshly.
(C) Although many students dislike studying, it must be a good way to achieve academic success because most students who study pass their courses.
(D) Although many film critics dislike horror films, such films are bound to be successful because a large number of people are eager to attend them.
(E) Although many people dislike feeling sleepy as a result of staying up late the previous night, such sleepiness must be acceptable to those who experience it because most people who stay up late enjoy doing so.

8. Working residents of Springfield live, on average, farther from their workplaces than do working residents of Rorchester. Thus, one would expect that the demand for public transportation would be greater in Springfield than in Rorchester. However, Springfield has only half as many bus routes as Rorchester.

Each of the following, if true, contributes to a resolution of the apparent discrepancy described above EXCEPT:

(A) Three-fourths of the Springfield workforce is employed at the same factory outside the city limits.
(B) The average number of cars per household is higher in Springfield than in Rorchester.
(C) Rorchester has fewer railway lines than Springfield.
(D) Buses in Springfield run more frequently and on longer routes than in Rorchester.
(E) Springfield has a larger population than Rorchester does.

9. People who need to reduce their intake of fat and to consume fewer calories often turn to fat substitutes, especially those with zero calories such as N5. But studies indicate that N5 is of no use to such people. Subjects who ate foods prepared with N5 almost invariably reported feeling hungrier afterwards than after eating foods prepared with real fat and consequently they ate more, quickly making up for the calories initially saved by using N5.

The reasoning in the argument is most vulnerable to criticism on the grounds that the argument fails to consider the possibility that

(A) many foods cannot be prepared with N5
(B) N5 has mild but unpleasant side effects
(C) not everyone who eats foods prepared with N5 pays attention to caloric intake
(D) people who know N5 contains zero calories tend to eat more foods prepared with N5 than do people who are unaware that N5 is calorie-free
(E) the total fat intake of people who eat foods prepared with N5 tends to decrease even if their caloric intake does not

10. Music historian: Some critics lament the fact that impoverished postwar recording studios forced early bebop musicians to record extremely short solos, thus leaving a misleading record of their music. But these musicians' beautifully concise playing makes the recordings superb artistic works instead of mere representations of their live solos. Furthermore, the conciseness characteristic of early bebop musicians' recordings fostered a compactness in their subsequent live playing, which the playing of the next generation lacks.

The music historian's statements, if true, most strongly support which one of the following?

(A) Representations of live solos generally are not valuable artistic works.
(B) The difficult postwar recording conditions had some beneficial consequences for bebop.
(C) Short bebop recordings are always superior to longer ones.
(D) The music of the generation immediately following early bebop is of lower overall quality than early bebop.
(E) Musicians will not record extremely short solos unless difficult recording conditions force them to do so.

GO ON TO THE NEXT PAGE.

11. Recent studies indicate a correlation between damage to human chromosome number six and adult schizophrenia. We know, however, that there are people without damage to this chromosome who develop adult schizophrenia and that some people with damage to chromosome number six do not develop adult schizophrenia. So there is no causal connection between damage to human chromosome number six and adult schizophrenia.

    Which one of the following most accurately describes a reasoning flaw in the argument above?

    (A) The argument ignores the possibility that some but not all types of damage to chromosome number six lead to schizophrenia.
    (B) The argument presumes, without providing evidence, that schizophrenia is caused solely by chromosomal damage.
    (C) The argument makes a generalization based on an unrepresentative sample population.
    (D) The argument mistakes a cause for an effect.
    (E) The argument presumes, without providing warrant, that correlation implies causation.

12. City councilperson: Many city residents oppose the city art commission's proposed purchase of an unusual stone edifice, on the grounds that art critics are divided over whether the edifice really qualifies as art. But I argue that the purpose of art is to cause experts to debate ideas, including ideas about what constitutes art itself. Since the edifice has caused experts to debate what constitutes art itself, it does qualify as art.

    Which one of the following, if assumed, enables the conclusion of the city councilperson's argument to be properly inferred?

    (A) Nothing qualifies as art unless it causes debate among experts.
    (B) If an object causes debate among experts, no expert can be certain whether that object qualifies as art.
    (C) The purchase of an object that fulfills the purpose of art should not be opposed.
    (D) Any object that fulfills the purpose of art qualifies as art.
    (E) The city art commission should purchase the edifice if it qualifies as art.

13. It is a given that to be an intriguing person, one must be able to inspire the perpetual curiosity of others. Constantly broadening one's abilities and extending one's intellectual reach will enable one to inspire that curiosity. For such a perpetual expansion of one's mind makes it impossible to be fully comprehended, making one a constant mystery to others.

    Which one of the following most accurately expresses the conclusion drawn in the argument above?

    (A) To be an intriguing person, one must be able to inspire the perpetual curiosity of others.
    (B) If one constantly broadens one's abilities and extends one's intellectual reach, one will be able to inspire the perpetual curiosity of others.
    (C) If one's mind becomes impossible to fully comprehend, one will always be a mystery to others.
    (D) To inspire the perpetual curiosity of others, one must constantly broaden one's abilities and extend one's intellectual reach.
    (E) If one constantly broadens one's abilities and extends one's intellectual reach, one will always have curiosity.

14. Theater managers will not rent a film if they do not believe it will generate enough total revenue—including food-and-beverage concession revenue—to yield a profit. Therefore, since film producers want their films to be shown as widely as possible, they tend to make films that theater managers consider attractive to younger audiences.

    Which one of the following is an assumption required by the argument?

    (A) Adults consume less of the sort of foods and beverages sold at movie concession stands than do either children or adolescents.
    (B) Movies of the kinds that appeal to younger audiences almost never also appeal to older audiences.
    (C) Food-and-beverage concession stands in movie theaters are usually more profitable than the movies that are shown.
    (D) Theater managers generally believe that a film that is attractive to younger audiences is more likely to be profitable than other films.
    (E) Films that have an appeal to older audiences almost never generate a profit for theaters that show them.

GO ON TO THE NEXT PAGE.

15. Almost all advances in genetic research give rise to ethical dilemmas. Government is the exclusive source of funding for most genetic research; those projects not funded by government are funded solely by corporations. One or the other of these sources of funding is necessary for any genetic research.

If all the statements above are true, then which one of the following must be true?

(A) Most advances in genetic research occur in projects funded by government rather than by corporations.
(B) Most genetic research funded by government results in advances that give rise to ethical dilemmas.
(C) At least some advances in genetic research occur in projects funded by corporations.
(D) No ethical dilemmas resulting from advances in genetic research arise without government or corporate funding.
(E) As long as government continues to fund genetic research, that research will give rise to ethical dilemmas.

16. Corporate businesses, like species, must adapt to survive. Businesses that are no longer efficient will become extinct. But sometimes a business cannot adapt without changing its core corporate philosophy. Hence, sometimes a business can survive only by becoming a different corporation.

Which one of the following is an assumption required by the argument?

(A) No business can survive without changing its core corporate philosophy.
(B) As a business becomes less efficient, it invariably surrenders its core corporate philosophy.
(C) Different corporations have different core corporate philosophies.
(D) If a business keeps its core corporate philosophy intact, it will continue to exist.
(E) A business cannot change its core corporate philosophy without becoming a different corporation.

17. A survey taken ten years ago of residents of area L showed that although living conditions were slightly below their country's average, most residents of L reported general satisfaction with their living conditions. However, this year the same survey found that while living conditions are now about the same as the national average, most residents of L report general dissatisfaction with their living conditions.

Which one of the following, if true, would most help to resolve the apparent conflict between the results of the surveys described above?

(A) Residents of area L typically value aspects of living conditions different from the aspects of living conditions that are valued by residents of adjacent areas.
(B) Between the times that the two surveys were conducted, the average living conditions in L's country had substantially declined.
(C) Optimal living conditions were established in the survey by taking into account governmental policies and public demands on three continents.
(D) Living conditions in an area generally improve only if residents perceive their situation as somehow in need of improvement.
(E) Ten years ago the residents of area L were not aware that their living conditions were below the national average.

GO ON TO THE NEXT PAGE.

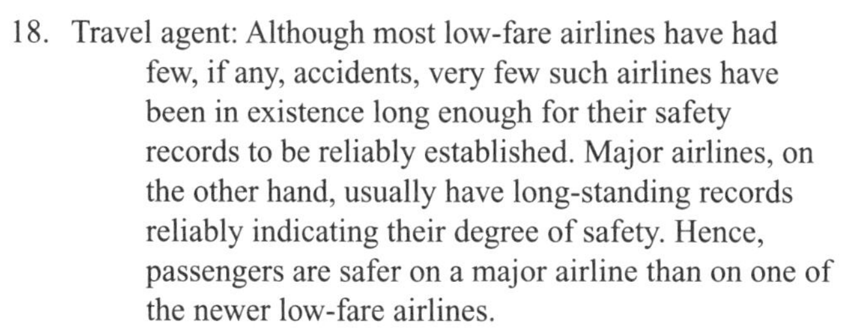

18. Travel agent: Although most low-fare airlines have had few, if any, accidents, very few such airlines have been in existence long enough for their safety records to be reliably established. Major airlines, on the other hand, usually have long-standing records reliably indicating their degree of safety. Hence, passengers are safer on a major airline than on one of the newer low-fare airlines.

    Of the following, which one is the criticism to which the reasoning in the travel agent's argument is most vulnerable?

    (A) The argument fails to address adequately the possibility that the average major airline has had a total number of accidents as great as the average low-fare airline has had.
    (B) The argument draws a general conclusion about how safe passengers are on different airlines on the basis of safety records that are each from too brief a period to adequately justify such a conclusion.
    (C) The argument fails to consider the possibility that long-standing and reliable records documenting an airline's degree of safety may indicate that the airline is unsafe.
    (D) The argument takes for granted that airlines that are the safest are also the most reliable in documenting their safety.
    (E) The argument fails to address adequately the possibility that even airlines with long-standing, reliable records indicating their degree of safety are still likely to have one or more accidents.

19. Economist: Our economy's weakness is the direct result of consumers' continued reluctance to spend, which in turn is caused by factors such as high-priced goods and services. This reluctance is exacerbated by the fact that the average income is significantly lower than it was five years ago. Thus, even though it is not a perfect solution, if the government were to lower income taxes, the economy would improve.

    Which one of the following is an assumption required by the economist's argument?

    (A) Increasing consumer spending will cause prices for goods and services to decrease.
    (B) If consumer spending increases, the average income will increase.
    (C) If income taxes are not lowered, consumers' wages will decline even further.
    (D) Consumers will be less reluctant to spend money if income taxes are lowered.
    (E) Lowering income taxes will have no effect on government spending.

20. A person with a type B lipid profile is at much greater risk of heart disease than a person with a type A lipid profile. In an experiment, both type A volunteers and type B volunteers were put on a low-fat diet. The cholesterol levels of the type B volunteers soon dropped substantially, although their lipid profiles were unchanged. The type A volunteers, however, showed no benefit from the diet, and 40 percent of them actually shifted to type B profiles.

    If the information above is true, which one of the following must also be true?

    (A) In the experiment, most of the volunteers had their risk of heart disease reduced at least marginally as a result of having been put on the diet.
    (B) People with type B lipid profiles have higher cholesterol levels, on average, than do people with type A lipid profiles.
    (C) Apart from adopting the low-fat diet, most of the volunteers did not substantially change any aspect of their lifestyle that would have affected their cholesterol levels or lipid profiles.
    (D) The reduction in cholesterol levels in the volunteers is solely responsible for the change in their lipid profiles.
    (E) For at least some of the volunteers in the experiment, the risk of heart disease increased after having been put on the low-fat diet.

GO ON TO THE NEXT PAGE.

21. Columnist: Although there is and should be complete freedom of thought and expression, that does not mean that there is nothing wrong with exploiting depraved popular tastes for the sake of financial gain.

Which one of the following judgments conforms most closely to the principle cited by the columnist?

(A) The government should grant artists the right to create whatever works of art they want to create so long as no one considers those works to be depraved.
(B) People who produce depraved movies have the freedom to do so, but that means that they also have the freedom to refrain from doing so.
(C) There should be no laws restricting what books are published, but publishing books that pander to people with depraved tastes is not thereby morally acceptable.
(D) The public has the freedom to purchase whatever recordings are produced, but that does not mean that the government may not limit the production of recordings deemed to be depraved.
(E) One who advocates complete freedom of speech should not criticize others for saying things that he or she believes to exhibit depraved tastes.

22. When a society undergoes slow change, its younger members find great value in the advice of its older members. But when a society undergoes rapid change, young people think that little in the experience of their elders is relevant to them, and so do not value their advice. Thus, we may measure the rate at which a society is changing by measuring the amount of deference its younger members show to their elders.

Which one of the following is an assumption on which the argument depends?

(A) A society's younger members can often accurately discern whether that society is changing rapidly.
(B) How much deference young people show to their elders depends on how much of the elders' experience is practically useful to them.
(C) The deference young people show to their elders varies according to how much the young value their elders' advice.
(D) The faster a society changes, the less relevant the experience of older members of the society is to younger members.
(E) Young people value their elders' advice just insofar as the elders' experience is practically useful to them.

23. Politician: We should impose a tariff on imported fruit to make it cost consumers more than domestic fruit. Otherwise, growers from other countries who can grow better fruit more cheaply will put domestic fruit growers out of business. This will result in farmland's being converted to more lucrative industrial uses and the consequent vanishing of a unique way of life.

The politician's recommendation most closely conforms to which one of the following principles?

(A) A country should put its own economic interest over that of other countries.
(B) The interests of producers should always take precedence over those of consumers.
(C) Social concerns should sometimes take precedence over economic efficiency.
(D) A country should put the interests of its own citizens ahead of those of citizens of other countries.
(E) Government intervention sometimes creates more economic efficiency than free markets.

24. The Kiffer Forest Preserve, in the northernmost part of the Abbimac Valley, is where most of the bears in the valley reside. During the eight years that the main road through the preserve has been closed the preserve's bear population has nearly doubled. Thus, the valley's bear population will increase if the road is kept closed.

Which one of the following, if true, most undermines the argument?

(A) Most of the increase in the preserve's bear population over the past eight years is due to migration.
(B) Only some of the increase in the preserve's bear population over the past eight years is due to migration of bears from other parts of the Abbimac Valley.
(C) Only some of the increase in the preserve's bear population over the past eight years is due to migration of bears from outside the Abbimac Valley.
(D) The bear population in areas of the Abbimac Valley outside the Kiffer Forest Preserve has decreased over the past eight years.
(E) The bear population in the Abbimac Valley has remained about the same over the past eight years.

GO ON TO THE NEXT PAGE.

25. If a wig has any handmade components, it is more expensive than one with none. Similarly, a made-to-measure wig ranges from medium-priced to expensive. Handmade foundations are never found on wigs that do not use human hair. Furthermore, any wig that contains human hair should be dry-cleaned. So all made-to-measure wigs should be dry-cleaned.

    The conclusion of the argument follows logically if which one of the following is assumed?

    (A) Any wig whose price falls in the medium-priced to expensive range has a handmade foundation.
    (B) If a wig's foundation is handmade, then it is more expensive than one whose foundation is not handmade.
    (C) A wig that has any handmade components should be dry-cleaned.
    (D) If a wig's foundation is handmade, then its price is at least in the medium range.
    (E) Any wig that should be dry-cleaned has a foundation that is handmade.

26. Philosopher: Wolves do not tolerate an attack by one wolf on another if the latter wolf demonstrates submission by baring its throat. The same is true of foxes and domesticated dogs. So it would be erroneous to deny that animals have rights on the grounds that only human beings are capable of obeying moral rules.

    The philosopher's argument proceeds by attempting to

    (A) provide counterexamples to refute a premise on which a particular conclusion is based
    (B) establish inductively that all animals possess some form of morality
    (C) cast doubt on the principle that being capable of obeying moral rules is a necessary condition for having rights
    (D) establish a claim by showing that the denial of that claim entails a logical contradiction
    (E) provide evidence suggesting that the concept of morality is often applied too broadly

S T O P

IF YOU FINISH BEFORE TIME IS CALLED, YOU MAY CHECK YOUR WORK ON THIS SECTION ONLY.
DO NOT WORK ON ANY OTHER SECTION IN THE TEST.

PREPTEST 58 LOGICAL REASONING SECTION I

1. C
2. D
3. E
4. E
5. A
6. A
7. B
8. E
9. E
10. B
11. A
12. D
13. B
14. D
15. D
16. E
17. B
18. C
19. D
20. E
21. C
22. C
23. C
24. E
25. A
26. A

PrepTest 58 Logical Reasoning Section I Explanations

Question #1: Assumption—SN. The correct answer choice is (C)

The commentator opens the stimulus with this premise: While today's freshwater supply is adequate to meet people's current needs, during the next few decades there will be an increase in human population, and a greater need for freshwater.

Based on this premise, the commentator concludes that water use restrictions will soon be necessary to meet people's freshwater needs. We should note this use of the term "necessary," as it might alert us to the fact that the commentator uses *conditional reasoning* in drawing his or her conclusion:

To continue to meet human freshwater needs, water use restrictions will be *necessary*:

Sufficient		Necessary
continue to meet freshwater needs	⟶	water use restrictions

In other words, if we are able to continue meeting our freshwater needs, that information is sufficient for us to conclude that water use restrictions have been implemented.

The contrapositive of the statement above tells us that without water restrictions, there is no way to continue to meet humankind's freshwater needs in the coming decades:

water use restrictions (negated) ⟶ continue to meet freshwater needs (negated)

The stimulus is followed by an Assumption question. In this case, the commentator asserts that the only way to continue meeting freshwater needs is through water use restrictions. The implicit presumption is that no other means of achieving this outcome will be effective.

Answer choice (A): The commentator does not discuss humans' wasteful use of other natural resources, and this assumption is not required by the commentator's argument.

Answer choice (B): The commentator asserts that a drastic population increase *in the future* will increase humans' need for freshwater. This argumnet does not rely on any assumptions about the supply of freshwater in the recent past.

Answer choice (C): This is the correct answer choice. The commentator asserts that water use restrictions will be an absolute necessity, implying that the problem cannot be solved by any other means. We can double check our answer to any Assumption question by applying the Assumption Negation technique: the negated version of the correct answer choice will weaken the author's argument.

If we negate (or take away) this assumption from the commentator, we are left with this: "The freshwater supply *will* increase sufficiently to meet the increased needs of humankind."

So, when we take away this assumption from the commentator, the argument fails, proving that this choice does provide an assumption that the commentator relies upon, and confirming this as the correct answer choice. We might also note the use of conditional language ("sufficiently")in this choice. In asserting that water use restrictions are *necessary*, the commentator implicitly asserts that no other means would be *sufficient.*

Answer choice (D): While this answer choice may look enticing at first, the commentator does not rely upon this argument. To confirm this point, we can again apply the Assumption Negation technique, take away this assumption, and note the effect, if any, on the strength of the argument in the stimulus: The negated version of this choice would say that "some attempt to synthesize water may have an appreciable effect on the supply." But does this cause the commentator's argument to fail? No; even if there were an appreciable increase from water synthesis, water use restriction might still be necessary (above and beyond any synthesis-based increases).

Answer choice (E): Like incorrect answer choice (B) above, this choice is only about the past, and is not an assumption required by the commentator's conclusion. Once again, if we wish to confirm this choice to be incorrect, we can apply the Assumption Negation Technique: the negated version of this choice ("some measure *previously* yielded an increase...") this does not weaken the commentator's argument, which regards only *future* human needs.

Question #2: Parallel Reasoning—PR. The correct answer choice is (D)

The argument presented here is quite straightforward. The single premise, introduced with the term *since*, is that often, the harder we try to remember a word, the less likely that word is to come to mind. The psychologist's conclusion: if you are having trouble remembering a certain word or name, the best solution is to occupy your mind with other things.

The question that follows requires us to find the answer choice that reflects the same general principle. In basic terms, the psychologist's argument is that sometimes, the harder we try to attain something, the more elusive it becomes, so the best solution is to change your focus. The correct answer choice should illustrate a similar principle.

Answer choice (A): The principle here is different from the one expressed in the stimulus. In this choice, the basic principle is that wealth and fame do not necessarily bring happiness, as evidenced by the existence of wealthy and famous people who are unhappy. This lacks the principle that "the harder you try, the more elusive your goal often becomes."

(As an aside, we might also note that this choice presents a fairly weak assertion; the fact that "there are" unhappy people who have both wealth and fame means only that at least one such person exists.)

Answer choice (B): Many parallel reasoning questions are followed by wrong answers that involve a similar topic, as is the case here. This choice deals with "not thinking about something," but the principle here involves avoidance of discouragement, which is not part of the psychologist's principle.

Answer choice (C): Whereas the principle in the stimulus concerns the best way to achieve a desired outcome, this choice deals with the best way to overcome a serious problem. These are very different principles.

Answer choice (D): This is the correct answer choice, as it is the one which reflects the same basic principle as the stimulus. While the psychologist in the stimulus discusses memory, this answer choice involves sleep, but the general principle common to both is that sometimes, the best way to achieve something, whether sleep or recall, is to focus your attention elsewhere.

Answer choice (E): The principle presented in the stimulus is that often the best way to achieve a desired outcome is to focus *elsewhere*. This choice says that the best way to achieve the goal of coping with sadness is to focus on even *greater* sadness.

Question #3: Strengthen. The correct answer choice is (E)

The facts presented in this letter to the editor may seem at first paradoxical: The Planning Department budget has increased from $100,000 to over $500,000 since 2001, yet it would be incorrect to say that the department now spends five times as much to perform the same duties. But is this a paradox? The department has a budget that is over five times as great as that of 2001—either the department won't necessarily spend its whole budget, or the department is not using the money to perform the same duties.

The question stem that follows the stimulus is a strengthen question, so we should look for the answer choice which lends the most credibility to the letter's argument—that the department is *not* spending five times as much to perform the same duties. If we want to prephrase this answer, there are two possible ways to strengthen this argument: either show that the department is not currently spending five times as much, or the department is not performing the exact same duties.

Answer choice (A): The budgets of other departments are irrelevant to the question of whether or not the Planning Department is spending five times as much to perform the same duties, so this answer choice does nothing to bolster the argument presented in the stimulus.

Answer choice (B): Since we are provided with no specific information about the department's various areas of expenditure, this choice does nothing to strengthen the author's argument.

Answer choice (C): Since the relevant comparison is between the 2001 budget and this year's budget, this information is irrelevant to the argument.

Answer choice (D): Even if there were such adjustments, the figures cited still show the current year's expenditures at over five times as much as those of 2001, so this choice does not strengthen the argument in the stimulus.

Answer choice (E): This is the correct answer choice. If a piece of 2003 legislation expanded the duties of the Planning Department, then this strengthens the argument from the stimulus that the department is not spending five times as much on performing the *same duties*.

Question #4: Must Be True—PR. The correct answer choice is (E)

The author here discusses the mock trial results of jury instructions given in legal terms, versus those given in clear, nontechnical language. When the jury instructions were more technical, the jury tended to side with the beliefs of the judge (which they were able to determine through nonverbal cues from the judge). When such instructions were more straightforward, however, with less technical legal jargon, jury members were more likely to go their own way.

The stimulus is followed by a Must question stem, so the correct answer choice will present a fact presented in the stimulus. The suggestion in this stimulus is that the manner in which jury instructions are delivered can apparently play some role in jury behavior: in cases where more technical language is used, the jury seems more likely to go along with the opinions of the judge.

Answer choice (A): The author does not mention the relative degree of precision in technical versus nontechnical language. Even if you generally think of technical language as more precise, this choice does not pass the Fact Test; because it is not confirmed by the facts in the stimulus, this cannot be the correct answer to this Must Be True question.

Answer choice (B): As with incorrect answer choice (A) above, this choice gives us a *could be true* answer, but not a *must* be true. It might be reasonable to believe that one's influence increases proportionally with one's status, but this is not part of the discussion presented in the stimulus. The issue of status is not discussed, and regardless, the judge maintains the same status in court no matter how jury instructions are presented.

Answer choice (C): This is an Opposite Answer; the stimulus specifically provides that the jury had become aware of the judge's non-verbal behavior (and more often took the judge's side when technical language was used in their instructions).

Answer choice (D): Although you may agree with this statement, the author never compares real and mock trials—real trials are not even mentioned. Since this answer fails the Fact Test, it cannot be correct.

Answer choice (E): This is the correct answer choice; based on the example in the stimulus it appears that members of a jury can be swayed by the type of language used in their instructions.

Question #5: Weaken. The correct answer choice is (A)

The doctor quoted here makes a questionable argument: many alternative medicine-used herbs are safe to consume, so they should always be allowed as prescribed remedies for serious illnesses, because they won't harm patients, and might help. We should note the doctor's use of strong language: the assertion is that alternative herb prescribed remedies should *always* be allowed.

The stimulus is followed by a weaken question, which means that we should look for the answer choice which weakens the doctor's conclusion. The correct answer choice will likely provide either a previously unstated detriment that goes along with the use of such herbs, or a benefit associated with their avoidance.

Answer choice (A): This is the correct answer choice, providing a previously unstated detriment associated with the use of such alternative medicine herbs. If the use of such herbs comes at the cost of effective conventional medicine, then patients might indeed be harmed (by not having access to conventional methods that have been proven effective).

Answer choice (B): This answer choice does not weaken the doctor's argument, which allows for the possibility that some are not effective, but concludes that their prescription should be allowed if they do no harm.

Answer choice (C): The doctor discusses herbs that have been proven safe to consume, so the fact that some people are allergic to some medicines does not weaken the doctor's argument, and this answer choice is incorrect.

Answer choice (D): The motivations of alternative medicine purveyors does not affect the strength of the doctor's conclusion, which is that such herbs should be allowed to be prescribed when they do no harm and may do some good.

Answer choice (E): This answer choice would not weaken the author's argument—it may strengthen the conclusion, providing a benefit of such herbs and making it more likely that they might help.

Question #6: Must Be True. The correct answer choice is (A)

In this stimulus, the author uses somewhat convoluted language to express the following conclusion in the opening sentence of the paragraph:

According to free market principles, a government on the brink of a financial crisis can limit the extent to which foreign investments and loans can be withdrawn in order to prevent economic collapse.

This conclusion is followed by a premise (introduced with the premise indicator "after all..."): Even the right to free speech is limited in some ways. The analogy is as follows: We are guaranteed the right to free speech, but that does not include the guarantee of the right to do potential damage, such as the common example of shouting "Fire!" in a crowded theatre.

In the same way that the right to yell "Fire" in a crowded theatre is not protected by the right to free speech, an unregulated ability for investors and lenders to withdraw funds, which might also cause serious damage, is not guaranteed by the right to a free market.

The stimulus is followed by a Must Be True question stem, so the correct answer choice will reflect something that the "argument does."

Answer choice (A): This is the correct answer choice. The argument in the stimulus shows the limitations on the principles of the free market through comparison to the limitations on the right to free speech. Neither, the author argues, dictates rights across the board; both are limited in extreme situations. The fire example could cause a literal rush that would be unsafe; allowing unfettered withdrawal by investors and lenders could cause a figurative rush that could lead to disaster of a different sort.

Answer choice (B): This rather awkwardly worded answer choice claims that the argument presumes the best explanation of observed facts to be the correct explanation. The author of the stimulus does not make this presumption, but rather draws the analogy to yelling "Fire" in a crowded theatre, and the limitations on the right to free speech.

Answer choice (C): Again, each incorrect answer to this Must Be True question stem will fail the Fact Test, and this incorrect choice is no exception. No experimental results are presented, so this answer cannot be correct.

Answer choice (D): No flawed explanation is discussed in the stimulus. The author simply points out a limitation on the rights implicit in a free market, through comparison to the limitation on the rights guaranteed by the right to free speech.

Answer choice (E): The author does not base the conclusion on an empirical generalization, but on a comparison to the similar case of the limited right to free speech.

Question #7: Parallel Flaw—CE, #%. The correct answer choice is (B)

The author of this stimulus concludes that negative political advertising is actually beneficial, despite objections by those who are the targets of such advertising. This questionable conclusion is based on the premise that most elections were won by candidates who had been the subjects of such negative advertising.

As with many flawed causal arguments, the author has mistaken a correlation for a causal relationship. Even if most election winners are negative ad targets, this does not necessarily support the conclusion that such ads provide any benefit—it is possible, for example, that those candidates won despite negative ads, rather than because of them.

The invalid Cause/Effect relationship is as follows:

C		E
Targeted by negative ads	⟶	Election wins

The stimulus is followed by a Parallel Flaw question stem, so we should look for the answer choice whose author notes a correlation and makes a similarly questionable causal presumption.

Answer choice (A): No correlation is presented here, and no causal conclusion is drawn, so this choice cannot parallel the flawed reasoning in the stimulus.

Premise:	Exercise is a good way to improve overall health.
Conclusion:	Therefore many should exercise, even if they dislike it.

Answer choice (B): This is the correct answer choice, which follows the same basic pattern of argumentation as that found in the stimulus: Harsh reviews are actually beneficial, the author concludes, even though many actors dislike them. This questionable conclusion is based on the premise that most prestigious acting awards have gone to actors who have received such harsh reviews. Much like the stimulus, the author of this choice notes the correlation between harsh reviews and winning awards, and jumps to the conclusion that the former must cause the latter. This conclusion, like the one drawn in the stimulus, is clearly flawed; another explanation of this observed correlation, for example, would be that the best known actors get the most reviews, some of which are likely to be harsh, and those same famous actors might also be the ones most likely to win awards.

Answer choice (C): Like incorrect answer choice (A) above, this choice cannot be correct because it presents a logical argument, so it cannot parallel the flawed argument in the stimulus. Based on the premise that most who study pass their courses, it is reasonable to conclude that studying must be a good way to achieve academic success, despite many students' dislike of doing so.

Answer choice (D): This choice provides a valid argument, so we can quickly rule it out as a contender for this Parallel Flaw question stem. The argument here is as follows:
Premise: A large number of people are eager to attend horror films.
Conclusion: Therefore such films are bound to be successful, despite the fact that many critics dislike such films.

Answer choice (E): The flaw found here is different from that presented in the stimulus. Again, the flaw in the stimulus is the mistaken conclusion that a noted correlation reflects a cause and effect relationship. The flawed reasoning here is as follows:

Premise:	Most people who stay up late enjoy doing so.
Conclusion:	Next day sleepiness must be acceptable to those who stay up late, despite the fact that many dislike the result of feeling sleepy.

Because this reasoning does not reflect the standard causal flaw found it the stimulus' reasoning, it cannot be the correct answer choice to this Parallel Flaw—CE question.

Question #8: Resolve the ParadoxX. The correct answer choice is (E)

The paradox presented here is fairly simple: In Springfield the average worker lives farther from work than in Rorchester, so we might expect Springfield to have a greater demand for public transportation. Yet Springfield has half as many bus routes as Rorchester.

This stimulus is followed by a ResolveX question stem. Thus, the four incorrect answer choices will help to resolve the apparent discrepancy discussed in the stimulus, and the correct answer we seek will fail to provide a resolution.

Answer choice (A): If the vast majority of Springfield's workforce is employed outside the city, then this would help to explain the lower number of bus routes necessary within the city—three quarters of the working population leaves the city on a daily basis.

Since this answer choice provides a reasonable resolution to the paradox presented in the stimulus, it cannot be the correct answer choice to this Resolve Except question.

Answer choice (B): Like incorrect answer choice (A) above, this choice also provides resolution to the apparent discrepancy: a greater average number of cars would make for less need for bus routes. Since this choice resolves the paradox, it must be one of the four incorrect answer choices here.

Answer choice (C): If Rorchester has fewer railway lines, and Springfield has a relatively greater number, this fact would help to explain why fewer bus routes would be necessary in Springfield, helping to provide resolution to the paradox presented in the stimulus. Since this choice does help resolve, it cannot be the correct answer choice.

Answer choice (D): Springfield's relatively smaller number of routes would be explained in part by routes of greater lengths and frequency. This answer choice helps to resolve the paradox, so it must be one of the four incorrect answer choices in this case.

Answer choice (E): This is the correct answer choice, as it is the only choice which fails to resolve the paradox presented in the stimulus. This answer actually expands the paradox, because a greater population in Springfield would give us even more reason to expect a higher demand for public transportation there, making Springfield's relatively low supply of busses that much greater a paradox.

Question #9: Flaw in the Reasoning. The correct answer choice is (E)

The author of this stimulus discusses N5, a non-caloric fat substitute. The conclusion is presented in the second sentence of the paragraph: "…N5 is of no use to such people." The author bases this conclusion on a single premise: N5 users, who continued to feel hungrier than they would have if they had they been eating real fat, ended up making up all of the calories saved by eating more.

There is a disconnect in this stimulus that we might notice: N5 is a fat substitute. The subjects made up for the calories they saved by eating more. As is common with regard to logical reasoning passages, the test makers hope that we will fail to note this subtle but important distinction.

The question stem which follows the stimulus in this case is, not surprisingly, a Flaw in the Reasoning question, so the correct answer choice will likely point out the difference between reduction of fat intake and reduction of total caloric intake.

Answer choice (A): The stimulus deals with people who use N5, so the existence of foods that cannot include N5 has no bearing on the author's argument, which deals with the usefulness of N5 for those who use it.

Answer choice (B): Since the important inquiry here deals with the usefulness of N5 for those who use it as a fat substitute, the existence or absence of mild side effects does not come into play (that is, N5 might still be useful even if its use brings mild side effects).

Answer choice (C): This answer choice provides us with a less straightforward version of the following: "some who use N5 don't care about caloric intake." This choice fails to point out the important distinction between fat intake and caloric intake, and, further, plays no role in the author's argument about the usefulness of N5 as a fat substitute.

Answer choice (D): Even if people who are aware of the fat substitute's benefits use more foods that include N5, this fails to point out a vulnerability in the author's argument that N5 is of no use as a fat substitute, so this answer choice cannot be correct.

Answer choice (E): This is the correct answer choice, and the one which points to the vital distinction between fat intake and caloric intake. If this answer choice is true, then the author's conclusion fails, because N5 appears to have value as a fat reducer even if users maintain caloric intake.

Question #10: Must Be True. The correct answer choice is (B)

The general argument used by the historian in this stimulus should probably look familiar by the time you've taken just a few practice LSAT Logical Reasoning sections:

> *"Some make a particular claim, but I question that claim."*

This general argumentative presentation is common among LSAT stimuli. In this instance, the specifics are as follows:

Historian: Some are dismayed by the fact that poor, post-war studios forced bebop musicians to record short solos, so that the recordings did not accurately reflect their normal musical style.

"But..." (this word, of course, indicates that the author is about to take the other side of the argument):

1. The concise style created works of art rather than simple artistic representations; and

2. The concise recordings led to more concise, compact live play.

The question stem which follows is a Must Be True, so we will be able to confirm the correct answer choice with the facts presented in the stimulus.

Answer choice (A): While the author implies that the works discussed were more valuable than "mere representations," there is no suggestion that solo representations are generally not *valuable* artistic works. Since this choice fails to pass the Fact Test, it cannot be the correct answer to this Must Be True question.

Answer choice (B): This is the correct answer choice. This is clearly an accurate reflection of the author's attitude, as well as the main point of the paragraph; while some complain about the limited length recordings, this historian lists two benefits that were derived as a result of this approach of post-war, impoverished recording studios.

Answer choice (C): Often an answer choice can be quickly eliminated based on a single word, and in this case that exceptionally strong word is *always*. While this author believes that there is some value in more concise, compact recordings, this choice is far too broad to be supported by the facts—the author makes no such claim, so this answer choice cannot be correct.

Answer choice (D): The only element that the historian discusses as having been lacking from the next generation was early bebop "compactness." This is only one factor, and the author does not reference "overall quality," so this answer choice is not supported by the statements presented.

Answer choice (E): If we reword this conditional "unless" statement, it becomes more transparently incorrect: "the only time that musicians will ever record extremely short solos is when difficult recording conditions force them to do so." The author discusses examples of musicians being *forced* by difficult conditions to record short solos, such musicians might also decide *on their own* to record short solos.

Question #11: Flaw in the Reasoning. The correct answer choice is (A)

The author of this stimulus draws a questionable causal conclusion based on two very limited premises: Studies show a correlation in humans between damage to chromosome number six and schizophrenia. But, the author points out that there are people who have the damaged chromosome without the disease, and there are people who have the disease without any damage to the chromosome. All that this actually proves is that there is not a perfect correlation between the two conditions, but the author incorrectly jumps to the conclusion that there can be *no causal connection* between the two.

The vagueness of the wording chosen by the author provides only that there are at least "some" (this might mean only one or two!) who have a damaged chromosome without having schizophrenia, and there are "some" who have the disease without damage to the chromosome. The existence of such people (who might just be *exceptions* to a general rule) does not prove that there is no causal link between the disease and chromosome number six—the disease and the chromosome may be very closely correlated, even if there do exist *some* people who have one without the other (even if there is not a *perfect* correlation).

The stimulus is followed by a Flaw in the Reasoning question, which should not be surprising, considering the weak argument presented in the stimulus. The correct answer choice will probably point out that the author incorrectly takes the existence of "some" exceptions as disproof of any causal relationship.

Answer choice (A): This is the correct answer choice. The author clearly believes that a causal link would require perfect overlap of the two attributes (the disease and the damaged chromosome). This answer presents another way to phrase this point: the author ignores the possibility that not *every* type of chromosome damage leads to schizophrenia—that there might be a causal relationship even if the two conditions will not always be linked

Answer choice (B): The author does not presume that chromosomal damage is the *only* cause of schizophrenia; the flaw in this stimulus is the author's conclusion that there is no causal link, just because there is not a perfect correlation.

Answer choice (C): There is no sample population discussed in this stimulus; the flaw here is not an unrepresentative sample. The author points to certain specific exceptions to the correlation between schizophrenia and a damaged chromosome (people who have one but not the other), but no sample population is presented or referenced.

Answer choice (D): While the flaw found in this stimulus does involve causal reasoning, the author does not mistake a cause for an effect. In fact, the author never specifies which of the two is believed to be the cause and which is believed to be the effect—only that there is not a perfect correlation between the two.

Answer choice (E): The author does not presume that correlation implies causation; in fact, this incorrect choice is very nearly an Opposite Answer, because the actual flaw in the author's reasoning is the mistaken presumption that any relationship short of perfect correlation cannot be a causal relationship. In reality, of course, there can be exceptions to general causal relationships.

Question #12: Justify the Conclusion—SN. The correct answer choice is (D)

Here the city council person discusses a disagreement as to whether or not a particular edifice qualifies as art, and thus whether the commission should make the proposed purchase. The author says that the purpose of art is to cause experts to debate, and the edifice has met that criterion. Thus, the council person concludes, the edifice does indeed qualify as art.

Without any additional premises or assumptions, the argument from this stimulus represents the following Mistaken Reversal:

Art must lead to debate: Art ⟶ Lead to debate

The edifice has led to debate, so it qualifies as art: Lead to debate ⟶ Art

Since the question stem which follows the stimulus requires us to Justify this Conclusion, however, we must find the answer choice which makes the council person's conclusion reasonable—this will be the answer choice that confirms the second conditional statement above (Lead to debate ⟶ Art).

Answer choice (A): The council person's argument is not justified by the conditional statement offered in this answer choice, which says, more simply, that if something is art it causes debate.

This can be diagrammed as follows: Art ⟶ causes debate

The council person has already established that the edifice in question causes debate; this choice does not justify the council person's conclusion that the edifice qualifies as art.

Answer choice (B): The council person's conclusion is that the edifice does qualify as art, so this choice would actually weaken that position, rather than justify the council person's conclusion.

Answer choice (C): The council person's argument deals only with whether the edifice in question qualifies as art. This answer choice doesn't even deal with the question of whether or not an item is art, but rather whether there should be opposition to a particular type of object (the type that fulfills the purpose of art). Since this choice fails to justify the conclusion from the stimulus, it cannot be the correct answer choice.

Answer choice (D): This is the correct answer choice. This choice provides the needed conditional rule—if something fulfills the purpose of art, it qualifies as art:

Fulfills purpose of art ⟶ qualifies as art

With the premise from the stimulus, and the additional premise supplied by this choice, the author can create the following conditional link:

Caused debate ⟶ fulfills purpose ⟶ qualifies as art

Answer choice (E): Like incorrect answer choice (C) above, this choice doesn't deal with the council person's conclusion that *the edifice qualifies as a work of art*. Whether or not the city should make the purchase is a separate question, so this choice does not justify the conclusion that the edifice is art, and this answer is incorrect.

Question #13: Main Point—SN. The correct answer choice is (B)

In this stimulus we are presented with several conditional statements:

In order to be an intriguing person, you must be able to inspire constant curiosity.

intriguing ⟶ able to inspire perpetual curiosity

If you are constantly broadening your abilities and extending your intellectual reach, you will be able to inspire that curiosity.

broadening ability and intellect ⟶ able to inspire perpetual curiosity

The final sentence begins with the word "For," which in this case is means "Because." So, here the author is actually presenting a premise: Constantly increasing your ability and intellect makes you impossible to totally understand, and thus a constant mystery to others:

broadening ability and intellect ⟶ constant mystery

Putting together the argument in retrospect: If you are constantly expanding, you are a constant mystery, and thus you are able to inspire perpetual curiosity:

broadening ability and intellect ⟶ constant mystery ⟶ able to inspire curiosity

The question which follows is a Main Point question, and we can prephrase an answer based on the discussion above: The author believes that a person who constantly increases his or her abilities and intellect is impossible to understand, is therefore a constant mystery, and is thus able to inspire perpetual curiosity.

We should note that even if one is able to inspire perpetual curiosity, we cannot assume that person will be intriguing—this would reflect a mistaken negation of the first sentence (what we know is that anyone who is intriguing can inspire such curiosity).

Answer choice (A): This choice, which restates the first sentence in the stimulus, can be diagrammed as follows:

intriguing ⟶ able to inspire perpetual curiosity

This does not express the conclusion of the argument, but rather the first premise presented, so this answer choice is incorrect.

Answer choice (B): This is the correct answer choice, and the one which restates the conclusion as prephrased above:

broadening ability and intellect ⟶ able to inspire curiosity

The author's conclusion is that if one is constantly expanding in ability and intellect, then one can remain mysterious, and this enables one to inspire perpetual curiosity in others.

Answer choice (C): This choice is a commonly chosen wrong answer, in part because it has information presented in the last sentence of the stimulus, but like incorrect answer choice (A) above, this is actually a supporting premise of the argument:

broadening ability and intellect ⟶ constant mystery

This premise lacks the important component of the ability to inspire perpetual curiosity, so it cannot represent the main conclusion of the argument.

Answer choice (D): This is another tricky wrong answer, mistaking a sufficient condition for a necessary one, provides the following *Mistaken Reversal*:

able to inspire curiosity ⟶ broaden ability and intellect

From the stimulus we know the reverse to be true: that if one can constantly broaden one's abilities, then one will be able to inspire perpetual curiosity.

Answer choice (E): This incorrect answer choice does not reflect the author's conclusion, nor is it even necessarily accurate according to the passage:

broadening ability and intellect ⟶ always have curiosity

The author tells us that a person who constantly broadens his or her abilities and intellect is able to inspire curiosity <u>in others</u>—not necessarily in his or her self.

Question #14: Assumption. The correct answer choice is (D)

The author begins by providing that if theater managers do not believe that a film will generate enough total revenue to make a profit (including food and beverage), they will not rent that film. In other words, they must believe that a film is likely to be profitable. The greater the perceived likelihood of profitability, then, the greater the chance that a manager will choose to rent a film.

Premise: **managers more likely to rent ⟶ greater likelihood of profitability**

The author then tells us about the producers' belief: If they create movies that are attractive to younger audiences, then the films will be more likely to be chosen by managers:

Conclusion: **attractive to younger audiences ⟶ managers more likely to rent**

The stimulus is followed by an assumption question, and the correct answer choice will need to link previously unconnected pieces in a way that allows for the author's conclusion to be logically possible. So as a prephrase, think about what is necessary for theater managers to be more likely to rent a film: if that film is likely to be profitable. So the connection of pieces should serve to satisfy that required idea, where movies that are attractive to younger audiences have a higher probability of being profitable:

Assumption: **attractive to younger audiences ⟶ greater likelihood of profit**

That also works beautifully from an Assumption Negation standpoint, as negating it to show that films attractive to younger audiences are NOT likely to be profitable would immediately invalidate this argument: if we remove profitability then we also reduce the likelihood of theater managers renting those films, which is the opposite of the author's belief in the stimulus.

Answer choice (A): Although there is discussion of the role of likelihood of overall profitability, the role played by concession stands is not specified, nor is the average consumption rate of adults versus children and adolescents. Regardless, this choice fails to provide the needed link, so it is incorrect.

Answer choice (B): There is no mention of whether movies that appeal to younger viewers might also appeal to an older audience, and this is not an assumption on which the argument relies.

Answer choice (C): The author only provides that concession sales are part of the overall profitability calculations, but offers no information about whether concessions or movie ticket sales are more profitable. Further, this choice fails to provide the prephrased link between attractiveness to younger viewers and likelihood of profitability.

Answer choice (D): This is the correct answer choice. This answer provides the needed link between younger viewers and increased profits. The key assumption of conditionality is always that the necessary condition is able to be fulfilled, as without it the sufficient cannot occur. In this case if we know that films that appeal to younger audiences are more likely to be profitable than other films, then the condition required for theater managers to rent those films (greater profit) is satisfied and the author's conclusion remains intact.

Answer choice (E): Like incorrect answer choice (B) above, this cannot be an assumption on which the argument relies, because no information is provided regarding films that appeal to older audiences (such films may or may not be the same films that appeal to younger crowds).

Question #15: Must Be True—SN, #%. The correct answer choice is (D)

In this stimulus we are presented with a fact set. To begin, most genetic research advances give rise to ethical dilemmas.

Genetic research —M→ give rise to ethical dilemmas

Further, most genetic research is funded solely by the government, the others are funded exclusively by corporations, and one of these two sources of funding is *necessary* for genetic research to take place:

Genetic research projects not funded by the government are funded by corporations:

funded by ~~government~~ ——→ funded by corporations

funded by ~~corporations~~ ——→ funded by government

For any genetic research one or the other source of funding is *necessary*:

government funding
genetic research ⟶ or
corporate funding

Thus:

government funding
and ⟶ genetic research
corporate funding

Again, this is a fact set, so we might expect the Must Be True question which follows. Only one answer choice will pass the Fact Test, and will be confirmed by the statements above.

Answer choice (A): The stimulus provides that the government is the source of funding for most genetic research, but the author says nothing about what source of funding more often leads to resulting advances. Since this choice cannot be confirmed by the facts in the stimulus, we can confidently rule it out.

Answer choice (B): Like incorrect answer choice (A) above, this choice cannot be confirmed with the facts provided in the stimulus. There is no information regarding what portion of government funded genetic advances lead to ethical dilemmas, there is no way to assess the accuracy of this statement, so it cannot be the correct answer choice.

Answer choice (C): The author tells us that genetic research which is not government-funded is funded by corporations, but provides no information regarding the success of corporate-funded research. Because the stimulus provides no confirmation that any such research (funded by corporations) leads, or has led, to any advances, this choice does not pass the Fact Test.

Answer choice (D): This is the correct answer choice; it can be confirmed with the second conditional contrapositive diagrammed above, replicated below:

government funding
and ⟶ no genetic research
corporate funding

Common sense dictates that if there is no genetic research there can be no ethical dilemmas which arise from advances in genetic research:

genetic research ⟶ resulting ethical dilemmas

Linking these two statements, we can confirm choice (D) to be the correct answer:

~~government~~ funding
and ⟶ genetic ~~research~~ ⟶ resulting ~~ethical~~ dilemmas
~~corporate~~ funding

With neither government nor corporate funding, there is no genetic research, and if there is no genetic research there can surely be no ethical dilemmas arising from advances in genetic research.

Answer choice (E): The author opens the stimulus with the fact that “Almost all advances in genetic research give rise to ethical dilemmas.” This statement provides no basis for the claim that this trend will continue indefinitely into the future.

Question #16: Assumption—SN. The correct answer choice is (E)

Here the author presents several conditional statements. When we diagram these conditional statements, we might note that the first two sentences are basically contrapositives of one another:

Corporate businesses *must* adapt to survive. So for survival, adaptation is *necessary*:

survive ⟶ adapt

If no longer efficient (don’t adapt) then businesses become extinct:

~~adapt~~ ⟶ ~~survive~~

But sometimes, a business cannot adapt without changing its core philosophy (that is, if a business is to adapt, it is *necessary* that the business change its core philosophy):

adapt ⟶ change core philosophy

Linking the diagram above with that of the first sentence, we arrive at the following:

survive ⟶ adapt ⟶ change core philosophy

The author then jumps to the conclusion (introduced by the common conclusion indicator "hence") that if a business wishes to survive, it must *become a different corporation*:

survive ⟶ different corporation

The stimulus is followed by an assumption question, and we should recognize it as a supporter assumption. The correct answer choice will likely provide a link between "change core philosophy" and "different corporation," and allow the author's conclusion to be properly drawn.

Answer choice (A): The author provides that *sometimes* survival requires a change in core corporate philosophy—there is no need to assume that this is always the case, and this choice does not provide the link discussed above, so this answer is incorrect.

Answer choice (B): Although inefficient businesses will become extinct, the argument presented in the stimulus does not require the presumption that inefficiency leads to a surrender of core corporate philosophies. Like incorrect answer choice (A) above, this choice fails to provide the needed link between a change in core philosophy and becoming a different corporation.

Answer choice (C): This choice may be tempting, because it deals with concepts that are closely related to the ones we are attempting to link. However, there is a subtle but important difference: this choice lacks the concept of *changing* core philosophies. The conclusion does not require the assumption that every corporation has a different core philosophy, and this choice does not fit our prephrase above.

Answer choice (D): The conditional statement provided by this incorrect answer choice can be diagrammed as follows:

core philosophy intact ⟶ continue to exist

This choice does not deal with becoming a different corporation and is not the prephrased assumption required by the author's conclusion.

Answer choice (E): This is the correct answer choice, and the one which provides the link prephrased in the discussion above. A business cannot *change its core philosophy* without *becoming a different corporation*. Another way to word this would be to say that if a business is to change its core philosophy, it is necessary to become a different corporation:

change core philosophy ⟶ become different corp.

This is the conditional statement that we can link to the premises from the stimulus, in order to arrive logically at the author's conclusion—that a business can survive only by becoming a different corporation:

survive ⟶ adapt ⟶ change core philosophy ⟶ become different corp

Question #17: Resolve the Paradox—#%. The correct answer choice is (B)

The author of this stimulus compares the results of two surveys taken of area L residents (surveys which were taken ten years apart).

In the survey from ten years ago, most residents were generally satisfied with their conditions, despite the fact that these conditions were slightly below average.

In the more recent survey, the living conditions in area L are more comparable to those of the nation as a whole, but most residents of the area now report general *dis*satisfaction with their living conditions.

The stimulus is followed by a Resolve the Paradox question, so we should look for the answer choice which explains the apparent discrepancy between higher relative living conditions (as compared to the country overall), and the greater dissatisfaction reported recently by the people of area L.

As is often the case with LSAT questions dealing with numbers and percentages, the information provided is limited; while the author provides information regarding the *relative* conditions of area L and the country as a whole—in the first survey the nation's average conditions were *better* than those in area L; in the second survey the nation's average conditions were *about the same* as those of area L. The problem is that without more specific information regarding the country's overall living conditions, there is really no way to tell whether living conditions in area L have improved, worsened, or stayed the same.

Not every Resolve answer can be easily prephrased, but in this case there appear to be two likely explanations: either the people have become more difficult to satisfy, or living conditions have actually gotten worse (in an absolute sense).

Answer choice (A): Different priorities would explain divergence between the opinions of area L residents and those of surrounding areas, but this choice fails to explain the dissatisfaction among the people of area L in response to higher *relative* conditions, so this cannot be the correct answer.

Answer choice (B): This is the correct answer choice. If the average living conditions in the country as a whole have substantially declined, then the conditions in area L (which are about the same as those of the country overall) may have declined as well. This answer matches one of our prephrased explanations from the discussion above, and does help to resolve the apparent discrepancy in the stimulus.

Answer choice (C): The manner in which optimal living conditions were assessed would not help to explain why the people of area L have become less satisfied with their living conditions over time, so this choice fails to resolve the stimulus' paradox.

Answer choice (D): This choice does not help to explain the increased level of dissatisfaction among the people of area L despite more equal conditions (as compared to the country as a whole).

Answer choice (E): This answer choice might help to resolve if area L residents were still living in conditions below those of the national average. But currently the living conditions of area L are comparable to those of the country overall, so this answer choice would not help to explain the people's more recent dissatisfaction.

Question #18: Flaw in the Reasoning. The correct answer choice is (C)

The travel agent quoted here makes the following questionable argument: Since most low fare airlines have not existed long enough to establish a record, major airlines which have had enough time to establish a safety record are *safer*. The problem with this argument is that just because a safety record has been *established* does not mean that it is a good one.

Answer choice (A): This is not the flaw found in the stimulus' argument, as there is no need to address this possibility. Incidentally, if the average major airline did have a total number of accidents as great as the average low-fare airline has had, that would still show the major airlines to be safer, since this would mean the same number of accidents over a longer period of time.

Answer choice (B): Since the major airlines are said to have long-standing records, this cannot be a description of the flaw from the stimulus.

Answer choice (C): This is the correct answer choice, which restates our prephrased description of the flaw in the discussion above: a long standing and reliable record does not guarantee that an airline is safe—on the contrary, such a record may reliably show an airline to be *unsafe*.

Answer choice (D): The travel agent does not presume that the safest airlines have the most reliable documentation, and this choice does not describe the flaw as prephrased above, so it cannot be the correct answer choice.

Answer choice (E): The discussion surrounds a comparison between the *relative* safety of major airlines as compared with low-fare airlines; it is irrelevant if all airlines are likely to have had one or more accidents, and there is no need for the argument to address this possibility.

Question #19: Assumption. The correct answer choice is (D)

Here the economist presents a causal argument, which we might recognize based on the use of words such as "result" and "cause." Basically, the economist says that factors such as high-priced goods and services cause consumers to be reluctant to spend, and this in turn causes our economy's weakness. The situation is made worse by a lower average income, so the author concludes that lower income taxes, though not a perfect solution, would cause the economy to improve.

How would lower income taxes cure the reluctance to spend? The author must assume that lower income taxes, meaning more money going back to consumers, would cause consumers to be less reluctant to spend.

The stimulus is followed by an assumption question; if lower taxes will reduce reluctance to spend, the presumption must be that the money consumers don't spend on taxes will be spent consuming (rather than saving or investing, for example).

Answer choice (A): This assumption is not required by the argument in the stimulus, because the conclusion is that the economy would improve, and this does not mean that prices would necessarily need to decrease.

Answer choice (B): This answer choice is incorrect for the same basic reason that answer choice (A) above is incorrect: Since the economist makes it clear that less spending reluctance will help the economy, the conclusion (that the economy will improve) does not require that average incomes increase when consumer spending does so.

Answer choice (C): The author's argument only deals with what will happen if income taxes *are* lowered; there is no reference to, or assumption about, what will happen if income taxes are *not* lowered, so this answer choice cannot be correct.

Answer choice (D): This is the correct answer choice. This choice presents exactly the Supporter Assumption that we seek, and the one which allows for the economist's conclusion to be properly drawn. If lower income taxes will cause consumers to be less reluctant to spend, then we can add this supporter assumption to the premises from the stimulus, and link the rogue elements to arrive at the economist's conclusion.

C E

Premise: less reluctance to spend ⟶ help economy

\+

Supporter Assumption: lower income taxes ⟶ less reluctance to spend

Conclusion: lower income taxes ⟶ less reluctance to spend ⟶ help economy

Answer choice (E): Like the other incorrect answer choices above, this choice is not required of the author's argument: regardless of any effects on government spending, the author only concludes that lowering the income tax will improve the economy.

Question #20: Must Be True—#%. The correct answer choice is (E)

Here information is provided about an experiment in which volunteers were placed on a low-fat diet. Those with a type B lipid profile have a higher risk for heart disease than those with type A, and the type B volunteers lowered their cholesterol levels during the experiment. The type A volunteers, on the other hand, experienced no benefits from the experiment, and 40 percent even became type B's (meaning that their risk of heart disease actually *increased*).

The stimulus is followed by a Must Be True question, so the correct answer choice can be confirmed by the information provided in the stimulus.

Answer choice (A): Since the stimulus provides no information regarding the portion of volunteers who saw some risk reduction, this choice fails the Fact Test, cannot be confirmed by the information provided, and must be incorrect.

Answer choice (B): The author provides that the type B volunteers lowered their cholesterol levels, but no information is provided to allow comparison of the cholesterol levels of the two groups.

Answer choice (C): We are provided with no information regarding any other aspects of the volunteers' lives, so this choice fails the Fact Test.

Answer choice (D): There is no specific explanation for the change in lipid profiles, and the group that experienced the cholesterol level decrease (type B) was different from the group that experienced changes in lipid profile (type A).

Answer choice (E): This is the correct answer choice. Since 40 percent of the type A volunteers shifted to type B, thus increasing their risk for heart disease, we know that at least some volunteers increased this risk. We might note in this case the somewhat counter intuitive link between lower fat and higher risk.

Question #21: Must Be True—PR. The correct answer choice is (C)

The columnist quoted in this stimulus might be a bit difficult to understand because of the use of a double negative, but the argument can be restated more simply as follows:

Thought and expression should be completely free, but that doesn't make it right to exploit depraved (i.e. corrupt, perverted, etc.) tastes for money.

The stimulus is followed by a Must Be True—Principle question, so we should seek the answer choice which follows the principle above.

Answer choice (A): This choice would put government limits on the freedoms of thought and expression, so this is not aligned with the principle from the stimulus.

Answer choice (B): The principle in the stimulus does not deal with the freedom to exploit depraved tastes and to refrain from such exploitation, so this cannot be the correct answer choice.

Answer choice (C): This is the correct answer choice. This answer perfectly follows the principle expressed by the author of the stimulus: with specific regard to books, thought and expression should not be restricted, but that does not mean that it is alright to exploit depraved tastes for gain.

Answer choice (D): This incorrect answer choice deals with limitations on depraved recordings, rather than freedom of thought or expression, so it does not conform to the principle in the stimulus and is incorrect.

Answer choice (E): The principle from the stimulus is that there should be freedom but that this does not justify the exploitation of depravity. This choice deals with criticism of others and exhibition, omitting any reference to the *exploitation* of depraved tastes.

Question #22: Assumption—CE. The correct answer choice is (C)

This stimulus presents the relationship between the rate of societal change and the degree to which young people value the advice of their elders. If societal change is slow, there is greater respect for the advice of elders, and, conversely, if societal change is more rapid, young people see less value in the advice of their elders. Based on these premises, the author jumps to the conclusion that the rate of societal change is reflected in the amount of deference (i.e. respect) which younger members of society show to older members.

Although it is somewhat subtle, we might note the leap from *valuing the advice* of elders, to *showing deference* to elders:

Premises: Slow societal change ⟶ greater value placed on elders' advice
Rapid societal change ⟶ lesser value placed on elders' advice

Conclusion: Rate of societal change is reflected in the deference shown to elders.

The stimulus is followed by an assumption question stem. Since there is a clear leap from greater *value* to greater *deference*, the correct answer choice will provide the Supporter Assumption which links these elements (the choice which links greater perceived value with greater deference).

Answer choice (A): This stimulus is not about whether or not society's young members can determine the rate of societal change, but rather whether the amount of respect that the youth have for their elders provides an accurate gauge of the societal rate of change. Since this choice fails to provide the Supporter Assumption required for the author's argument to be properly drawn, this answer choice is incorrect.

Answer choice (B): This choice provides a clever wrong answer. We need to link deference with how the young *assess* the value of their elders' advice. This choice instead links deference with how much actual value is provided by the elders. Because of this subtle but important distinction, this choice is incorrect.

Answer choice (C): This is the correct answer choice; it is the one which links the rogue elements as prephrased in our discussion above. If deference for elders and valuing of their advice vary together, then this allows the argument in the stimulus to be properly drawn:

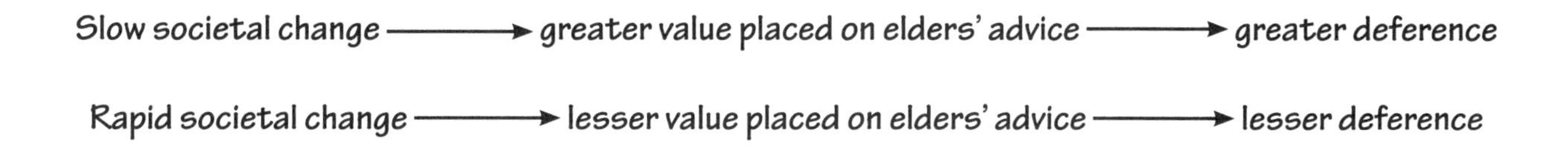

Between the premises presented in the stimulus, and the Supporter Assumption provided by this answer choice, the author's argument (that degree of deference for elders provides an accurate gauge of the societal change rate) is properly drawn.

Answer choice (D): This is another clever incorrect answer choice. The argument is that a faster changing society leads the youth to *assess* elders' advice as less relevant. This does not require the assumption provided here, which is that the *experience* of the elders *is* less relevant in a faster changing society.

Since this choice doesn't even reference the degree of deference that the youth have for their elders, it cannot link the needed elements from the stimulus and thus cannot be the Supporter Assumption that we are looking for.

Answer choice (E): This choice links the value that young people place on the advice of elders with the practical value that this advice holds for them. This does not provide the needed link between young peoples valuation of elders' advice and their degree of deference for elders, so this choice is incorrect.

Question #23: Must Be True—PR, CE. The correct answer choice is (C)

In this stimulus, the politician's conclusion is presented in the first sentence:

> Imported fruit should be taxed so that it is more expensive than domestic fruit.

The politician follows this conclusion with supporting premises—a discussion of what a tariff might avoid. Otherwise, the politician argues, other countries' cheaper fruit will put domestic fruit farmers out of business, farmland will be used for more lucrative industry, and a unique way of life (fruit farming) will disappear.

Considering that the argument is in favor of taxing foreign fruit, the politician clearly believes that domestic fruit farming is worth saving—despite the fact that industrial uses would apparently bring greater financial benefit. In other words, the politician favors a policy that would preserve this unique way of life, even though that policy does not maximize financial exploitation of the land involved.

Answer choice (A): While one incidental outcome of the suggested fruit tariff might be placing the politician's own country's economic interests above that of others, the central idea from the stimulus is that a unique lifestyle should be preserved—even if fruit growing is not the most lucrative way to use the land.

Answer choice (B): Like incorrect answer choice (A) above, this choice conforms to a principle that is rather different from the principle suggested by the politician. The politician does not reference producers in general, and does not weigh the interests of producers' against those of the consumers; rather, the politician's recommendation puts the interests of the domestic fruit growers ahead of those of maximization of financial gain.

Answer choice (C): This is the correct answer choice. The principle presented in this choice is aligned with the stand taken by the politician and discussed above—that saving domestic fruit farming is worthwhile, even if it is not the most economically efficient outcome—that is, regardless of the fact that it does not maximize financial gains.

Answer choice (D): Like the other answer choices which present slightly different groups whose interests are being weighed, this choice is incorrect. The politician does not suggest that the interests of one's own citizens should take priority—the politician is merely suggesting that protection of domestic fruit growers is more important than profit maximization.

Answer choice (E): This answer choice cannot be correct, because the politician's suggestion actually *reduces* economic efficiency. If free markets were allowed to reign, the foreign fruit growers would have the advantage, and bring in cheaper fruit, putting the domestic growers out of business, and the domestic land would then be converted for more lucrative use—thus government intervention as suggested in this case would actually *decrease* efficiency.

Question #24: Weaken—#%. The correct answer choice is (E)

Like many questions that deal with numbers and percentages, this one can be tricky if we don't have a strong grasp on the information provided. The premises are as follows: The Kiffer Forest Preserve is the portion of the Abbimac Valley most populated with bears. During the past eight years, the main road through the preserve has been closed, and the bear population in the preserve has doubled.

Based on the premises listed above, the author concludes that if the road remains closed, the bear population of the *whole valley* will increase. As with many of the LSAT's number/percentage stimuli, this one provides limited information; we know that the bear population in the preserve (which is, after all, only a *portion* of the Valley) has doubled over the past eight years, perhaps based on the road closing, but we have no information about what's been happening around the *rest* of the Valley. If the overall, Valley-wide bear population has been increasing, then the author's argument becomes stronger.

If the overall population has not also seen an increase over the past eight years, the author's conclusion is then provided significantly less support. We should keep this in mind, since the question stem requires us to find the answer that weakens the argument.

Answer choice (A): Regardless of whether the changes in the *preserve*'s bear population were attributable to migration, this choice fails to weaken the author's argument, which regards the bear population of the whole valley.

Answer choice (B): This answer choice provides very limited information. If "some" were from other areas within the valley, this means "at least one" bear had migrated from elsewhere. This choice does not weaken the argument from the stimulus.

Answer choice (C): This answer choice is limited in the same way as incorrect answer choice (B) above. The information that "some" of the bears migrated from outside the valley does not weaken the author's argument, which is that an increase in the *valley*'s bear population is to be expected based on the increases in the *preserve*'s bear population.

Answer choice (D): This choice provides us with another vague piece of information, of limited usefulness. Perhaps the bear population in other areas has decreased by *one* over the past 8 years. Without more information about the increase in the preserve and in the valley overall, this choice does not weaken the argument in the stimulus and thus cannot be the correct answer choice.

Answer choice (E): This is the correct answer choice. If the overall Valley population of bears has not increased, the author's argument is seriously undermined. The conclusion that the Valley's bear population will increase is based on the increased population in the preserve. If the overall population has not increased, this means that the bears that arrived in the preserve had come from nearby, within the very same valley. If this is the case, there is far less reason to believe the author's conclusion, so this must be the correct answer to this weaken question.

Question #25: Justify the Conclusion—SN. The correct answer choice is (A)

This stimulus provides a series of conditional statements, listed below with diagrams:

If a wig has any handmade components, it is more expensive than one with none:

Handmade components ⟶ more expensive than none

If a wig is made to measure, it ranges from medium priced to expensive:

Made to measure ⟶ medium- to high-priced

Handmade foundations are never found on wigs that don't use human hair. In other words, handmade foundations are found *only* on wigs that do use human hair.

Handmade foundations ⟶ wigs with human hair

Any wig that contains human hair should be dry-cleaned:

Wig with human hair ⟶ should be dry-cleaned

Based on the above premises, the author draws the following conclusion:
All made-to-measure wigs should be dry-cleaned:

Made to measure ⟶ should be dry-cleaned

Based on the information provided in the stimulus, all we really know about made-to-measure wigs is that they are medium- to high- priced. The Justify question stem requires that we somehow tie in the rogue element, "should be dry-cleaned." The correct answer choice will provide a premise which, when added to those provided in the stimulus, allows the author to conclude that made to measure wigs should be dry-cleaned.

Answer choice (A): This is the correct answer choice. This answer provides that if a wig is medium to high-priced, it has a handmade foundation:

medium- to high- priced ⟶ handmade

And, the stimulus says that handmade foundations can only be found in wigs with human hair (in other words, handmade foundations always have human hair):

medium to high ⟶ handmade ⟶ human hair

The author also provides that human-hair wigs should all be dry-cleaned:

medium to high ⟶ handmade ⟶ human hair ⟶ dry-cleaned

...And, according to the stimulus, made-to-measure wigs are always medium- to high- priced:

made to measure ⟶ medium to high ⟶ handmade ⟶ human hair ⟶ dry-cleaned

As reflected in the diagram once we link the relevant conditions, this choice justifies the author's conclusion that all made-to-measure wigs should be dry-cleaned:

made to measure ⟶ dry-cleaned

Answer choice (B): This choice provides the following conditional statement:

Handmade foundation ⟶ more expensive than non-hand-made

Since this choice does not allow us to link the rogue element "should be dry-cleaned," it does not justify the argument in the stimulus.

Answer choice (C): This answer can be diagrammed as follows:

Has handmade components ⟶ should be dry-cleaned

This choice might be appealing at first, because it does involve the needed element "should be dry-cleaned." However, the stimulus provides no link between a wig having hand-made components and being made-to-measure, so this choice does not justify the author's conclusion.

Answer choice (D): The conditional statement provided by this answer choice can be diagrammed as follows:

Handmade foundation ⟶ medium-priced or higher

Based on the information in the stimulus we already knew that wigs with handmade foundations are more expensive than those without; this choice expands somewhat on that information, providing that such wigs are always medium-priced or higher. Since this choice fails to link the condition "made to measure" with the condition "should be dry-cleaned," it cannot be the correct answer choice to this Justify question.

Answer choice (E): This choice provides that if a wig should be dry-cleaned, it has a foundation that is handmade:

Should be dry-cleaned ⟶ foundation that is handmade

Question #26: Method of Reasoning. The correct answer choice is (A)

Here the philosopher points out that among wolves, it is intolerable for one wolf to attack another that has already shown submission, and the same goes for foxes and domesticated dogs.

In a convoluted final sentence, the author draws the following conclusion: therefore it would be wrong to deny animal rights based on the claim that humans are the only ones who can follow a moral code.

In other words, the information provided about wolves, foxes, and dogs, is intended to show that these breeds are able to obey a moral code, so a supposed inability to follow such a code should not be used to deny their rights.

The question is followed by a Method of Reasoning question, so the correct answer choice will describe the philosopher's approach—to provide information that refutes a claim.

Answer choice (A): This is the correct answer choice. The philosopher's counterexamples of wolves, foxes, and dogs are provided to refute the claim that animals cannot follow a moral code—this refuted claim might otherwise be used as basis for the conclusion that animals should be denied their rights.

Answer choice (B): The philosopher's argument deals with only three breeds, implying nothing about all animals.

Answer choice (C): The argument is not intended to question whether the ability to follow a moral code is necessary, but rather to show that this ability is present is some animals, so even if it is not necessary some animals still shouldn't be denied their rights on this basis.

Answer choice (D): The philosopher seeks to refute a claim, rather than to establish one, by showing that its supposed basis is inaccurate.

Answer choice (E): The philosopher does not suggest that the concept of morality is often defined too broadly, but rather that some animals can follow a moral code.

6

Chapter Six: PrepTest 58 Logical Reasoning Section II

6

Chapter Six: PrepTest 58 Logical Reasoning Section II

POWERSCORE
BY BARBRI

PrepTest 58
Logical Reasoning Section II

SECTION V
Time—35 minutes
25 Questions

Directions: The questions in this section are based on the reasoning contained in brief statements or passages. For some questions, more than one of the choices could conceivably answer the question. However, you are to choose the best answer; that is, the response that most accurately and completely answers the question. You should not make assumptions that are by commonsense standards implausible, superfluous, or incompatible with the passage. After you have chosen the best answer, blacken the corresponding space on your answer sheet.

1. Automated flight technology can guide an aircraft very reliably, from navigation to landing. Yet this technology, even when functioning correctly, is not a perfect safeguard against human error.

Which one of the following, if true, most helps to explain the situation described above?

(A) Automated flight technology does not always function correctly.
(B) Smaller aircraft do not always have their automated flight technology updated regularly.
(C) If a plane's automated flight technology malfunctions, crew members have to operate the plane manually.
(D) Some airplane crashes are due neither to human error nor to malfunction of automated flight technology.
(E) Automated flight technology invariably executes exactly the commands that humans give it.

2. To keep one's hands warm during the winter, one never needs gloves or mittens. One can always keep one's hands warm simply by putting on an extra layer of clothing, such as a thermal undershirt or a sweater. After all, keeping one's vital organs warm can keep one's hands warm as well.

Which one of the following, if true, most weakens the argument?

(A) Maintaining the temperature of your hands is far less important, physiologically, than maintaining the temperature of your torso.
(B) Several layers of light garments will keep one's vital organs warmer than will one or two heavy garments.
(C) Wearing an extra layer of clothing will not keep one's hands warm at temperatures low enough to cause frostbite.
(D) Keeping one's hands warm by putting on an extra layer of clothing is less effective than turning up the heat.
(E) The physical effort required to put on an extra layer of clothing does not stimulate circulation enough to warm your hands.

3. The reason music with a simple recurring rhythm exerts a strong primordial appeal is that it reminds us of the womb environment. After all, the first sound heard within the womb is the comforting sound of the mother's regular heartbeat. So in taking away from us the warmth and security of the womb, birth also takes away a primal and constant source of comfort. Thus it is extremely natural that in seeking sensations of warmth and security throughout life, people would be strongly drawn toward simple recurring rhythmic sounds.

Which one of the following most accurately expresses the main conclusion drawn in the reasoning above?

(A) The explanation of the strong primordial appeal of music with a simple recurring rhythm is that it reminds us of the womb environment.
(B) The comforting sound of the mother's regular heartbeat is the first sound that is heard inside the womb.
(C) Birth deprives us of a primal and constant source of comfort when it takes away the warmth and security of the womb.
(D) People seek sensations of warmth and security throughout life because birth takes away the warmth and security of the womb.
(E) The comforting sound of the mother's regular heartbeat is a simple recurring rhythmic sound.

GO ON TO THE NEXT PAGE.

4. Linguist: Most people can tell whether a sequence of words in their own dialect is grammatical. Yet few people who can do so are able to specify the relevant grammatical rules.

Which one of the following best illustrates the principle underlying the linguist's statements?

(A) Some people are able to write cogent and accurate narrative descriptions of events. But these people are not necessarily also capable of composing emotionally moving and satisfying poems.
(B) Engineers who apply the principles of physics to design buildings and bridges must know a great deal more than do the physicists who discover these principles.
(C) Some people are able to tell whether any given piece of music is a waltz. But the majority of these people cannot state the defining characteristics of a waltz.
(D) Those travelers who most enjoy their journeys are not always those most capable of vividly describing the details of those journeys to others.
(E) Quite a few people know the rules of chess, but only a small number of them can play chess very well.

5. Company president: For the management consultant position, we shall interview only those applicants who have worked for management consulting firms generally recognized as in the top 1 percent of firms worldwide. When we finally select somebody, then, we can be sure to have selected one of the best management consultants available.

The company president's reasoning is most vulnerable to criticism on the grounds that it

(A) takes for granted that only the best management consultants have worked for the top management consulting firms
(B) generalizes from too small a sample of management consulting firms worldwide
(C) takes for granted that if something is true of each member of a collection, then it is also true of the collection as a whole
(D) presumes, without providing warrant, that persons who have worked for the top companies will accept a job offer
(E) presumes, without providing justification, that highly competent management consultants are highly competent at every task

6. Beginners typically decide each chess move by considering the consequences. Expert players, in contrast, primarily use pattern-recognition techniques. That is, such a player recognizes having been in a similar position before and makes a decision based on information recalled about the consequences of moves chosen on that prior occasion.

Which one of the following is most strongly supported by the information above?

(A) Beginning chess players are better at thinking through the consequences of chess moves than experts are.
(B) A beginning chess player should use pattern-recognition techniques when deciding what move to make.
(C) One's chess skills will improve only if one learns to use pattern-recognition techniques.
(D) In playing chess, an expert player relies crucially on his or her memory.
(E) Any chess player who played other games that require pattern-recognition skills would thereby improve his or her chess skills.

7. Farmer: Because water content is what makes popcorn pop, the kernels must dry at just the right speed to trap the correct amount of water. The best way to achieve this effect is to have the sun dry the corn while the corn is still in the field, but I always dry the ears on a screen in a warm, dry room.

Which one of the following, if true, most helps to resolve the apparent discrepancy between the farmer's theory and practice?

(A) The region in which the farmer grows popcorn experiences a long, cloudy season that begins shortly before the popcorn in fields would begin to dry.
(B) Leaving popcorn to dry on its stalks in the field is the least expensive method of drying it.
(C) Drying popcorn on its stalks in the field is only one of several methods that allow the kernels' water content to reach acceptable levels.
(D) When popcorn does not dry sufficiently, it will still pop, but it will take several minutes to do so, even under optimal popping conditions.
(E) If popcorn is allowed to dry too much, it will not pop.

GO ON TO THE NEXT PAGE.

8. Factory manager: One reason the automobile parts this factory produces are expensive is that our manufacturing equipment is outdated and inefficient. Our products would be more competitively priced if we were to refurbish the factory completely with new, more efficient equipment. Therefore, since to survive in today's market we have to make our products more competitively priced, we must completely refurbish the factory in order to survive.

The reasoning in the factory manager's argument is flawed because this argument

(A) fails to recognize that the price of a particular commodity can change over time
(B) shifts without justification from treating something as one way of achieving a goal to treating it as the only way of achieving that goal
(C) argues that one thing is the cause of another when the evidence given indicates that the second thing may in fact be the cause of the first
(D) recommends a solution to a problem without first considering any possible causes of that problem
(E) fails to make a definite recommendation and instead merely suggests that some possible course of action might be effective

9. Two months ago a major shipment of pythons arrived from Africa, resulting in a great number of inexpensive pythons in pet stores. Anyone interested in buying a python, however, should beware: many pythons hatched in Africa are afflicted with a deadly liver disease. Although a few pythons recently hatched in North America have this disease, a much greater proportion of African-hatched pythons have it. The disease is difficult to detect in its early stages, and all pythons die within six months of contracting the disease.

Which one of the following statements can be properly inferred from the statements above?

(A) Some pythons hatched in North America may appear fine but will die within six months as a result of the liver disease.
(B) Pythons that hatch in Africa are more susceptible to the liver disease than are pythons that hatch in North America.
(C) Any python that has not died by the age of six months does not have the liver disease.
(D) The pythons are inexpensively priced because many of them suffer from the liver disease.
(E) Pythons hatched in neither Africa nor North America are not afflicted with the liver disease.

10. Nutritionists believe that a person's daily requirement for vitamins can readily be met by eating five servings of fruits and vegetables daily. However, most people eat far less than this. Thus, most people need to take vitamin pills.

Which one of the following statements, if true, most seriously weakens the argument?

(A) Even five servings of fruits and vegetables a day is insufficient unless the intake is varied to ensure that different vitamins are consumed.
(B) Certain commonly available fruits and vegetables contain considerably more nutrients than others.
(C) Nutritionists sometimes disagree on how much of a fruit or vegetable constitutes a complete serving.
(D) Many commonly consumed foods that are neither fruits nor vegetables are fortified by manufacturers with the vitamins found in fruits and vegetables.
(E) Fruits and vegetables are also important sources of fiber, in forms not found in vitamin pills.

11. Researcher: This fall I returned to a research site to recover the armadillos I had tagged there the previous spring. Since a large majority of the armadillos I recaptured were found within a few hundred yards of the location of their tagging last spring, I concluded that armadillos do not move rapidly into new territories.

Which one of the following is an assumption required by the researcher's argument?

(A) Of the armadillos living in the area of the tagging site last spring, few were able to avoid being tagged by the researcher.
(B) Most of the armadillos tagged the previous spring were not recaptured during the subsequent fall.
(C) Predators did not kill any of the armadillos that had been tagged the previous spring.
(D) The tags identifying the armadillos cannot be removed by the armadillos, either by accident or deliberately.
(E) A large majority of the recaptured armadillos did not move to a new territory in the intervening summer and then move back to the old territory by the fall.

GO ON TO THE NEXT PAGE.

12. Sahira: To make a living from their art, artists of great potential would have to produce work that would gain widespread popular acclaim, instead of their best work. That is why governments are justified in subsidizing artists.

    Rahima: Your argument for subsidizing art depends on claiming that to gain widespread popular acclaim, artists must produce something other than their best work; but this need not be true.

    In her argument, Rahima

    (A) disputes an implicit assumption of Sahira's
    (B) presents independent support for Sahira's argument
    (C) accepts Sahira's conclusion, but for reasons different from those given by Sahira
    (D) uses Sahira's premises to reach a conclusion different from that reached by Sahira
    (E) argues that a standard that she claims Sahira uses is self-contradictory

13. Adult frogs are vulnerable to dehydration because of their highly permeable skins. Unlike large adult frogs, small adult frogs have such a low ratio of body weight to skin surface area that they cannot survive in arid climates. The animals' moisture requirements constitute the most important factor determining where frogs can live in the Yucatán peninsula, which has an arid climate in the north and a wet climate in the south.

    The information above most strongly supports which one of the following conclusions about frogs in the Yucatán peninsula?

    (A) Large adult frogs cannot coexist with small adult frogs in the wet areas.
    (B) Frogs living in wet areas weigh more on average than frogs in the arid areas.
    (C) Large adult frogs can live in more of the area than small adult frogs can.
    (D) Fewer small adult frogs live in the south than do large adult frogs.
    (E) Small adult frogs in the south have less permeable skins than small adult frogs in the north.

14. Editorial: A recent survey shows that 77 percent of people feel that crime is increasing and that 87 percent feel the judicial system should be handing out tougher sentences. Therefore, the government must firmly address the rising crime rate.

    The reasoning in the editorial's argument is most vulnerable to criticism on the grounds that the argument

    (A) appeals to survey results that are inconsistent because they suggest that more people are concerned about the sentencing of criminals than are concerned about crime itself
    (B) presumes, without providing justification, that there is a correlation between criminal offenders being treated leniently and a high crime rate
    (C) fails to consider whether other surveys showing different results have been conducted over the years
    (D) fails to distinguish between the crime rate's actually rising and people's believing that the crime rate is rising
    (E) presumes, without providing justification, that tougher sentences are the most effective means of alleviating the crime problem

15. Proofs relying crucially on computers provide less certainty than do proofs not requiring computers. Human cognition alone cannot verify computer-dependent proofs; such proofs can never provide the degree of certainty that attends our judgments concerning, for instance, simple arithmetical facts, which can be verified by human calculation. Of course, in these cases one often uses electronic calculators, but here the computer is a convenience rather than a supplement to human cognition.

    The statements above, if true, most strongly support which one of the following?

    (A) Only if a proof's result is arrived at without the help of a computer can one judge with any degree of certainty that the proof is correct.
    (B) We can never be completely sure that proofs relying crucially on computers do not contain errors that humans do not detect.
    (C) Whenever a computer replaces human calculation in a proof, the degree of certainty provided by the proof is reduced.
    (D) If one can corroborate something by human calculation, one can be completely certain of it.
    (E) It is impossible to supplement the cognitive abilities of humans by means of artificial devices such as computers.

GO ON TO THE NEXT PAGE.

16. Madden: Industrialists address problems by simplifying them, but in farming that strategy usually leads to oversimplification. For example, industrialists see water retention and drainage as different and opposite functions—that good topsoil both drains and retains water is a fact alien to industrial logic. To facilitate water retention, they use a terrace or a dam; to facilitate drainage, they use drain tile, a ditch, or a subsoiler. More farming problems are created than solved when agriculture is the domain of the industrialist, not of the farmer.

The situation as Madden describes it best illustrates which one of the following propositions?

(A) The handling of water drainage and retention is the most important part of good farming.
(B) The problems of farming should be viewed in all their complexity.
(C) Farmers are better than anyone else at solving farming problems.
(D) Industrial solutions for problems in farming should never be sought.
(E) The approach to problem solving typical of industrialists is fundamentally flawed.

17. Critic: Works of modern literature cannot be tragedies as those of ancient playwrights and storytellers were unless their protagonists are seen as possessing nobility, which endures through the calamities that befall one. In an age that no longer takes seriously the belief that human endeavors are governed by fate, it is therefore impossible for a contemporary work of literature to be a tragedy.

Which one of the following is an assumption required by the critic's argument?

(A) Whether or not a work of literature is a tragedy should not depend on characteristics of its audience.
(B) The belief that human endeavors are governed by fate is false.
(C) Most plays that were once classified as tragedies were misclassified.
(D) Those whose endeavors are not regarded as governed by fate will not be seen as possessing nobility.
(E) If an ignoble character in a work of literature endures through a series of misfortunes, that work of literature is not a tragedy.

18. Despite the efforts of a small minority of graduate students at one university to unionize, the majority of graduate students there remain unaware of the attempt. Most of those who are aware believe that a union would not represent their interests or that, if it did, it would not effectively pursue them. Thus, the graduate students at the university should not unionize, since the majority of them obviously disapprove of the attempt.

The reasoning in the argument is most vulnerable to criticism on the grounds that the argument

(A) tries to establish a conclusion simply on the premise that the conclusion agrees with a long-standing practice
(B) fails to exclude alternative explanations for why some graduate students disapprove of unionizing
(C) presumes that simply because a majority of a population is unaware of something, it must not be a good idea
(D) ignores the possibility that although a union might not effectively pursue graduate student interests, there are other reasons for unionizing
(E) blurs the distinction between active disapproval and mere lack of approval

19. Anyone who believes in democracy has a high regard for the wisdom of the masses. Griley, however, is an elitist who believes that any artwork that is popular is unlikely to be good. Thus, Griley does not believe in democracy.

The conclusion follows logically if which one of the following is assumed?

(A) Anyone who believes that an artwork is unlikely to be good if it is popular is an elitist.
(B) Anyone who believes that if an artwork is popular it is unlikely to be good does not have a high regard for the wisdom of the masses.
(C) If Griley is not an elitist, then he has a high regard for the wisdom of the masses.
(D) Anyone who does not have a high regard for the wisdom of the masses is an elitist who believes that if an artwork is popular it is unlikely to be good.
(E) Unless Griley believes in democracy, Griley does not have a high regard for the wisdom of the masses.

GO ON TO THE NEXT PAGE.

20. A recent study confirmed that salt intake tends to increase blood pressure and found that, as a result, people with high blood pressure who significantly cut their salt intake during the study had lower blood pressure by the end of the study. However, it was also found that some people who had very high salt intake both before and throughout the study maintained very low blood pressure.

Which one of the following, if true, contributes the most to an explanation of the results of the study?

(A) Study participants with high blood pressure who cut their salt intake only slightly during the study did not have significantly lower blood pressure by the end of the study.
(B) Salt intake is only one of several dietary factors associated with high blood pressure.
(C) For most people who have high blood pressure, reducing salt intake is not the most effective dietary change they can make to reduce their blood pressure.
(D) At the beginning of the study, some people who had very low salt intake also had very high blood pressure.
(E) Persons suffering from abnormally low blood pressure have heightened salt cravings, which ensure that their blood pressure does not drop too low.

21. The odds of winning any major lottery jackpot are extremely slight. However, the very few people who do win major jackpots receive a great deal of attention from the media. Thus, since most people come to have at least some awareness of events that receive extensive media coverage, it is likely that many people greatly overestimate the odds of their winning a major jackpot.

Which one of the following is an assumption on which the argument depends?

(A) Most people who overestimate the likelihood of winning a major jackpot do so at least in part because media coverage of other people who have won major jackpots downplays the odds against winning such a jackpot.
(B) Very few people other than those who win major jackpots receive a great deal of attention from the media.
(C) If it were not for media attention, most people who purchase lottery tickets would not overestimate their chances of winning a jackpot.
(D) Becoming aware of individuals who have won a major jackpot leads at least some people to incorrectly estimate their own chances of winning such a jackpot.
(E) At least some people who are heavily influenced by the media do not believe that the odds of their winning a major jackpot are significant.

GO ON TO THE NEXT PAGE.

22. A book tour will be successful if it is well publicized and the author is an established writer. Julia is an established writer, and her book tour was successful. So her book tour must have been well publicized.

    Which one of the following exhibits a pattern of flawed reasoning most closely parallel to the pattern of flawed reasoning exhibited by the argument above?

    (A) This recipe will turn out only if one follows it exactly and uses high-quality ingredients. Arthur followed the recipe exactly and it turned out. Thus, Arthur must have used high-quality ingredients.
    (B) If a computer has the fastest microprocessor and the most memory available, it will meet Aletha's needs this year. This computer met Aletha's needs last year. So it must have had the fastest microprocessor and the most memory available last year.
    (C) If cacti are kept in the shade and watered more than twice weekly, they will die. This cactus was kept in the shade, and it is now dead. Therefore, it must have been watered more than twice weekly.
    (D) A house will suffer from dry rot and poor drainage only if it is built near a high water table. This house suffers from dry rot and has poor drainage. Thus, it must have been built near a high water table.
    (E) If one wears a suit that has double vents and narrow lapels, one will be fashionably dressed. The suit that Joseph wore to dinner last night had double vents and narrow lapels, so Joseph must have been fashionably dressed.

23. Eight large craters run in a long straight line across a geographical region. Although some of the craters contain rocks that have undergone high-pressure shocks characteristic of meteorites slamming into Earth, these shocks could also have been caused by extreme volcanic events. Because of the linearity of the craters, it is very unlikely that some of them were caused by volcanoes and others were caused by meteorites. Thus, since the craters are all different ages, they were probably caused by volcanic events rather than meteorites.

    Which one of the following statements, if true, would most strengthen the argument?

    (A) A similar but shorter line of craters that are all the same age is known to have been caused by volcanic activity.
    (B) No known natural cause would likely account for eight meteorite craters of different ages forming a straight line.
    (C) There is no independent evidence of either meteorites or volcanic activity in the region where the craters are located.
    (D) There is no independent evidence of a volcanic event strong enough to have created the high-pressure shocks that are characteristic of meteorites slamming into Earth.
    (E) No known single meteor shower has created exactly eight impact craters that form a straight line.

GO ON TO THE NEXT PAGE.

24. The genuine creative genius is someone who is dissatisfied with merely habitual assent to widely held beliefs; thus these rare innovators tend to anger the majority. Those who are dissatisfied with merely habitual assent to widely held beliefs tend to seek out controversy, and controversy seekers enjoy demonstrating the falsehood of popular viewpoints.

    The conclusion of the argument follows logically if which one of the following is assumed?

    (A) People become angry when they are dissatisfied with merely habitual assent to widely held beliefs.
    (B) People who enjoy demonstrating the falsehood of popular viewpoints anger the majority.
    (C) People tend to get angry with individuals who hold beliefs not held by a majority of people.
    (D) People who anger the majority enjoy demonstrating the falsehood of popular viewpoints.
    (E) People who anger the majority are dissatisfied with merely habitual assent to widely held beliefs.

25. Claude: When I'm having lunch with job candidates, I watch to see if they salt their food without first tasting it. If they do, I count that against them, because they're making decisions based on inadequate information.

    Larissa: That's silly. It's perfectly reasonable for me to wear a sweater whenever I go into a supermarket, because I already know supermarkets are always too cool inside to suit me. And I never open a credit card offer that comes in the mail, because I already know that no matter how low its interest rate may be, it will never be worthwhile for me.

    The two analogies that Larissa offers can most reasonably be interpreted as invoking which one of the following principles to criticize Claude's policy?

    (A) In matters involving personal preference, performing an action without first ascertaining whether it is appropriate in the specific circumstances should not be taken as good evidence of faulty decision making, because the action may be based on a reasoned policy relating to knowledge of a general fact about the circumstances.
    (B) In professional decision-making contexts, those who have the responsibility of judging other people's suitability for a job should not use observations of job-related behavior as a basis for inferring general conclusions about those people's character.
    (C) General conclusions regarding a job candidate's suitability for a position should not be based exclusively on observations of the candidate's behavior in situations that are neither directly job related nor likely to be indicative of a pattern of behavior that the candidate engages in.
    (D) Individuals whose behavior in specific circumstances does not conform to generally expected norms should not automatically be considered unconcerned with meeting social expectations, because such individuals may be acting in accordance with reasoned policies that they believe should be generally adopted by people in similar circumstances.
    (E) Evidence that a particular individual uses bad decision-making strategies in matters of personal taste should not be considered sufficient to warrant a negative assessment of his or her suitability for a job, because any good decision maker can have occasional lapses of rationality with regard to such matters.

S T O P

IF YOU FINISH BEFORE TIME IS CALLED, YOU MAY CHECK YOUR WORK ON THIS SECTION ONLY.
DO NOT WORK ON ANY OTHER SECTION IN THE TEST.

PREPTEST 58 LOGICAL REASONING SECTION II

1. E	8. B	15. B	22. C
2. C	9. A	16. B	23. B
3. A	10. D	17. D	24. B
4. C	11. E	18. E	25. A
5. A	12. A	19. B	
6. D	13. C	20. E	
7. A	14. D	21. D	

PrepTest 58 Logical Reasoning Section II Explanations

Question #1: Resolve the Paradox. The correct answer choice is (E)

This stimulus presents us with the following paradox: even though automated flight technology can reliably guide every part of an airplane's flight, this technology is still subject to human error.

The question stem requires that we find the answer choice which best explains the apparent paradox. The correct answer choice will be the one that explains how a properly functioning, reliable technology, which is capable of guiding a plane from navigation to landing, still fails to provide a completely reliable guard against human error.

Answer choice (A): The author tells us that the technology is not a perfect safeguard *even when functioning correctly*. This choice fails to explain this fact, so it cannot be the correct answer to this Resolve the Paradox question.

Answer choice (B): This answer choice, like incorrect answer choice (A) above, fails to resolve the paradox: a lack of updates is irrelevant, because the technology is not a perfect safeguard against human error, even when that technology is functioning correctly.

Answer choice (C): This choice, which discusses a malfunction scenario, is irrelevant to the question of why *properly functioning* technology of this sort is vulnerable to human error. Like incorrect answer choices (A) and (B) above, this one fails to address the issue of well functioning automated flight technology.

Answer choice (D): The paradox presented in the stimulus, the fact that well functioning automated flight technology is vulnerable to human error, is not explained by this choice, which deals with problems that are caused by neither the flight technology nor human error.

Answer choice (E): This is the correct answer choice, explaining why the technology described in the stimulus is still subject to human error. If automated flight technology invariably executes exact commands, then the technology is only as good as the human in command. If a human makes an error, the automated flight technology is programmed to perfectly execute the flawed command.

Question #2: Weaken. The correct answer choice is (C)

Here the author begins by pointing out that to keep your hands warm, you don't ever absolutely need gloves or mittens. You can keep your hands warm by wearing a thermal undershirt or a sweater, since keeping your vital organs warm can keep your hands warm as well. Putting the argument in a more straightforward order:

> You can keep your hands warm by keeping your vital organs warm.
>
> Therefore you can keep your hands warm by wearing a thermal undershirt or sweater.
>
> Therefore gloves or mittens are never an absolute necessity in keeping your hands warm.

The argument is followed by a weaken question stem, so the correct answer choice will effectively attack part or all of the argument presented above.

Answer choice (A): The author makes no claims about which part of the body it is more important to keep warm, so this answer choice has no effect on the argument presented.

Answer choice (B): The author presents no information about the best type of layering for keeping warm, so this choice plays no role in the argument and thus cannot weaken.

Answer choice (C): This is the correct answer choice. If wearing an extra layer of clothing does not, at certain temperatures, keep your hands warm, then this disproves the premise that you can *always* keep your hands warm with an extra layer of clothing.

Answer choice (D): The author does not claim that wearing an extra layer of clothing is the *best* way to keep warm—only that it is one effective way to do so. Even if turning up the heat is more effective, this does not weaken the author's somewhat limited claim about wearing an extra layer.

Answer choice (E): There is no suggestion in the stimulus that the warmth is derived in the process of *putting on* an extra layer of clothes, but rather that *wearing* an extra layer can be an effective way to keep warm.

Question #3: Main Point. The correct answer choice is (A)

In this case the main conclusion is presented in the opening sentence of the paragraph: Music with a strong rhythm is primordially appealing because it is reminiscent of the womb environment. This conclusion is immediately followed by the premise (introduced with the indicator "after all") that the first sound we hear is the comforting sound of the mother's heartbeat. The author asserts that birth removes this constant source of comfort, leaving us in search of warmth and security, which can come in the form of rhythmic sounds.

The stimulus is followed by a Main Point question, and the first sentence of the paragraph provides a nice prephrase for this answer: recurring rhythm has appeal because it reminds us of the womb environment.

Answer choice (A): This is the correct answer choice. This answer perfectly expresses the main conclusion of the paragraph, as prephrased above. The author believes that the reason we find primal appeal in recurring rhythm is found in its similarity to the womb environment.

Answer choice (B): Although this choice is accurate according to the stimulus, it is not the main point of the argument but rather a supporting premise.

Answer choice (C): Much like incorrect answer choice (B) above, this choice provides a premise in support of the main conclusion, rather than the main point of the argument itself.

Answer choice (D): This choice, like the other incorrect answer choices above, accurately presents information from the stimulus; according to the argument, people do seek warmth and security after it has been taken away at birth, but this is not the author's main conclusion. The main point is that people often find this warmth and security in recurring rhythms, which remind them of the womb, *which is the reason that music with a simple recurring rhythm has a strong primordial appeal.*

Answer choice (E): This choice provides yet another important part of the argument presented, but does not express the main point. Rather, this is a premise which provides support for the main conclusion—that we are drawn to simple recurring rhythms because they remind us of the secure, warm environment that we lose in birth.

Question #4: Must Be True—PR. The correct answer choice is (C)

The linguist in this stimulus presents an interesting contrast: although most people can tell when a sentence in their first language is grammatically correct, not many know the specific underlying grammatical rules.

The question requires that we identify the answer choice which best illustrates the principle from the stimulus, which is basically this: many can recognize an attribute (in the stimulus' case, grammatical correctness) without necessarily knowing what defines that attribute.

Answer choice (A): This choice illustrates a different principle—that the ability to create an accurate narrative is different from the ability to create a moving poem.

Answer choice (B): This answer choice is incorrect, as it draws a comparison that is quite different from that in the stimulus. Rather than the recognition of an attribute without the ability to fully define it, the principle in this answer choice is that those who apply certain technologies in some cases require more knowledge than those who discovered the principles at work.

Answer choice (C): This is the correct answer choice because it manifests the principle from the stimulus, in a slightly different context. Most people know a waltz when they hear it, despite the fact that most do not know exactly what defines a waltz.

Answer choice (D): This answer choice is similar to incorrect answer choice (A) above. Rather than presenting the principle reflected in the stimulus—the distinction between recognition and complete understanding—the dichotomy drawn here is between the ability to enjoy one's journeys and the ability to vividly describe them.

Answer choice (E): This choice may look appealing at first because of the reference to an understanding of rules. In the stimulus, though, the author tells us that most people can recognize a particular attribute, yet few understand all of the underlying rules defining that attribute. This answer choice provides an idea that is slightly different: Most people know the rules, but few are good at the game.

Question #5: Flaw in the Reasoning—#%. The correct answer choice is (A)

Here the "company president" presents a plan whose stated goal is to select one of the best management consultants available. To achieve this end, the president has decided to limit interviews to only those who have worked for management consulting firms which are considered to be in the top 1% of firms around the world.

The question stem requires us to find the vulnerability in this plan. If the goal is to select one of the best management consultants available, then the president appears to presume that having worked for a top 1% consulting firm provides such a guarantee. In other words, the president must assume that every consultant who has worked for a top 1% firm could be described as one of the best consultants in the country.

Answer choice (A): This is the correct answer, restating our prephrase from the discussion above, in slightly different terms. Assuming that only the best management consultants work at the top 1% firms is the same as assuming that every consultant at those top firms could accurately be described as one of the best in the country.

Answer choice (B): The president specifically states that the candidates are to come from firms generally considered to be in the top 1% worldwide. This is a stringent criterion, not a generalization based on too small a sample.

Answer choice (C): This answer choice may have drawn your attention, but it is incorrect because there is no such presumption implied in the plan from the stimulus. The president does not imply that the firms are good because those working for them are good, but rather the opposite: the president's assumption is that the consultants who work for the top firms must each individually be among the best.

Answer choice (D): There is no presumption that everyone who receives an offer will accept a job—the president is discussing *selection* in this stimulus, not acceptance of the offer.

Answer choice (E): The firm is looking for talented management consultants—there is no presumption that these applicants are competent at every task.

Question #6: Must Be True. The correct answer choice is (D)

The author of this stimulus discusses the difference between the chess play of typical beginners and that of typical experts. Beginners tend to look at moves one at a time, considering the consequences of each. Expert players, on the other hand, typically look at the bigger patterns, recognizing potential consequences from similar scenarios from the past.

This stimulus is followed by a Must Be True question, so the correct answer choice will pass the Fact Test; the right answer choice can always be confirmed by the information provided in the stimulus.

Answer choice (A): This answer choice mischaracterizes a tendency among beginners to make chess decisions move by move. This tendency is more likely based on an inability to recognize the patterns noted by the more experienced players, rather than a sign of being better at thinking through consequences.

Answer choice (B): Although the author tells us that experts tend to use this strategy, this does not necessarily mean that beginners would be well advised to take the same approach—given a beginners lack of experience and of previous patterns to recognize, it would seem that this approach would require some degree of experience with the game.

Answer choice (C): Although we know that pattern recognition is an approach that is more common among expert chess players, we cannot reasonably conclude that the use of pattern recognition is a *necessary condition* for improvement.

Answer choice (D): This is the correct answer choice. Since expert players tend to rely on recognition of patterns from past scenarios, an expert player most certainly relies on his or her memory.

Answer choice (E): Although we know that expert chess players primarily employ pattern recognition techniques, and there might be some benefit for many such players to practice with other pattern-recognition games, we cannot leap to the conclusion that *Any* chess player would definitely improve his or her chess skills by playing other pattern recognition games.

Question #7: Resolve the Paradox. The correct answer choice is (A)

Popcorn kernels need to dry at the proper speed to trap water, which is necessary to make popcorn pop. The farmer quoted in this stimulus always dries the ears of corn in a warm, dry room, despite the fact that the best way to trap the right amount of water is to let the sun dry the corn while it is still in the field.

Not surprisingly, the passage is followed by a Resolve the Paradox question, so we should look for the answer choice which explains the Farmer's unexplained preference. The correct answer choice will most likely either present a detriment or problem associated with the dry-in-the-field method, or a benefit or need associated with the Farmer's preferred method of drying the corn in a warm dry room.

Answer choice (A): This is the correct answer choice. Although the ideal situation might be to allow the corn to dry in the field, this choice explains why this farmer's situation makes such a plan impractical. If the farmer's land is in a region that experiences a long cloudy season just before the popcorn would normally begin to dry, then the rain might spoil the intended effects of leaving the corn in the field. Thus the indoor method of corn-drying would appear to be the better approach in this case.

Answer choice (B): Rather than resolving the paradox, this answer choice would actually expand it; this choice provides yet another benefit of drying corn in the fields, which makes the farmer's preference for indoor drying that much more paradoxical.

Answer choice (C): Since the farmer has already presented two different approaches to the drying of popcorn, this answer choice provides no new information, and fails to explain why the farmer dries corn inside in spite of the fact that sun drying is the best way for the corn to trap the right amount of moisture.

Answer choice (D): The stimulus deals with ideal drying times for popcorn, and drying the corn inside versus outside. The effects of insufficient drying, as presented in this answer choice, are irrelevant to the question of why the farmer chooses the indoor method.

Answer choice (E): Like incorrect answer choice (D) above, this choice discusses the effects of improper corn drying. This information is irrelevant to the farmer's chosen method, so this choice cannot be correct.

Question #8: Flaw in the Reasoning. The correct answer choice is (B)

The factory manager quoted in this stimulus notes that the products produced at the factory are expensive, which is at least partly attributable to its outdated, inefficient manufacturing equipment. The manager then suggests one possible solution: the factory's products could be more competitively priced if the factory were refurbished with newer, more efficient equipment.

At this point, the manager has identified the problem (the factory's products are expensive), has noted one solution (newer equipment), and has then gone on to draw a very questionable conclusion: since the factory's survival depends on its products' being more competitively priced, "we <u>must</u> completely refurbish the factory in order to survive." (emphasis added).

The stimulus is followed by a Flaw in the Reasoning question. If after reading the stimulus, you didn't happen to notice any flaw, this question should lead you to reconsider the passage. What was the flaw, or the logical leap, in the factory manager's argument? The assertion that the factory <u>must</u> be completely refurbished, despite the fact that other potential solutions may exist.

Answer choice (A): There is no indication that the manger fails to recognize this fact; changing commodity prices are not relevant to the manager's flawed reasoning—that the factory must be refurbished if the company wishes to price its products more competitively.

Answer choice (B): This is the correct answer choice. The factory manager suggests only one single solution to the factory's problems (completely refurbishing the factory), and then leaps to the assertion that this solution <u>must</u> be implemented.

Answer choice (C): This answer choice describes a causal flaw, but it does not describe the problem with the factory manager's argument as discussed above.

Answer choice (D): The problem with the stimulus is not that the manager fails to consider any possible causes—rather, the flaw is that the manager recommends one solution and then leaps to the conclusion that it must be implemented, before considering any other <u>solutions</u>.

Answer choice (E): This answer choice is incorrect, because the factory manager does not fail to make a definite recommendation, and instead suggest one possible course of action: rather, the factory manager makes <u>too</u> definite a recommendation based on the consideration of only one course of action.

Question #9: Must Be True. The correct answer choice is (A)

In this stimulus the author warns of one potential hazard that has emerged with a recent shipment of pythons from Africa: a deadly liver disease, difficult to detect in its early phases, contracted by a few of these snakes that have hatched in North America, and a much greater proportion of those hatched in Africa. All pythons die within six months of contracting this disease.

The stimulus is followed by a Must Be True question, so the correct answer choice must pass the Fact Test, and be confirmed by the information provided in the stimulus.

Answer choice (A): This is the correct answer choice, since it is confirmed by the information from the stimulus. We know that a few of the pythons hatched in North America have this disease, which means that they will surely be dead within six months. We also know that the disease can be difficult to detect in its early stages, so if any of the pythons were stricken with the disease recently, those pythons may still appear fine.

Answer choice (B): All that we know about pythons that hatch in North America versus those that hatch in Africa is that a greater proportion of African hatched pythons have the disease. Because we have limited information, we cannot conclude from this that African hatched pythons have a greater general susceptibility.

Answer choice (C): The liver disease under discussion kills all pythons within six months of contracting the disease—not within six months of life. Thus this answer choice is incorrect.

Answer choice (D): All we know about the python pricing is that a large shipment of them has resulted in a great number of inexpensive pythons in pet stores. We cannot presume that the low prices are based on their suffering from the liver disease—perhaps the prices are based solely on the great supply that came with the recent shipment. In any case, since the author neither states nor implies that the pythons are cheap because of the liver disease, this choice is unsupported.

Answer choice (E): The stimulus provided information about some pythons hatched in Africa, and some hatched in North America. Since we are provided with no information about pythons hatching on any other continent, this cannot be the correct answer to this Must Be True question.

Question #10: Weaken. The correct answer choice is (D)

This simple stimulus provides two pieces of basic information (premises), followed by a conclusion:

According to nutritionists, people can meet their daily vitamin needs by eating five servings of fruit and vegetables per day. Most people eat far less than the required five servings.

Conclusion: Most people need to take vitamin pills.

For some reason, the author assumes that the only alternative to the five recommended servings would be vitamin pills. Since the question which follows is a Weaken, perhaps we should look for an answer choice which provides another option that allows people to follow the nutritionists' recommendation.

Answer choice (A): If even five servings of fruits and vegetables would sometimes be insufficient, this increases the need for some substitute source of vitamins.

Answer choice (B): The fact that there is a wide variety of vitamin-levels among fruits and vegetables does not weaken the argument that most people should be taking vitamin pills, since the problem is that most people eat far less than five servings of fruits and vegetables per day.

Answer choice (C): Even if there is some disagreement as to what constitutes a complete serving, this does not weaken the simple argument in the stimulus: since most eat far less than the recommended five servings per day, most should take vitamin pills.

Answer choice (D): This is the correct answer choice, as it provides another possible source of necessary vitamins, beyond those of fruits, vegetables, and vitamin pills. If many common foods are vitamin fortified, then this provides another option, weakening the argument that most people need to take vitamin pills.

Answer choice (E): The argument from the stimulus regards fruits, vegetables, and *vitamins*. Even though this choice provides a benefit of food that is unavailable in vitamin pills, fiber is not mentioned in the stimulus, so this answer choice does not weaken the author's conclusion.

Question #11: Assumption. The correct answer choice is (E)

The researcher here tagged a number of armadillos during one spring and returned to the research site the next fall. Based on the fact that a large majority of the tagged armadillos could be found within a few hundred yards of their initial tagging, the researcher has concluded that armadillos do not quickly move into new territories.

An assumption question follows. Since there is no clear "gap" between the premises and the conclusion, this looks like a Defender Assumption question; application of the Assumption Negation technique can turn a difficult Assumption question into a simpler Weaken question. The correct answer choice, when negated, will weaken the argument in the stimulus.

Answer choice (A): This choice provides that the researcher tagged most of the armadillos in the area the previous spring ("few were able to avoid being tagged"). The argument does not rely on this assumption, because the researcher is discussing the group that were captured *this* fall. In other words, the researcher does not need to have tagged any particular number or portion the previous spring in order to draw the conclusion presented in the stimulus.

Answer choice (B): If the majority of tagged armadillos got away and were not recaptured, this would weaken the researcher's conclusion that armadillos do not move quickly into new territories. Since this choice would actually hurt the researcher's argument, it cannot be an assumption on which the researcher relies.

Answer choice (C): The researcher's conclusion does not presume that the armadillos were safe from predators.

For confirmation, if we apply the Assumption Negation technique to this answer choice, we arrive at the statement "predators *did* kill some of the tagged armadillos." This does not weaken the researcher's argument, so this answer choice can be ruled out.

Answer choice (D): This is a fairly common type of wrong answer choice. It is nice that the tags are reliable, but if they weren't, the researcher's argument would not be weakened, because the conclusion is based on the portion that did have tags.

Answer choice (E): This is the correct answer choice. Again, we are looking for the choice which, when negated, will weaken the researcher's argument that armadillos are slow movers. When we negate this choice, we get the following: "A large majority of the recaptured armadillos *did* move to a new territory in the intervening summer and then move back to the old territory in the fall." This negated version would certainly weaken the author's argument, so this must be an assumption on which the researcher's argument relies.

Question #12: Method of Reasoning. The correct answer choice is (A)

Sahira argues that governments are justified in subsidizing artists (this is the main conclusion of her argument), because without such subsidies, she asserts, artists with great potential would have to create popular works "instead of their best work." Sahira's clear implication here is that the popular works created would not represent such artists' best work.

Rahima points out that the above conclusion depends on a questionable notion: that talented artists' popular creations would represent something other than their best work. Rahima says that this is not necessarily the case.

The dialogue between Sahira and Rahima is followed by a Method of Reasoning question, so we should prephrase the answer if possible: In her argument, Rahima questions Sahira's implication that popular works would not represent these artists' best work.

Answer choice (A): This is the correct answer choice. Rahima's response is to question Sahira's assumption that appealing to the masses would lead to something other than the best work from artists of great potential.

Answer choice (B): Rahima disagrees with Sahira; she does not present independent support for Sahira's argument but rather takes issue with it.

Answer choice (C): Rahima questions Sahira's conclusion because it is based on a questionable notion. Since Rahima does not accept Sahira's conclusion, this answer choice cannot be correct.

Answer choice (D): Rahima does not "use" Sahira's premises; instead, she questions an unstated premise (i.e., an *assumption*) of Sahira's argument.

Answer choice (E): Rahima asserts that one of Sahira's assumptions may be invalid—Rahima does not claim that there has been any self-contradiction.

Question #13: Must Be True. The correct answer choice is (C)

Here the author simply presents information, drawing no conclusions:

Adult frogs have thin skin, so they're vulnerable to dehydration.

Small adult frogs cannot survive in arid areas (because their ratio of body weight to skin surface area is too low). In this regard, small adult frogs are "unlike large adult frogs." Since the author is not explicit, we should note the implication, which is that large adult frogs can live in arid areas.

Finally, we are informed that the frogs' need for water is the most important factor determining where they can live in the Yucatan peninsula, where it is arid in the north and wet in the south.

The stimulus is followed by a Must question stem, so the information presented in the stimulus will confirm the correct answer choice.

Answer choice (A): Although both large and small adult frogs are discussed, there is no mention of an inability to coexist in wet areas. Since this choice fails the Fact Test, this answer is incorrect.

Answer choice (B): The passage suggests that only large adult frogs can live in arid areas, which would mean that the small adult frogs in the area would be relegated to the wet areas. Since this would *decrease* the average weight of frogs in the wet areas, this is an Opposite Answer and thus incorrect.

Answer choice (C): This is the correct answer choice. The frogs' moisture requirements determine where they can live in the area, and small adult frogs cannot live in arid areas—unlike adult frogs, which the author suggests *can* live in arid areas. If this is the case, then large adult frogs have more options in the Yucatan than young adult frogs.

Answer choice (D): All we know of the south is that it is a wet area, where both large and small adult frogs can live. The author provides no information regarding the respective numbers of large and small frogs, so this choice is not confirmed in the stimulus.

Answer choice (E): All adult frogs have permeable skin, but the author provides no information about varying degrees of permeability, so this choice fails the Fact Test.

Question #14: Flaw in the Reasoning. The correct answer choice is (D)

This editorial's conclusion is based on the results of a recent survey, in which the majority of people "feel that crime is increasing," and the majority of people believe that sentences should be tougher. The author concludes that "the government should firmly address the rising crime rate."

The problem is that the author quickly jumps to the conclusion that the survey results accurately represent reality. Just because most people *feel* that crime is increasing, does that mean that it really is?

The question stem asks for the flaw in the author's reasoning, which is the author's acceptance of survey opinions as fact.

Answer choice (A): Although the percentages are not exactly the same for the two specific results presented, this is not an inconsistency, because there is no reason to presume a perfect correlation. In other words, there is no inconsistency in feeling that crime is increasing without believing that sentences should be tougher, and there is nothing inherently inconsistent about believing that sentences should be tougher without necessarily believing the crime is increasing.

Answer choice (B): There is no such presumption. The author presents survey results about the perceived crime rate increase and the perceived need for tougher sentences, but there is no correlation suggested.

Answer choice (C): This is not a flaw, because the author does not need to consider other such surveys taken over the years. The problem is that the survey results presented do not necessarily reflect the actual state of affairs. If such surveys do not accurately reflect reality, then their results don't provide support for the author's conclusion, regardless of when the surveys were taken.

Answer choice (D): This is the correct answer choice. The survey results presented reflect only popular opinion, but the author appears to believe that perception equals reality. Because the author fails to consider that popular opinion is not necessarily accurate, this argument is flawed.

Answer choice (E): The author does not presume that tougher sentences are the best way to reduce crime. The conclusion is that the government must firmly address the problem, but the author does not discuss or imply the *best* way to reduce crime.

Question #15: Must Be True. The correct answer choice is (B)

The discussion here involves proofs and the need for computers. Proofs that are completely reliant on computers provide us with less certainty, because we cannot "check their work," so to speak, or verify their findings on our own, independently, without the use of computers.

This is distinguishable from proofs that do not rely on computers—basic operations in math, for example, can be calculated by computer and verified by human calculation. The author points out that calculators are often used for convenience, but such cases are different, because the calculator is used for convenience (and not out of necessity).

A Must question stem follows, so we should look for the choice that can be confirmed with the information provided by the author.

Answer choice (A): The language used in this choice is far stronger than justified by the stimulus. The bold claim in this choice is that any help from computers will make it impossible to judge a proof with *any degree of certainty*. The stimulus provides only that the level of certainty is *decreased* where results cannot be independently verified.

Answer choice (B): This is the correct answer choice. The problem with computer reliant proofs, according to the author, is that humans cannot verify their accuracy—thus the need for computers. Such proofs provide less certainty because humans cannot verify their accuracy (some mistakes might be undetectable).

Answer choice (C): This choice is disproved with the author's discussion of the use of calculators. The author provides that a calculator is often used even though humans can verify the results; in such cases the degree of certainty is not reduced, because the computer is not an absolute necessity, but rather a convenience, and the results can still be verified independently.

Answer choice (D): Like incorrect answer choice (A), the strong language used in this choice takes it out of contention. The author's point is that when independent human verification is possible, we can be *more* certain than when such independent verification is impossible. This is not the same, however, as claiming that human verification equates to *complete* certainly. Because of the strength of the language used in this choice, it is incorrect.

Answer choice (E): The creation of proofs that rely crucially on computers is an example of computers supplementing the cognitive abilities of humans. Since this supplementing of our cognitive abilities is clearly possible according to the author, this cannot be the correct answer choice.

Question #16: Must Be True. The correct answer choice is (B)

Madden's argument is basically that industrialists address problems with simplification. When applied to farming, Madden asserts, this approach often turns into oversimplification. For example, this overly simplistic industrialist perspective sees the retention of water and the drainage of water as opposites, missing the fact that good topsoil can both drain and retain water.

Instead of seeing the simplest solution, industrialists use two distinct approaches—one for the purpose of draining and another for retaining. To aid retention, a dam or terrace is used, and for drainage a tile, ditch or subsoiler is used. In sum, Madden believes that putting the overly simplistic industrialists in charge of agricultural decisions (rather than the farmers) creates more problems than solutions.

The question stem requires us to find among the answers the best illustration of Madden's argument. The correct answer choice will probably deal with the problems of farming and how industrialists see things too simply.

Answer choice (A): The problems of water retention and drainage are not presented as the *most* important part of good farming—these issues are intended to exemplify the overly simplistic approach that industrialists take to the problems of farming.

Answer choice (B): This is the correct answer choice, confirmed by Madden's assertion that the industrialist approach tends to oversimplify the problems of farming. Clearly, Madden believes that farming problems should be seen in all their complexity.

Answer choice (C): The language used in this answer choice should allow us to quickly rule it out. The claim is not that farmers are the *best* at solving problems—just that industrialists who try to solve farming problems tend to create more problems than solutions.

Answer choice (D): Like incorrect answer choice (C), the strong language used takes this answer choice out of contention. The author does not take the bold stand that industrial solutions should *never* be sought for farming problems. The author says that the simplistic industrialist approach usually (but perhaps not always) leads to oversimplification.

Answer choice (E): The author believes that industrialists' solutions are too simplistic to be successfully applied to agricultural problems such as water retention and draining. However, that is not the same as saying that the typical industrialist's approach is "fundamentally flawed"—just that it should not be applied to agricultural issues. Since this choice makes a bold claim that is not supported by the stimulus, it fails the Fact Test and should be ruled out of contention in response to this question.

Question #17: Assumption—SN. The correct answer choice is (D)

This critic provides several conditional statements, in the form of two very long sentences. The first is that modern literary works cannot be tragedies like those from the past, unless their characters are seen as having enduring nobility. In order to diagram this sentence, we can apply the Unless Formula, which provides that the condition which follows the word "unless" is the necessary condition, and the other condition must be negated and becomes the sufficient.

In this case, modern works cannot be tragedies like the ancient ones unless their characters are seen as noble:

modern tragedies ⟶ characters possess nobility

The contrapositive of this statement, diagrammed below, tells us that if characters cannot be seen as possessing nobility, then there can be no modern tragedies:

characters possess nobility ⟶ modern tragedies

The critic goes on to say that in this age, we know longer believe that humans are bound by fate, so it is impossible for a modern work to be a tragedy:

believe humans bound by fate ⟶ modern tragedies

Considering the two conditional statements above, we might note a "leap" from the premise to the conclusion: If characters cannot be seen as possessing nobility, there can be no modern tragedies. Thus, since we no longer believe that humans are bound by fate, there can be no modern tragedies.

If we notice the missing link in these conditional statements, we should not be surprised to see the stimulus followed by an assumption question. To answer this supporter assumption question, the correct choice will link the two "rogue elements"—the condition that "characters cannot possess nobility", and the condition that "humans are not seen as being bound by fate."

Answer choice (A): The word "should" in this answer choice would reflect a value judgement, and the author makes no such assertion in the stimulus.

Answer choice (B): This choice uses the word "false," which is a stronger claim than the author makes in the stimulus. The stimulus provides only that the no one takes this belief seriously, which is not the same as claiming that the belief is absolutely false.

Answer choice (C): The author does not claim that past tragedies have been misclassified, but rather that modern plays cannot be properly characterized as tragedies, because we no longer seriously believe in fate, so we no longer see characters as possessing nobility.

Answer choice (D): This is the correct answer choice, which links the rogue elements as required by the question. This choice says that if one is not seen as having his or her endeavors guided by fate, one will not be seen as possessing nobility. When this is diagrammed and combined with the information from the stimulus, we can see that this is the needed assumption:

Premise: characters ~~possess~~ nobility ⟶ modern ~~tragedies~~

\+ Assumption: believe humans ~~bound~~ by fate ⟶ characters ~~possess~~ nobility

Conclusion: believe humans ~~bound~~ by fate ⟶ characters ~~possess~~ nobility ⟶ modern ~~tragedies~~

Answer choice (E): The author actually lists such endurance as a required part of possessing nobility, so this answer choice is not accurate.

Question #18: Flaw in the Reasoning—#%. The correct answer choice is (E)

In the first sentence of this stimulus we are told that there is a small minority of graduate students at a particular university interested in unionizing, while the majority of students are completely unaware of these efforts. Among the *minority* of students who are aware of these efforts, most feel that a union would not represent or pursue their interests.

From this information the author jumps to the conclusion that "the majority of them *obviously* disapprove of the attempt," and based on this faulty conclusion, the author asserts that the students should not unionize.

What is the problem with the conclusion that the majority of students disapprove of the effort? We were told from the outset that the majority of students at the university were entirely unaware of the efforts to unionize. If this is true, then the author cannot logically conclude that the majority *disapprove*. This should be expressed in the correct answer to the flaw question that follows the stimulus.

Answer choice (A): The author makes no mention of a long standing practice in support of the conclusion drawn. Rather, the conclusion is based on the students' lack of approval, misconstrued by the author as disapproval.

Answer choice (B): There is no discussion of the reasons behind students' approval or disapproval of the plan. Since no such reasons are discussed, the failure to consider alternative explanations is not a flaw, and this answer choice cannot be correct.

Answer choice (C): This incorrect answer choice might be appealing, but the author does not make any such value judgements. There is no discussion about whether or not unionization is a good idea—just about whether or not the students at the university are in support of the idea.

Answer choice (D): Like incorrect answer choice (B) above, this choice deals with the reasons for unionizing or not unionizing. The author's conclusions are based on student support, or lack thereof, but the author does not discuss the underlying reasons for these decisions.

Answer choice (E): This is the correct answer choice. The author makes the claim that the majority of students actively disapprove of the plan to unionize, although the passage has already established that the majority of students at the university don't know anything about it. If this is the case, then those students did not approve of the plan, but they did not disapprove either.

Question #19: Justify the Conclusion—SN. The correct answer choice is (B)

Here we are presented with several conditional statements, including a conclusion that must be justified. The first statement is that if you believe in democracy, you respect the wisdom of the masses:

believe in democracy ⟶ respect wisdom of masses

The contrapositive of this statement tells us that if you don't respect the wisdom of the masses, then you do not believe democracy:

respect wis~~do~~m of masses ⟶ believe i~~n d~~emocracy

The next statement concerns Griley, who believes popular artwork is unlikely to be good. From this premise the author concludes that Griley does not believe in democracy:

popular artwork is unlikely to be good ⟶ believe i~~n d~~emocracy

Considering the above two conditional statements, we can clearly see the logical "leap" to the conclusion:

If you don't respect the wisdom of the masses, then you don't believe in democracy.
Thus, if you believe popular art is unlikely to be good, then you don't believe in democracy. The author sees Griley's popular art criticism as reflecting a lack of respect for the wisdom of the masses.

Having noted this missing link in the author's conditional reasoning chain, we should not be surprised to see a Justify question stem follow.

The correct answer choice will be the one that effectively links the "rogue elements" discussed above: a lack of confidence in the quality of popular artwork and a failure to respect the wisdom of the masses.

Answer choice (A): The author does say that Griley is an elitist, but this fact is not a component of any of the conditional rules presented. Further, this choice fails to link the rogue elements from the stimulus, so this choice cannot justify the conclusion drawn by the author.

Answer choice (B): This is the correct answer choice. It is the only choice which links the rogue elements from the stimulus and allows the author's conditional conclusion to be properly drawn, as we can see by diagramming the relevant statements:

Premise (contrapositive): respect wisdom of masses ⟶ believe in democracy
\+ Answer choice: believe pop artwork unlikely good ⟶ respect wisdom of masses

pop artwork unlikely good ⟶ respect wisdom of masses ⟶ believe in democracy

The conditional chain above illustrates how this answer choice justifies the author's conclusion: If Griley believes that popular artwork is unlikely to be good, then he does not respect the wisdom of the masses. Thus, he does not believe in democracy.

Answer choice (C): The stimulus provides that Griley *is* an elitist, so this choice provides no useful information—there is no reason to consider what happens if Griley is not an elitist, and no way that this statement can justify the author's conclusion. And although this choice includes the condition "high regard for the wisdom of the masses," it does not link it to beliefs about popular artwork, so it cannot be the right answer choice.

Answer choice (D): In order to justify the author's conclusion about Griley, we need to assume that people who are skeptical about the quality of popular art (such as Griley) do not have enough respect for the wisdom of the masses. This choice reverses this condition, so it cannot justify the author's conclusion.

Answer choice (E): This choice says that respect for the wisdom of the masses requires a belief in democracy. This choice does not provide the needed link to Griley's beliefs about popular art, so it does not justify the author's conclusion that Griley doesn't believe in democracy.

Question #20: Resolve the Paradox. The correct answer choice is (E)

This passage presents the results of a study of the relationship between salt intake and high blood pressure. Heavy salt intake tends to increase blood pressure. Predictably, many high blood pressure sufferers experienced a blood pressure decrease when they cut their salt intake. There were also participants, however, who had heavy salt intake throughout the study and yet were able to somehow maintain low blood-pressure.

The passage is followed by a Resolve question stem, so the correct answer choice will provide some explanation of those who, contrary to normal expectations, had high salt intake throughout and maintained low blood pressure regardless.

Answer choice (A): The study participants who create the paradox are those who had low blood pressure despite maintaining high levels of salt intake throughout the study. This choice deals with a different group, and does not resolve the discrepancy.

Answer choice (B): Even if there are other factors associated with high blood pressure, this does not explain the fact that, despite a general correlation between heavy salt intake and higher blood pressure, some participants had consistently high salt intake and consistently low blood pressure.

Answer choice (C): Just because salt reduction is not the best way to reduce high blood pressure, salt reduction is still one approach that we would expect to be effective. We would still expect those who eat a lot of salt generally to have higher blood pressure, so this choice fails to resolve the paradox.

Answer choice (D): Much like incorrect answer choice (A) above, this choice deals with the wrong population. The author presents the paradoxical case of study participants who ate a lot of salt and still maintained high blood pressure. This choice deals with the opposite: those who have low salt intake and high blood pressure. If anything this would actually broaden the apparent discrepancy, making the study results more puzzling, so it cannot be the correct answer choice.

Answer choice (E): This is the correct answer choice. This choice describes a group who could have low blood pressure despite high salt intake. This is a group of people who suffer from abnormally low blood pressure, and crave a lot of salt just to keep their blood pressure levels high enough. For such people, we might expect the otherwise paradoxical results from the study.

Question #21: Assumption. The correct answer choice is (D)

Although one is very unlikely to win the lottery, the few who do win receive significant media attention. And most people are aware of the issues that get significant attention from the media. From these two premises, the author concludes that many people greatly overestimate their chances of winning the lottery. The author has not explicitly said so, but clearly believes that many people's awareness of lottery wins equates with many people's overestimation of their own chances of winning:

Premise:	Lottery winners get a lot of media attention.
Premise:	Most people are aware of big media stories.
Conclusion:	Therefore many people overestimate their own chances of winning.

The unstated premise—the supporter assumption, in this case—will likely tie the awareness of big winners to overestimation of one's chances to win.

Answer choice (A): The author makes no mention of the media's downplaying the odds of winning, and this choice fails to provide the supporter assumption prephrased above.

Answer choice (B): There is no discussion of the other parties who receive significant media attention, and this choice is not an assumption on which the author's argument depends.

Answer choice (C): The author does not say or imply that the media is the sole reason for people's overestimation of their chances, so the argument does not depend on this assumption.

Answer choice (D): This is the correct answer choice. This answer links the elements which were not explicitly linked in the stimulus: awareness of others' big wins must lead some to overestimate their own prospects for such a win.

To test this choice, we can apply the Assumption Negation Technique, negating the answer choice to see if taking away the assumption will weaken the author's argument. The negated version of this answer choice is "Becoming aware of major jackpots leads no one to overestimate his or her own chances to win." This negated version would certainly weaken the author's conclusion, confirming this to be the correct answer choice.

Answer choice (E): The only group mentioned in this context is that of the people who greatly overestimate their own chances to win the lottery. There is no discussion about those who do not overestimate their chances.

Question #22: Parallel Flaw. The correct answer choice is (C)

The conditional statements here lead the author to a unique kind of mistaken conclusion. The first conditional statement: if a book is well publicized and the author is established, then a book tour will be successful:

well publicized book tour
and ⟶ book tour successful
well established author

Next, we are told that Julia is an established writer and her book tour was successful. Based on the diagram above, these two pieces of information do not lead to any logical conclusion. However, the author incorrectly concludes that Julia's book tour must have been well-publicized. The author appears to mistakenly think that if any two conditions are met, the third one is met as well.

The question that follows is, not surprisingly, a parallel flaw question, which means that the correct answer choice will reflect the same **mistaken** notion—that if one of two sufficient conditions is met, and the sole necessary condition is met, this must mean that the second sufficient was met as well.

Answer choice (A): This clever wrong answer choice might have been appealing at first, but here we have two necessary conditions and one sufficient:

This recipe will turn out only if it is followed exactly and high quality ingredients are used:

followed exactly
recipe will turn out ⟶ and
high quality ingredients

All we need to know is that the recipe turned out in order to logically conclude that high quality ingredients were used. Since the conclusion here is valid, this choice cannot parallel the flaw.

Answer choice (B): Although this choice does illustrate flawed logic, it is not precisely the same type. This answer choice presents something that looks almost like a standard mistaken reversal, but adds an additional error as well:

If a computer has the fastest microprocessor and the most memory available, it will meet Aletha's needs *this* year:

fastest microprocessor available
and ⟶ meet Aletha's needs this year
most memory available

The computer Aletha used met her needs last year, so it must have had the fastest microprocessor and the most memory available last year:

met Aletha's needs last year ⟶ fastest microprocessor available and most memory available

Again, this looks almost like a straightforward mistaken reversal, but this statement adds the additional error of basing a conclusion about *last* year on a conditional statement about *this* year.

Answer choice (C): This is the correct answer choice. As prephrased above, this choice provides a conditional statement with two sufficient conditions and one necessary, making the exact same mistake as that in the stimulus: If cacti are kept in shade and watered more than twice per week, they die:

kept in shade and watered more than twice per week ⟶ die

Based on the fact that a particular cactus was kept in the shade and is now dead, this choice concludes that it must have been watered more than twice per week. Exactly like the flawed logic from the stimulus, this choice illogically presumes that meeting one of two sufficient conditions, along with the necessary condition, will assure that the second sufficient condition was met as well.

Answer choice (D): This incorrect choice might look good at first, because it deals with two sufficient conditions and one necessary condition. The problem is that it uses valid logic:

A house will suffer from dry rot and poor drainage only if it is built near a high water table:

dry rot and poor drainage ⟶ built near high water table

This house has suffered from dry rot and poor drainage, so it must have been built near a high water table. This logic is valid as shown by the diagram above, so it cannot parallel the flawed logic from the stimulus.

Answer choice (E): Much like incorrect answer choice (D), this choice might have initial appeal because it presents two sufficient conditions and one necessary. The problem, as with answer choice (D), is that this answer reflects valid logic. In this choice, we are first told that if you wear a suit with double vents, and it has narrow lapels, then you will be fashionably dressed:

suit with double vents
and ——→ fashionably dressed
suit has narrow lapels

Thus it is valid to conclude that if Joseph was wearing a suit with double vents and narrow lapels that Joseph must have been fashionably dressed. Since this choice uses valid logic it cannot parallel the flawed logic found in the stimulus.

Question #23: Strengthen. The correct answer choice is (B)

Here we learn about eight craters that might have been caused by meteorites, or may have been caused by volcanic events. Some of the craters contain rocks that could have been the result of crashing meteorites, but these same craters also could have resulted from volcanic events. The craters are lined up so perfectly that it is unlikely that some were caused by volcanoes and others by meteorites (the perfect alignment of the craters was not likely the product of coincidence). Further, the craters are different ages. Since they were not all created at the same time, the author concludes, the craters were probably produced by volcanic activity, as opposed to several meteors hitting the earth at different times to produce a perfect line of craters.

The question which follows requires us to find the answer choice which most strengthens the author's argument. This means that the right answer can specifically strengthen the conclusion that volcanoes were responsible for creating the craters, or weaken the argument that meteorites were their source.

Answer choice (A): The craters described in the stimulus are all different ages, and they create a much longer line of craters, which are both reasons that the author is convinced they were the result of volcanic activity. The craters mentioned in this answer choice make a shorter line and are all the same age, creating an entirely different scenario.

Answer choice (B): This is the correct answer choice. In order to strengthen the author's argument, we can bolster the idea that volcanoes created the craters, or somehow refute the notion that meteorites were the cause. This answer choice achieves the latter. If there is no known cause in nature that might lead to eight different aged meteorite craters in perfect alignment, that makes it less likely that meteorites were actually the cause. By ruling out one possible alternative cause, this answer choice strengthens the argument that volcanic activity was the actual cause of the nicely aligned craters.

Answer choice (C): A lack of outside evidence for either possible cause would not strengthen the author's argument, so this choice cannot be correct.

Answer choice (D): This choice provides some support to the argument that meteorites caused the craters, so this choice could not strengthen the argument that volcanic activity was the cause.

Answer choice (E): The craters discussed in the stimulus were different ages, so they could not have come from a single meteor shower, so the fact that no such formation has come from a single meteor shower is irrelevant.

Question #24: Justify the Conclusion—SN. The correct answer choice is (B)

In this stimulus the author presents a series of conditional statements, concluding that innovators anger the majority. The conditional statements are diagrammed below:

A real creative genius is one who is not content to simply accept widely held beliefs:

real creative genius ⟶ content to ~~accept~~ wide beliefs

Thus, the author concludes, such *real creative geniuses tend to anger the majority*. This conclusion is followed by further conditional statements:

Those not content to accept others' beliefs seek out controversy:

content to ~~accept~~ wide beliefs ⟶ seek controversy

...and those who seek controversy enjoy showing how popular views are wrong:

seek controversy ⟶ like to demonstrate popular falsehoods

Putting this conditional chain together, we arrive at the following:

real genius ⟶ content ~~w/~~ wide beliefs ⟶ seek controversy ⟶ demonstrate popular falsehoods

As we can see from the diagram, there is no reference to angering the majority, yet the author's conclusion is that real creative geniuses tend to anger the majority. Since the question stem requires us to justify the conclusion, the tendency to anger the majority must be somehow linked to the conditional chain above.

Answer choice (A): The conclusion that we must justify in this stimulus is that real creative geniuses, who are dissatisfied with merely habitual assent to widely held beliefs tend to anger *the majority.* This choice provides that the geniuses get angry *themselves*. This does not justify the conclusion as needed.

Answer choice (B): This is the correct answer choice. This answer provides that people who like to demonstrate the falsehoods of popular viewpoints anger the majority:

demonstrate popular falsehoods ⟶ anger majority

So we can link this to the end of the conditional chain provided in the stimulus:

real genius ⟶ not content w/ wide beliefs ⟶ seek controversy ⟶ demonstrate pop. falsehoods ⟶ anger majority

Based on the conditional diagram above, we can see that this answer choice allows us to logically draw the conclusion that real creative geniuses tend to anger the majority.

Answer choice (C): This choice is close, but this answer provides that people get angered when people hold different beliefs themselves. This is subtly different from the link we need, which is that people get angry when others *demonstrate* the falsehood of commonly held beliefs.

Answer choice (D): This answer provides the mistaken reversal of the link we actually need. This choice says that if you anger the majority, then you enjoy demonstrating the falsehood of commonly held beliefs:

anger the majority ⟶ enjoy demonstrating popular false beliefs

The link that we need is the exact reverse—that those who enjoy demonstrating popular false beliefs tend to anger the majority:

enjoy demonstrating popular false beliefs ⟶ anger the majority

This is the link provided by the correct answer choice, (B).

Answer choice (E): Much like incorrect answer choice (D), this choice provides the mistaken reversal of a conditional statement that would logically justify the author's conclusion. Here we are provided with the following: if you anger the majority, then you are not content just accepting widely held beliefs:

anger the majority ⟶ content to accept widely held beliefs

This choice does not provide the needed link, because it cannot be added to the author's conditional chain to justify the author's conclusion.

If this choice had provided the opposite statement, it would be the correct answer choice—if we knew that all those not content to accept widely held beliefs tended to anger the majority, then we could logically draw the author's conclusion as follows:

real creative genius ⟶ content to accept wide beliefs ⟶ anger the majority

Question #25: Method of Reasoning—PR. The correct answer choice is (A)

Here we are presented with a dialogue between Claude and Larissa regarding job candidates who salt their food before tasting it. Claude sees this as a fault, because he believes such decisions are made without adequate information. Larissa disagrees, comparing the salting with two types of decisions she commonly makes without much consideration. Before walking into a supermarket she puts on a sweater, and before opening credit card offers she throws them away. Both are decisions she believes have been justifiably made, based on the ability to predict an outcome based on past experience.

The stimulus is followed by a Method Principle question, and this answer can be effectively prephrased. Larissa's response is to present two scenarios in which she also makes decisions without complete information. She disagrees with Claude's assertion that such decisions are ill-informed. She feels that decisions like these are justified, because they are more generally supported by information from past experience.

Answer choice (A): This is the correct answer choice. The general principle advanced in Larissa's argument is that where personal preference is concerned, it is sometimes acceptable to make a specific decision even without all of the facts surrounding that particular instance. Larissa believes that making such a decision does not necessarily reflect poor decision making, because more general information about such circumstances might be sufficient.

Answer choice (B): This choice's principle is that when it comes to professional decision making, one should not consider job-related behavior in drawing general conclusions about a person's character. Neither speaker brought up the issue of character judgement in the stimulus. Additionally, both Claude and Larissa discuss non-job related behavior, so this choice fails on at least two counts.

Answer choice (C): The two speakers do discuss behavior that is not directly job-related, but they both appear to agree that the behaviors discussed might indicate a pattern. Claude believes that this pattern (of making decisions in particular instances of imperfect information) reflects poorly on one's decision making abilities, and Larissa disagrees). Since this choice deals specifically with behavior that does not indicate a pattern, this cannot be the principle reflected in Larissa's response.

Answer choice (D): The dialogue presented is not about adherence to social norms, but rather about decision making in instances where not all information has been considered. There is no indication that any of the behaviors discussed in the stimulus would be non-conforming, so this choice can be ruled out as well.

Answer choice (E): This choice is incorrect because Larissa does not agree that Claude's scenario exemplifies bad judgement. Only Claude believes that salting untasted food equates to poor decision making, so this choice does not describe the principle advanced by Larissa in her response.